D0217102

Cases for
TEACHER
DEVELOPMENT

For the teachers in Ontario, Canada,
whose commitment to teaching continues to
reflect the knowledge, skills, and values of the profession

—W. Douglas Wilson
Registrar and Chief Executive Officer,
Ontario College of Teachers

Cases for
TEACHER
DEVELOPMENT

PREPARING FOR THE CLASSROOM

EDITORS

PATRICIA F. GOLDBLATT
Ontario College of Teachers

DÉIRDRE SMITH
Ontario College of Teachers

SAGE Publications
Thousand Oaks ■ London ■ New Delhi

For information:

Sage Publications, Inc.
2455 Teller Road
Thousand Oaks, California 91320
E-mail: order@sagepub.com

Sage Publications Ltd.
1 Oliver's Yard
55 City Road
London EC1Y 1SP
United Kingdom

Sage Publications India Pvt. Ltd.
B-42, Panchsheel Enclave
Post Box 4109
New Delhi 110 017 India

Printed in the United States of America

Library of Congress Cataloging-in-Publication Data

Cases for teacher development: Preparing for the classroom/edited by Patricia F. Goldblatt and Déirdre Smith (Ontario College of Teachers).
     p. cm.
Includes bibliographical references and index.
ISBN 1-4129-1366-7 (cloth) — ISBN 1-4129-1367-5 (pbk.)
   1. Teaching—Case studies. 2. Teachers—Training of. I. Goldblatt, Patricia F. II. Smith, Déirdre. III. Ontario College of Teachers.
LB1025.3.C39 2005
371.102—dc22   2004025365

This book is printed on acid-free paper.

05   06   07   08   09   10   9   8   7   6   5   4   3   2   1

Acquiring Editor:	Diane McDaniel
Editorial Assistant:	Marta Peimer
Production Editor:	Beth Bernstein
Copy Editor:	Taryn L. Bigelow
Typesetter:	C&M Digitals (P) Ltd.
Indexer:	Teri Greenberg
Cover Designer:	Michelle Lee-Kenny

Contents

Acknowledgments

This book became a reality because teachers thought about, talked about, and wrote about their practice. They were willing to share their knowledge, their experiences, and their insights with other teachers and the public. They invite you to join their learning community.

The names of the individual teachers who wrote their stories are not listed here. This was their request. Names, locations, contexts, and dilemmas have been modified and changed for the purpose of confidentiality. It was the desire of these writers that the unique quality of their voices would represent a sampling of the myriad practitioners in the teaching profession. By offering their cases of practice, the writers hoped to inspire their colleagues to reflect on their own teaching experiences.

This book became a reality through the vision and the support of the members of the Standards of Practice and Education Committee of the Ontario College of Teachers. Committee members recognized that the standards of practice are most effectively described through the voices of teachers and college members sharing their experiences in classrooms, schools, and educational systems.

The Standards of Practice and Education Committee members include Ernie Checkeris, Karl Dean, Suzanne De Froy, Margaret Dempsey, Audrey Hadfield, Nancy Hutcheson, Martin Kings, Diane Leblovic, Karen Mitchell, Harry Mulvale, Iain Munro, Janet Ouellette, Jennifer Pitt, Don Watson, and Lila Mae Watson.

This book was developed through the hard work, perseverance, and belief in teachers in the province of Ontario by staff members in the Standards of Practice and Education Committee of the Ontario College of Teachers. Dr. Patricia F. Goldblatt assumed the lead role in facilitating, writing, and coordinating the work of the teacher contributors, editing the material, and preparing the manuscript for publication.

This is a book that strives to deepen understanding about the standards of practice while providing a venue for the experiences and challenges facing teachers. Many of the college's educational partners supported and contributed to this project. Their efforts have established a new medium for professional learning.

The many teachers and commentators who contributed their time and knowledge to this casebook have helped demonstrate the meaning and relevance of case methodology in teacher education. Patricia F. Goldblatt and Déirdre Smith, the editors of this casebook, also acknowledge the following reviewers: Christopher Blake, Mount St. Mary's College, Emmitsburg, Maryland; Allan Cook, University of Illinois, Springfield; Andrew C. Kemp, University of Louisville, Kentucky; Delores D. Liston, Georgia Southern College in Statesboro; Suzanne M. Miller, Buffalo State University (SUNY); Georgianna Short, Ohio State University, Columbus; Carol Wareing, Merrimack College, North Andover, Massachusetts; Carolyn Tighe Wemlinger, Dominican University, River Forest, Illinois; and Jamie Whitman-Smithe, Wesley College, Dover, Delaware; and Dr. Linda Grant, former coordinator of professional affairs at the Ontario College of Teachers. Also, we must thank Suzanne Baril for her expertise, patience, and support throughout this entire project.

Increased understanding of principles of practice as described in the Ontario College of Teachers' *Standards of Practice for the Teaching Profession* (2002) and the *Ethical Standards for the Teaching Profession* (2000) and—just as important—the need to create communication for shared professional inquiry resulted from the case writers' efforts. The collaborative culture of educators who participated in the global discourse in this book celebrates an authentic presence—of teachers everywhere whose ongoing and self-directed learning speaks to professionalism in and out of the classroom.

Introduction

Using Cases to Understand
What It Means to Be a Teacher

*"T*his is going to be fun! Scott is in our class."

My ears prick up. This is an early warning sign of an interesting classroom challenge.

"It's the school's fault!"

It was not the first time that I had heard Mr. Russell blame the school for his son's difficulties. I was sure it was not the school's fault; if it were, that would mean that it was my fault, at least in part, since I was the child's teacher!

There was an uneasy silence that punctuated the empty classroom. Mel looked downward before she spoke.

"I need to talk."

There was a tremor in her voice, and I knew something important was to follow.

These introductory sentences alert you to the dilemmas that will unfold in a particular setting. The place is school. The writers are teachers, grappling with real issues that they have encountered in their profession. Immediately, we recognize the authenticity of the scenarios. The uneasy silence, the inner thoughts, the ponderous sense of responsibility foreshadows the serious nature of the stories selected for inclusion in this book.

The cases in the book reflect the experiences that teachers encounter in their careers. Each story represents a teaching tension in an educator's career, an event that, even years after its occurrence, continues to concern the writer. These narratives document the initiation, entrance, development, and commitment of teachers in their profession. Situated in recognizable contexts, replete with emotional struggles and questions, each telling is an unraveling thread that addresses the complex question, *what does it mean to be a teacher?*

The readers and users of this book are privileged to enter the classrooms and psyches of educators to confront issues that may also arise in their own professional careers. Like practitioners of medicine, social work, and architecture, teachers function in specific contexts in practical and meaningful ways (Madfes & Shulman, 2002). Cases impart meaning to theory through vivid descriptions that depend on the time, place, teacher, and student need. This vicarious entry into the teaching profession introduces a realm of complexity as one dilemma unfolds that is hinged on many others.

In the last few years, cases have been considered one of the most promising avenues toward reform in teacher education and staff development (Doyle, 1990; Hutchings, 1993; Merseth, 1991; Shulman, 1986; Sykes & Bird, 1992).

Cases have been used at both the undergraduate and graduate levels in general methods, foundations of education, and ethical dimensions of education courses. Cases are appearing in current trends in education courses, teacher research, and introduction to teaching seminars. And cases are a staple in action research and clinical practice seminars. Whether for the purpose of personal reflection, a focused assignment, or an offering to colleagues for analysis and evaluation, the intent is clear: to promote thoughtful, penetrating conversations and insights among teachers who are ready to pause, reflect, and critically consider the complex educational issues that exist in all classrooms.

This book, therefore, may be used in many ways: in classes, in discussion groups, as practicum, and for self-study. The goals of the text are to provide a path for your exploration as an educator and to facilitate your growth in the teaching profession.

This introduction will provide you with an overview of the text. By describing what a case is and what its uses and benefits are, we establish grounding for the commentaries, the pedagogy, the matrix, and the Connecting Questions provided within the pages of this book. The development of a case as a teaching tool supports our contention that the teachers whose narratives appear in this book *know what teachers need to know*. It is through their stories that you will encounter and puzzle over the dilemmas that teachers face daily. In reading and vicariously experiencing those challenges, you will participate and engage in teaching conversations that will deepen your awareness and understanding of issues pertinent to your profession.

Each chapter is structured to facilitate the examination of professional practice through individual and/or collective inquiry. This format includes a case, commentaries, and pedagogical processes designed to engage the reader in critical reflection. The case is both content and pedagogy that will facilitate your development as a teacher. The commentaries that follow each case are a unique feature of this book. They deepen pedagogical reflection by inviting examination of the assumptions, understandings, and practices of teachers. The commentaries, written by experts in the field, explore the different educational issues raised by the cases.

❖ WHAT IS A CASE?

A case is an opportunity to learn how to think like a teacher to develop the mindful habits that exemplify the skills, traits, and dispositions of professional practitioners. A case also acknowledges a variety of perspectives that come into play in any conflict. Set in recognizable contexts that are integral to the problem, the case poses no easy answers. Rather, it is the ambiguity, complexity, and possibility of alternative solutions to the dilemma described that position the case as the beginning of a deep inquiry. Much like a narrative but more than just an interesting anecdote, these cases are real-life stories that draw on teachers' unique problems in practice.

Cases provide a framework into which teachers can insert themselves. The ambiguity of a situation offers a gap, an opening that allows an individual to ponder or connect to a similar professional experience with the depiction in the case. Through analysis and reflection, "teachers recognize specific events as problematic, gain an understanding of them, [while considering] the consequences of action and devis[ing] sensible, moral and educative ways of acting" (Harrington & Garrison, 1992, p. 718). Although case situations re-create the rich, varied, and individual contexts of teaching, cases are at the same time indicative of the collective experience of the profession.

Through discussion of real-life cases, teachers prepare as professionals for adverse situations that may arise by extending and testing strategies before problems occur. Engaging with the issues in a case therefore allows teachers to carefully contemplate the impact of a specific strategy and establish a pattern of reflection and culture of inquiry. Through discussion, teachers are afforded the opportunity to listen and respond to the voices of their colleagues, but negotiate for themselves ways to build new information onto old ways of thinking.

❖ THE BENEFITS OF USING CASES

Cases are unique because they allow students to observe how theory actually looks in practice. The cases in this book make the interior of the classroom visible. Readers can enter, pause, reflect, and stop time by puzzling over issues of classroom management, collegial relations, or student behavior. The casebook's format facilitates the entry into educational milieus.

Readers vicariously experience with each case writer the complexity of a unique educational environment. Then, they can step beyond the boundaries of the case itself to query and pose questions about teacher thinking, student behavior, parental relations, and classroom management and to connect to their own emerging experiences. As they are thrust into familiar tensions, demands, and needs that must be addressed on an hourly or even minute-to-minute basis, readers will participate in a "reflective practicum" (Schön, 1987), moving between the inner realm of story and the external realm of critic.

Cases are open discourses upon which readers can build or construct new levels of meaning, enveloping each dilemma in each case with greater understanding. In this way, commentaries also provide and encourage readers to engage in conversations that focus on myriad topics related to the cases. While considering suggestions and possible solutions, testing hypotheses and examining consequences of proposed strategies and actions, or connecting educational themes among cases, readers reflect, analyze, frame, and reframe issues from multiple and diverse perspectives. Through this process, assumptions held for many years are reexamined and new ways to think about old experiences may occur.

❖ HOW THE CASES WERE DEVELOPED: AUTHENTIC TEACHER VOICES

Our initial purpose in developing this book was to find a way to investigate the nature of teachers' professional knowledge and teaching practice. Interested in how educators continually work to support student learning in a variety of contexts, we deliberately identified educators from a wide range of backgrounds and locales as case writers. The case writers are new and experienced teachers, principals, and retirees. While investigating the complexities of each case, you will become aware of the issues that encompass the challenging profession of teaching in school communities today.

The cases were created when 20 practitioners gathered for several days to engage in studying the tenets of the case genre. After writing a "case seed," participants further developed their stories in conjunction with their colleagues and with us. More rounds of reflection, review, and revision followed. At no time did we direct the educators about what they should write. Rather, we set the scene for respectful, thoughtful, open discussion of issues that mattered to each person present. We viewed ourselves as facilitators in support of the process. In this way, all writers' words and thoughts are unique and authentic, unscripted by us.

❖ WHAT ROLE DO COMMENTARIES PLAY?

A commentary is a response made to a case. It could be an echo of an experience reframed and reinterpreted years later. It might be the illumination of a teaching principle that suddenly reveals a crucial decision point. It might be a personal story similar to those in the casebook. Commentaries raise salient questions, possibilities for action, contemplation, and interpretation. They often surprise and delight, making us aware of new paths or responsibilities. They may even challenge how we think about traditional situations and assumptions, causing us to revisit our assumptions and respond to personal professional resonance. Commentaries are stimulating, useful catalysts that foster deeper meaning. As tools for exciting debate or quiet reverie, commentaries propel cases into fresh arenas for learning.

Our cases provide three to five commentaries (occasionally from opposing points of view) on the same topic. They are reflections on, rarely resolutions to, the issues presented in the case.

The commentaries are written by a diverse group of educational experts familiar with the issues embedded within the cases. Their reflections and insights suggest alternative perspectives that may foster your exploration of issues in practice. The commentators have responded to case scenarios, connecting with their own experiences as academic scholars, researchers, teacher-educators, practitioners, or administrators. Each commentator shared her or his interpretation based on professional knowledge and extensive lived experience in the field of teacher education.

Commentators enrich and enhance our understanding of cases. Their responses provide connections with their own psyches, and we borrow their lenses to share in their insights and epiphanies. We benefit from their wisdom, their speculations, and their years of experience. Commentators open new doors of understanding and encourage us to walk in their shoes.

❖ PEDAGOGY

This book is organized around a variety of pedagogical features that were designed to help you engage effectively with the cases and to facilitate your understanding of the educational issues raised by the cases and the commentaries. Each chapter begins with a brief introduction that describes the focus of the case and the details of the commentaries that follow it. Next, **Thinking Ahead** draws your attention to the areas of teacher knowledge and context that will underpin your understanding of the case.

Following each case, we have included a feature entitled **Exploring the Case**, which is designed to facilitate a discussion that will enhance your understanding of the situation (Shulman, Whittaker, & Lew, 2002). The use of "she and he," while it may appear awkward to the reader, is intended to ensure the absence of gender bias. It begins with an **Identification** section that asks you to recognize and illuminate the factual elements presented in the case. Next, we provide a guide for you to form your own **Analysis** of the key issues raised. From here, we move on to an **Evaluation** of the protagonist's strategies for handling the problems as they appear in the narrative. You can then generate **Alternative Solutions** to those dilemmas while considering the problem from a diversity of perspectives. After you work through a discussion of the details, dilemmas, and solutions of the case, you can contemplate the narrative's conclusion with a **Reflection** on the story's resolution.

We then bring the discussion back to you, personally, challenging you to consider if reading and discussing the case results in **Changing Opinions**. To conclude the discussion, **Synthesis** asks you to consolidate your understanding of the cases into a single statement. Before examining the commentaries, we leave you with the question, "*What is this a case of?*" Cases must represent instances of a larger class, *a case of something* (Shulman, 1996), a situation that occurs frequently in schools or classrooms. Teaching cases allows for an investigation of those thoughts, behaviors, relationships, tensions, and interactions that are identifiable to those belonging to the teaching profession. When analyzing a case and considering "what is this a case of?" one's answers will vary and be dependent on the lens through which one views the case. Responses will guide you inward toward your own experiences, actual or vicarious, but also outward toward the broad educational arenas and themes that underpin all teaching situations.

Following each commentary, **Exploring the Issues** challenges you to discuss, engage with, and question the commentators' responses and reactions to the issues raised by the case. At the close of all the commentaries is a final set of questions, **Engaging With the Commentaries**, which offers you an opportunity to compare and contrast the commentators' responses to the case. Finally, in the **Additional Readings** section, we provide a brief case-related annotated bibliography to allow you to explore issues even further.

❖ INTRODUCTION TO THE MATRIX

This book of cases was designed to be used flexibly in a variety of courses. As a tool for tailoring the contents of the book to your needs, we have created a matrix (see Figure I.1) that identifies the educational level, chapter focus, and primary and secondary issues of the case. For students, it can be used as a brief pre-reading overview. For instructors, the chart will help to identify how to integrate the cases into their courses.

(*Text continues on page 12*)

Figure I.1 Case Matrix

Chapter	Title	Level	Focus	Primary Issues	Secondary Issues	Commentators
1	Dealing With Religious Intolerance	Elementary	A principal faced with issues of diversity looks to the school's mission statement for inspiration.	• Religious diversity • School policies • Multiple perspectives • Ethical decision making	• Conflict resolution • Assumptions • Collaboration and leadership	• Judith Lessow-Hurley • Lyn Miller-Lachmann • Poonam C. Dev • Harold Brathwaite
2	Is the Teacher's Gender an Issue in a Kindergarten Classroom?	Elementary	A young teacher wonders if the problems he encounters are gender related.	• Gender issues • Stereotyping • Relationships between teacher and student • Support for new teachers	• School policies • Student learning • Power struggles	• Ellen Moir • Barbara B. Levin • Kristopher Wells • Jerry Lee Rosiek and Becky M. Atkinson • Paul Axelrod
3	Working With a Challenging Student and His Family	Elementary	A teacher works hard to meet the target needs of a challenging child and his father.	• Student behavior • Parental relations • Programming • Teacher self-image	• Schools in society • Support and resources • Developing trust	• Deborah J. Trumbull • David Booth • Peter McLaren and Nathalia Jaramillo • David E. Wilson and Joy S. Ritchie • Janna Dresden

Figure I.1 (Continued)

Chapter	Title	Level	Focus	Primary Issues	Secondary Issues	Commentators
4	Negotiating Different Styles When Two Teachers Share a Class	Elementary	Two teachers who share a classroom have differing approaches to instruction and classroom management.	• Teaching styles • Power struggles • Classroom management • Student culture	• Teacher isolation • Communication breakdown • School policies	• Rita Silverman • Ron Wideman • Cheryl J. Craig
5	Managing Conflict When Working With Educational Partners	Elementary	A teacher finds her or his teaching strategies are challenged by a tutoring company and the parents of a child with special needs.	• Trust relationships • Teacher identity • Strategies and assessments for students with special needs	• Power struggles • Communication	• Becky Wai-Ling Packard • Nancy L. Hutchinson • Anne Jordan
6	A Student Teacher Faces the Challenges of the Classroom	Middle	When a mentor teacher is absent from class, a teacher candidate gains insight into students, colleagues, and herself.	• Classroom management • Identity issues • Power struggles • Support for new teachers	• Gender issues • Communication • Mentoring	• Tom Russell • William J. Hunter • D. Jean Clandinin • Janet L. Miller
7	Engaging in Action Research in the Classroom	Middle	A teacher reflects on the effect an action research project has on a class.	• Student behavior • Teacher support • Action research • Power struggles	• Teacher self-confidence • Reflection • Student behavior under diverse conditions	• Robert E. Stake • Stefinee Pinnegar • Andrea K. Whittaker

Figure I.1 (Continued)

Chapter	Title	Level	Focus	Primary Issues	Secondary Issues	Commentators
8	Evaluating a Teacher's Classroom Management Strategy	Secondary	A teacher's classroom management strategies are questioned when she applies for a permanent teaching credentials.	• Teaching strategies • Relationships with students and colleagues • New teacher support • Classroom management	• Reflection • Teacher self-confidence • Multiple intelligence theory	• Elizabeth Campbell • Iain Munro • Frances Squire • Jay Martin
9	Balancing the Needs of All Students in an Inclusive Classroom	Secondary	An experienced teacher must decide how to balance the needs of all her or his students when one boy presents a challenge.	• Working with students with special needs • Classroom management • Reflection • Teacher support	• Inclusion issues • Privacy issues • Partnerships	• Anna Ershler Richert • Lynne M. Cavazos • Tania Madfes • Linda F. Rhone
10	Implications of Student Cheating for the Teaching Community	Secondary	When a teacher is alerted to evidence of cheating in class, she or he finds that solutions can be complicated.	• School policies • Ethical decision making • Collegial relationships • Power struggles	• Teacher responsibilities • Teacher support	• Jean McNiff • Aria Razfar • Michael Manley-Casimir • James McCracken
11	Challenges Teachers Face When Reentering the Classroom	Secondary	A teacher returning to teaching unexpectedly receives support from a student.	• Classroom dynamics • Teacher confidence • Support networks • Effective teaching	• Teacher self-esteem • Diversity • Communication	• Patrick M. Jenlink • Margaret Olson • A. G. Rud

Figure I.1 (Continued)

Chapter	Title	Level	Focus	Primary Issues	Secondary Issues	Commentators
12	Developing Appropriate Boundaries With a Troubled Student	Secondary	A teacher considers the role she or he plays in the life of a troubled student.	• Professional conduct • Student expectations • Teacher-student relationships	• Gifted students • Student responsibility • Teacher roles • Trust	• John Loughran • Ardra L. Cole • Allen T. Pearson • Janine Remillard
13	School Politics Divide a Community	All levels	The closing of a school causes a superintendent to question the role politics plays in her or his town.	• School policies • School politics • Community partnerships • Ethical decision making • Professional integrity	• Political slogans • Leadership • Reflection	• Michael Dale • Elizabeth Jordan • Fred MacDonald • Ron McNamara

❖ INTRODUCTION TO THE CONNECTING QUESTIONS

Every case in this book is underpinned by a variety of educational issues. The **Connecting Questions** bring forth common themes that are woven throughout several chapters and provide an opportunity to explore the connections among the unique situations presented in the cases.

Connecting Questions

1. Teachers new to the profession will face unexpected challenges. Consider Ms. Wright in "A Student Teacher Faces the Challenges of the Classroom," Pam in "Evaluating a Teacher's Classroom Management Strategy," and the new teacher in "Is the Teacher's Gender an Issue in a Kindergarten Classroom?" Are similar newcomer traits responsible for the difficulties each teacher experiences? Explain your answer and propose what might help each teacher. Determine who was most successful in overcoming the barriers that confronted each teacher.

2. Not all people will share the same set of ethics. The educators in "Implications of Student Cheating for the Teaching Community," "Dealing With Religious Intolerance," and "School Politics Divide a Community" act ethically in difficult situations. In spite of their best efforts, each finds her- or himself at odds with educational partners. What ethical issues come to the forefront and how could the educators have prevented any stakeholder from being left out of the decision-making process?

3. Effective classroom management is the result of many components. Compare and evaluate the teaching strategies in "Challenges Teachers Face When Reentering the Classroom," "Negotiating Different Styles When Two Teachers Share a Class," and "Evaluating a Teacher's Classroom Management Strategy." Consider the reasons for difficulties encountered by each teacher. Consider whether the teachers had fully prepared for their classes and why neither supports nor resources, nor colleagues, ameliorated the situations described.

4. Teaching students responsibility should be a goal of every teacher. In "Implications of Student Cheating for the Teaching Community," "Balancing the Needs of All Students in an Inclusive Classroom," and "Engaging in Action Research in the Classroom," the teachers

involved model exemplary behavior for their classes, yet problems occur. Identify the problems, why they occurred, and what was the long-term impact on students in each case.

5. Collegial relations can put additional strain on teachers. By examining staff relationships in "Challenges Teachers Face When Reentering the Classroom," "A Student Teacher Faces the Challenges of the Classroom," and "Developing Appropriate Boundaries With a Troubled Student," determine why team efforts at the schools benefited (or did not benefit) the teachers described.

6. Students with special needs face unique educational challenges, as do their teachers. The students in "Working With a Challenging Student and His Family," "Managing Conflict When Working With Educational Partners," "Balancing the Needs of All Students in an Inclusive Classroom," and "Developing Appropriate Boundaries With a Troubled Student" must confront unique difficulties because they each have special needs. Examine and evaluate the measures taken by the teacher in each story to meet the needs of Marc, Annie, Scott, and Mel. How does each teacher feel about her or his efforts with the student? Consider the ways that inclusive classrooms are beneficial for all of the students named.

7. Classroom decisions and students can be affected by factors outside of the classroom. Examine those factors in "Negotiating Different Styles When Two Teachers Share a Class," "Managing Conflict When Working With Educational Partners," "Working With a Challenging Student and His Family," and "Is the Teacher's Gender an Issue in a Kindergarten Classroom?" and explain how each factor affects the teacher and the students. Evaluate the teacher's ability to deal effectively (or not) with those elements.

8. Schools are usually structured with policies and rules. In "A Student Teacher Faces the Challenges of the Classroom," "Is the Teacher's Gender an Issue in a Kindergarten Classroom?" and "Implications of Student Cheating for the Teaching Community," identify the school's defining structures and consider why the teachers and students in each case confront difficulties because of them.

9. In deciding whose rights must predominate, it is often necessary that hard choices be made. In "School Politics Divide a Community," "Dealing With Religious Intolerance," and "Balancing the Needs of All Students in an Inclusive Classroom," educators find themselves

at odds—with their communities, with parents, with themselves. Describe and explain these tensions.

10. The teachers in the following cases exhibit particular skills and abilities for coping and thinking about their teaching situations: "Developing Appropriate Boundaries With a Troubled Student," "Managing Conflict When Working With Educational Partners," and "Engaging in Action Research in the Classroom." What qualities are revealed by all of the teachers? What practical steps did each take to deal with the dilemmas he or she faced and to resolve conflicts? Did their special qualities or skills affect their abilities to address tensions?

11. Principals are usually considered to be school leaders; however, leadership can occur at every level. In "Negotiating Different Styles When Two Teachers Share a Class," "Dealing With Religious Intolerance," and "Evaluating a Teacher's Classroom Management Strategy," school administration appears to support teacher autonomy. How valid is this contention in each of the named cases? Has collaboration also been encouraged? If not, why not?

1

Dealing With Religious Intolerance

I n this case, a principal faced with issues of diversity looks to the
school's traditions and its mission statement for inspiration.
Commentators Judith Lessow-Hurley, Lyn Miller-Lachmann, Poonam
C. Dev, and Harold Brathwaite examine issues of religious diversity,
school policies, equity, and parental communication. Although a principal should be a strong leader, collaboration must be an essential element in creating meaningful educational partnerships.

❖ THINKING AHEAD

As you read this chapter, reflect on the following questions and issues:

- Consider the attitudes, skills, and experience of the principal in
  this case.
- What dilemmas occur at this school?

The use of "she and he," while it may appear awkward to the reader, is intended
to ensure the absence of gender bias.

- Consider the diverse cultures in the school, and explain what significant role they play in the formation of the dilemmas in the case.
- What are the pressure points in the case? Why do they occur?

"Jesus Christ is a wicked man," announces one student to another. "Yeah, and Allah is evil; He kills people," is the immediate response. Cindy Greenshaw overhears two fourth-grade elementary students arguing and preparing to fight—students who are usually best friends. Shocked, Cindy freezes in her shoes. She cannot believe what she has just witnessed. In an environment where inclusion of all cultures and faiths is honored, a school where students are taught to celebrate and respect one another, these exclamations surprise, alarm, and anger her. She reflects that these statements are certainly not about peace on earth and goodwill to all people. She stops and ponders for a moment— What season is this? It is, indeed, the end of Ramadan, marked by the celebration of Eid ul-Fitr, and the beginning of Christmas, the Festival of Lights season.

I put down the phone in my office, after having had a rather lengthy conversation with the chair of the Parent Advisory Council about the tenets of Islam, equity, and the curriculum. I feel confident about the conversation. I know my knowledge is grounded in school governance, and I feel reassured and satisfied with my response to her queries.

Interrupting my thoughts, a familiar knock on my office door breaks into my reverie. I hear, "Have you got a minute?" I look up to see the faces of two very concerned teachers. Having been an administrator for more than 8 years, I immediately know the underlying meaning of "Have you got a minute?" It translates into "I need you for an hour or three!"

The two teachers, Mrs. Greenshaw and Mrs. Bhadra, are visibly upset. Mrs. Greenshaw begins, "We need to talk to you about a problem. I overheard Roberta and Mohammed in Miss Wong's class, and I was disturbed by their conversation." She relates the confrontation she observed. For a moment, the room is silent, but Mrs. Greenshaw's trembling voice gives her away as she looks at me for support. "I don't know what to do."

Mrs. Bhadra adds, "I, too, had a rather disturbing conversation with one of our volunteer moms, Mrs. Ali, Rose's mom. She came to see me today, and she was furious because I was teaching Rose Christmas carols. I tried to explain to her that for the Festival of Lights assembly, each grade presents a different festival to the rest of the school, and this year the second graders were doing Christmas. I stressed that the staff endeavor to teach from an antiracist perspective to ensure that all the students can experience a variety of cultural experiences. I showed her how we embed diversity into the curriculum, allotting time equally so that no one culture is left out or elevated more than another. Therefore, during the month of December, we are busy every day with preparations and presentations for Diwali, Christmas, Ramadan and Eid ul-Fitr, Posada, Hanukkah, and Kwanzaa celebrations, and each grade takes responsibility to teach and inform the rest of the school about one particular culture."

"I outlined our integrated approach that links all the areas of the curriculum. I even elaborated how students and teachers invite prominent people from each culture to come in and speak in-depth to the students. For example, we had invited an Imam to visit during Ramadan. The Muslim parents in the community even worked with the school to organize a big Eid ul-Fitr luncheon. And we brought in Jewish storytellers to tell the story of Hanukkah. As a school, we go beyond the eating of ethnic foods, listening to ethnic music, and the wearing of ethnic clothing. We certainly go way beyond the 'holidays and heroes' approach so our students can begin to comprehend diversity."

"I even reminded her that last year, when the second grade's festival was Ramadan, she had come in and helped me with the preparations." Mrs. Bhadra, who speaks with such passion, is almost in tears. "My goodness, Mrs. Ali was so hostile." I could tell that Mrs. Bhadra felt her belief and value system was under attack.

Every year around Christmastime, as the school population increases and the demographics change, we fall into the routine of this sort of tension. Lately, religion takes center stage as the initiator of conflicts. I think about the list of complaints: Muslin parents refusing to send their children to school to celebrate Christmas; one critic returning his son's weekly spelling list because the sheet was decorated with a Santa Claus; others complaining about carol singing, especially if Jesus's name is mentioned. Yet, for many of the students, especially the Spanish-speaking students whose families celebrate Posada, the baby Jesus plays a big part in their tradition. So how could we even consider censoring his name?

I glance across my desk to see two good women, fine and admirable teachers, so angry, so frustrated, now depleted, and at a loss for words. As I listen to their concerns, I realize the potential of this problem.

As a staff, we are all committed to having a strong sense of equity and social justice. It is embedded in our mission statement and in everything that we value as a staff, hence the teachers' frustration. As a Band-Aid solution to reassure them that our value system is not faulty, I engage the teachers in a dialogue about equity and commitment. Mrs. Greenshaw, a new teacher, looks puzzled and unsure as she makes this comment: "Are we really doing the right thing?" I quote from the school's mission statement to support the position we take at our school.

Commitment to equitable and respectful treatment is very important in a school like ours, as the ethnic, religious, linguistic, and cultural backgrounds are as diverse as the United Nations. We have students from Somalia, the English-speaking Caribbean, South and Southeast Asia, Latin America, Europe, Kuwait, Iraq, Afghanistan, Ukraine, and Russia. There are over 25 different nationalities! Interestingly, 85 percent of our students are born to immigrant parents. Fifteen percent of our students are themselves immigrants or refugees, newly arrived and intending to become citizens when their residency period has been fulfilled. We celebrate diversity daily.

On most days, I know that our students get along fairly well. My mind moves from the students to the staff as I question how well prepared the staff members were to manage this kind of direct attack on diverse values, curriculum expectations, teaching practice, and students' learning. I exhale slowly and review our teaching strategies.

We believe in the teaching of inclusion from all aspects. The staff takes pride in ensuring that the students see themselves not only in the classroom, but also in the curriculum. We use materials and human resources that reinforce and validate our students' life experiences. We take great care to make certain that learning experiences are relevant and connected to the students' lives. With that philosophical approach, how can this conversation be taking place among my students at this particular school? I ruminate. Where is this coming from? What or who is fueling this kind of intolerance?

My mind races back to the potential "forest fire" that I might be facing. To calm myself, I reflect on the players who have perpetuated this dilemma. I could imagine Rose's parents, who are devoutly religious, asking, "Has Allah ever been insulted?" I could imagine the diatribe of Mrs. Cortez, the chair of the Parent Advisory Council, if she got wind that Jesus's name was being defamed. My mind's eye captures her, always handing out Christian pamphlets to the secretaries and the teachers. She prides herself on knowing her rights and taking every opportunity to let the staff know that she has the ears of the school trustee and superintendent and intends to act when she thinks that she has a cause to complain, complain, complain.

This situation troubles me further. If it had occurred under my former superintendent, I would not have felt overly concerned. She understood the complexities of equity, poverty, and the ongoing tensions of managing a diverse school. She had expressed her support, and I had earned her respect and trust. She would say, "I have confidence in your abilities and skills as an educational leader." I wondered, however, about the present superintendent, brand new to the family of schools, what would her reaction be? I doubt that she will laugh it off, asserting her trust in my reputation and ability. Perhaps she will also be terrified of provoking a forest fire and micromanage, undermining my management skills. I feel the weight of the world on my shoulders. There is no way of knowing how she will react.

I slump down in my chair, refocusing not on the complaints but on our guiding philosophy, one I truly believe in. We live in a multicultural society. We have to model respect for all human beings. Children, I believe, are capable of acknowledging other religions, without feeling they are being converted.

In spite of my lofty aspirations, I wondered, how then does a school cope with this kind of intolerance when it comes from the home? How can public schools adequately prepare children to live in a global society?

❖ EXPLORING THE CASE

A principal with 20 years of experience wrote this case.

Identification

Identify the key facts of this case. What factual events are central to understanding the situation? Identify the dilemmas and tensions in this case. Explore the main aspects of each dilemma and tension.

Analysis

Analyze the issue(s) from the viewpoints of the different people in the case. Identify and compare the clash between parental and school values. Why is it important for the principal to present strong leadership?

Evaluation

Examine critically the principal's strategies for handling the challenge(s). Does the principal depicted fulfill, fall short of, or surpass your notion of the role of a community leader?

Alternative Solutions

Were there alternative solutions or strategies available to deal with the school's dilemmas? Generate alternative solutions to the ones presented in the narrative. Take into consideration risks, benefits, and long- and short-term consequences of each proposed action.

Reflection

The principal is very philosophical at the end of the story, moving outwards to thoughts on diversity and its place in the larger scheme of life. Has anything been resolved or learned through the school's experience?

Changing Opinions

Consider your thoughts and assumptions at the beginning of the chapter. Who or what has caused you to consider a new way of thinking? How strongly do you still feel about your previous assumptions?

Synthesis

Synthesize your understanding of this case into a statement. What is this a case of?

Case Commentary by Judith Lessow-Hurley

Bullivant (1993) suggests that human beings construct culture to respond to physical, social, and metaphysical environments. Adaptations to the metaphysical environment, which include our religious assumptions and practices, are perhaps the deepest and most difficult to discern. This case explores the conflicts that can arise when public school assumptions and practices conflict with those deeply held value systems.

The case raises a key dilemma: If, indeed, religion is an essential adaptation to a particular environment, in other words, if religion is an essential aspect of culture, is it possible to create a school environment that is reflective of and responsive to diverse communities without some acknowledgment of religion? For example, is a classroom for students with Mexican heritage truly responsive if it denies the Virgin of Guadalupe, patron saint of Mexico? On the other hand, can the curriculum acknowledge religion in the classroom without promoting one faith tradition over another, or without promoting religion in general?

The principal and school in this case have acknowledged that it is important to teach students about religious traditions. This is most appropriately addressed with sensitivity in the social studies, art, and music. Bringing in community members and clerics, however, to describe their faith traditions is problematic. There is always a risk that even well-briefed speakers will promote or be perceived as promoting their particular faiths.

Religion in American Life (Butler, Wacker, & Balmer, 2003) is an excellent series of books designed for middle school and secondary students that includes nine volumes about significant world religions. *Taking Religion Seriously Across the Curriculum* (Nord & Haynes, 1998) offers thoughtful guidelines and useful guidelines about how to incorporate religion into the curriculum in manners that are both content and age appropriate.

Despite a stated desire to avoid the "tacos and chitlins" approach to multiculturalism, this school overemphasizes holidays, and in doing so, has opened itself to justifiable criticism and controversy. In their approach, the principal and teachers are making assumptions about what constitutes normal assumptions and practice. For example, December is not everyone's "holiday season." To assume so is to engage in a subtle but important form of "Christo-centricity." Jews, for example, celebrate the High Holy Days of Rosh Hashanah and Yom Kippur in the fall. Because of the nature of the lunar calendar and the way Muslims keep time, Ramadan can occur in any season. The principal's perspective is restated in a comment later in the discussion: "Every year around Christmastime . . . we fall into the routine of this sort of tension." The principal appears unaware that it's not Christmastime for everyone.

Also, the nature of the holiday celebration in the school suggests erroneous assumptions about the comparable magnitude and nature of various celebrations. For example, whereas Hanukkah has taken on greater significance in recent years, it is still considered a minor festival. If the school were to oblige a Jewish holiday with significance comparable to that of Christmas, it would probably be Rosh Hashanah, the Jewish New Year. Any attempt to honor holiday celebrations in the curriculum must be based in true understanding of the meaning and importance of those celebrations.

Responding to a parent's concern about the use of an image of Santa Claus on a child's paper, the principal expresses surprise that a parent might take offense. Although Santa Claus is certainly a secular figure, there can hardly be any doubt that the image is associated with Christmas. This approach is insensitive to the experience of a member of a minority faith community in December, when the world is awash in images of Christmas, which is, ultimately, a religious holiday.

This school's administration and faculty might consider rethinking their approach to introducing religion into the curriculum. To that end, they might

- Reflect on the ways that they introduce religion covertly. Considering religious traditions only in December is one example; marking papers with Santa Claus images, another. It's easy to imagine that these are but two of many ways that this school communicates an exclusionary point of view.
- Consider how to carefully introduce religion overtly, in the social studies, music, and art curricula.
- Work on strategies for introducing religious traditions to young students. Although best practice suggests experiential learning, role-playing and acting out religious practices can be controversial, and hands-on activities have to be approached with caution.
- Move away from holiday celebrations and discussion of traditions in keeping with holiday calendars and encourage teaching about religion, as it is relevant to historical and social content.
- Develop a basic understanding of the world's major religious traditions, as well as any religious traditions represented in the school population. It is almost impossible to develop in-depth knowledge of faith traditions without years of study, but familiarity will assist teachers in avoiding pitfalls and engage students in learning about religion in positive and useful ways.

Finding Common Ground (Haynes & Thomas, 2001) is written from the perspective of the United States Constitution and in the context of schooling in the United States, but it provides a good overview of the issues. Given the protections for freedom of conscience and religion in Canada, it might be an excellent framework for professional development.

❖ EXPLORING THE ISSUES

Religious Diversity

Lessow–Hurley says, "This case explores . . . value systems." She juxtaposes the notions of schools being responsive to *or* reflecting diverse religions. In this situation, which is the case: responsive or reflective, both, or neither? Why is either stance problematic for multi-cultural groups?

Collaboration

Lessow–Hurley provides many suggestions for bringing together the school community; however, the students appear to be left out of the debate on religious diversity. How could they become educational partners and have their learning impacted at the same time? What model could be created that could benefit student learning?

Multiple Perspectives

Lessow–Hurley provides several resources to remedy the conflict in her commentary. How could these resources contribute to conversations on a parents' night or even stimulate a resolution of school conflicts? How would resources such as these begin to explore "erroneous assumptions?"

Case Commentary by Lyn Miller-Lachmann

At present, 10 percent of Americans and 18 percent of Canadians were born abroad; the percentage is far higher in urban areas. Schools have responded to this increasing diversity in different ways. Many have chosen what James Banks terms the "contributions" approach, emphasizing ethnic foods, heroes, and holidays without changing the content or structure of the curriculum or involving students and parents in the decision-making process (Banks, 2003). The principal in this case study has consciously gone beyond the "holidays and heroes" approach in creating a multicultural curriculum; ironically, it is the celebration of a holiday season that brings out suspicion, intolerance, and conflict.

Those who seek to restrict multicultural education to "contributions" invite this kind of situation, for even holidays or heroes can tap into deeply held beliefs that come into conflict. In spite of the young children's remarks, both Muslims and Jews consider Jesus Christ a great man if not the Messiah, and Allah is the Arabic word for God. Still, one cannot blame a newcomer parent, or a member of a cultural or religious minority, for feeling threatened when his or her child is being led to celebrate a holiday that may run counter to fundamental beliefs.

The principal has created a school climate that respects diversity and models that respect through the way the staff members treat each other, children, and parents as well as through a curriculum that is inclusive. But the principal's shock and dismay points to the fact that the school cannot control everything about a student's life. The school did not contribute to the circumstances that drove the family from its country of origin, and it did not force the family to adapt to life in a community very different from the one it left. However, schools and other community institutions have become the often-contested territory where people with widely divergent values meet.

The principal seeks to "model respect for all human beings" and believes that "children . . . are capable of acknowledging other religions, without feeling they are being converted." But the malleability and natural acceptance that characterize young children are a source of concern for their parents. Immigrant parents like Mrs. Ali and Mrs. Cortez fear their children will be converted or otherwise estranged from the family and its values in a new country, and they do what they do to hold on to their children and their culture at a time in which they have already given up so much.

In creating a climate that accepts and promotes diversity, teachers and administrators must be sensitive to the concerns of immigrant parents and parents who may perceive themselves as members of a beleaguered minority. This does not imply giving space to expressions of intolerance. Rather, administrators, as educational leaders, must work with other community organizations—churches, synagogues, mosques, public libraries, social service agencies, and political leaders, among others—to help newcomers adjust to a society often far more diverse and very different from the ones they left. This means helping parents find a place within the school and coming to an understanding that regardless of our cultural and religious differences, "we are all in this together," building lives and communities and raising children in a new land.

❖ EXPLORING THE ISSUES

School Policies

From the narrative, Miller-Lachmann points out that the principal has gently put into place policies that should promote diversity and respect. Although, as the principal writes, "the school climate . . . respects diversity and models respect," what does the conversation between the two fourth graders reveal about the principal's knowledge of the success of school policies? What does Miller-Lachmann suggest to apprise oneself of the success or failure of school policies and programs?

Collaboration

In her commentary, Miller-Lachmann addresses the principal's lofty goals for the school. As a way to deal with societal conflict, however, school may become the battlefield. How might a school prepare for dealing with changing attitudes that might not be in sync with parental religious views before problems occur?

Leadership

Miller-Lachmann points out the need to be sensitive to diversity. How can a principal showcase respect for multiculturalism? Consider what leadership means for teachers and school administration in dealing with immigrant families. Why is it important to model leadership at multiple levels for students?

Multiple Perspectives

Miller-Lachmann comments on the multicultural populations that create schoolyards of diversity and refers to Banks's criticism of the "contribution" approach. Why might a school population reject or accept policies or even mission statements? What role could a school community play in these areas?

Case Commentary by Poonam C. Dev

What do diversity and inclusion really mean? The context as well as one's experiences and philosophies are sure to play a significant role in how these two terms are defined. These terms are sometimes overused and popular in documents across educational institutions today. Schools and other academic institutions usually have a "diversity statement" in student or parent handbooks, statements that have probably been crafted after much deliberation by a group of well-meaning individuals. Administrators are usually quick to show such statements—sometimes with pride—to employees and students as well as to parents anytime the issues of diversity and inclusion are raised, however informal the conversation might be.

In the case—written from the point of view of a school administrator—the principal reflects upon issues of diversity and inclusion as well as what they mean for the school. The principal is asked to assist with a situation faced by two teachers. The administrator clearly feels that the teachers have taken every step necessary to make all the children in the school feel that they belong by planning numerous activities related to a variety of cultures, for example, celebrating religious festivals. Although clearly with the best of intentions, this principal, like many administrators, seems to focus more on treating all cultures equally than on one of the main tenets of antiracist behavior, that of equity. Although the principal discusses equity and social justice with the teachers, she or he admits that the action taken is only a tactic to patch the situation and not a permanent solution. This would have been the ideal context in which to facilitate a discussion and encourage reflection upon what the school's mission statement means to the teachers. What does it mean to a teacher when school personnel, parents, or students raise issues related to inclusion and diversity? How are cultures defined? Are religious and ethnic groups the only cultural groups in schools? What about children who have special physical, intellectual, or emotional challenges? What about those who are considered radical thinkers or whose families are not considered typical in their school?

The principal says that "equitable and respectful treatment is very important" but seems satisfied with the superficial level of cultural understanding prevalent at this school. The school's focus seems to be on tolerating rather than respecting differences in individuals, and the differences seem to be based primarily on ethnic and religious backgrounds, rather than any other characteristics. Teachers and administrators would be more effective in promoting an atmosphere of mutual respect and understanding by focusing on each individual student, parent, and school employee, rather than on just a few characteristics that make each individual whole. They could help facilitate a deeper understanding of the impact of one's culture on behaviors, learning styles, and perspectives among all members of the school community.

The scenarios described by the principal would be ideal prompts for engaging teachers in discussions—among themselves as well as among their students—about how each person is different and yet similar to others in so many ways and what that means for everyone. Celebrating various religious festivals; meeting people from various ethnic, religious, linguistic, and other backgrounds; eating a variety of cuisines; and similar situations are only starting points for creating awareness and enhancing understanding about differences in all of us. It cannot be the only strategy used for preparing children or anyone else to communicate effectively and succeed in a global society. Words and tone of voice used by teachers as well as their interactions with visibly different students are noted by students themselves and can play a major role in influencing student behaviors.

As we all know, one learns best by doing, especially if the activity or topic is personally or professionally relevant. Hence, just writing or talking about diversity and inclusion is not enough to truly reflect on the terms and what they mean for individuals as well as for society. Instances described by this principal could have been and should be used as teaching moments by the teachers, parents, and students involved to help them effectively examine and perhaps resolve their own philosophies and beliefs. Frequent introspection as well as ongoing reflection and discussion on diversity and inclusion by all individuals in the learning community would also help enhance understanding of and respect for one another. The principal seems to have the students' best interest at heart and to truly believe in the benefits of a multicultural society; but the whole school would benefit if these beliefs could be incorporated at a deeper level in the curriculum and communicated effectively to all students and parents as well as school employees.

❖ EXPLORING THE ISSUES

Communication

Dev alludes to the way in which slogans and words become meaningless. How can the words from a school's mission statement be made real and observable in the school?

Equity

Dev seems to draw our attention to the difference between *tolerating* and *respecting* differences in an education community. How might *teaching* and *reflection* add important dimensions to the aim of imparting equity and social justice in a school environment?

Case Commentary by Harold Brathwaite

I will adopt an unusual approach to this case study, one that more accurately reflects what I suspect many of us do as we read a case study. We have immediate reactions and then, later, we engage in a more broad-based, in-depth analysis.

The title, "Dealing With Religious Intolerance," immediately influences my mind-set, and yet the opening paragraph is paradoxical: Two fourth-grade students seemingly denounce the spiritual leaders of other's religions, a teacher appears not to know what to do, and there are references to an inclusive school environment in which of all faiths and cultures are honored. The first questions that come to mind are these:

- What are the real issues between the students (friends) that led to name-calling, and is this really an issue of intolerance or one of students knowing which buttons to push?
- Why did teacher Cindy Greenshaw not intervene immediately?
- Did her failure to do so reflect a lack of skill or training in how to handle unacceptable, antisocial behavior?
- Was her incapacity due to fear of racist or cultural overtones?
- The second paragraph, in which the principal refers to her or his conversation with the chair of the School Advisory Council, is also troubling, and gives rise to the following questions:

Why is the principal having such a heavy-duty conversation on the telephone?

Why not face-to-face where a more intercultural exchange could occur, thus reducing the chance of a misunderstanding?

What is the context of the principal's queries?

Is this the first time the chairperson of the council (in the context of this school) has engaged in a discussion about Islam, equity, and so on?

A further concern is the principal's assertion that "I know my knowledge is grounded in school governance." This is more than a matter of governance; it involves human rights, it involves an understanding of what's needed for social cohesion in the school and community. It is more than feeling "satisfied with my response to her queries." More important, does the chairperson understand and is she satisfied with the responses to her queries? Recourse to governance and regulations rarely provide an adequate solution.

The entry of the two teachers, Mrs. Greenshaw and Mrs. Bhadra, adds a bit of context but raises the level of concern even further. Since we now learn that the incident occurred in Miss Wong's class, was she aware of it, or did Mrs. Greenshaw bring it to her attention? Why are they discussing Mrs. Greenshaw's problem with the principal before or without involving Miss Wong?

Attention now shifts to Mrs. Bhadra's recent experience with Mrs. Ali. Mrs. Bhadra's description of her classroom practice appears to be exemplary, but what leaps to mind is the following:

- What prior communication has occurred with the parents of her students about the curriculum content and classroom activities involving cross-cultural practices?
- Were parents informed at the beginning of the year about the board and school philosophy?
- Were parents invited to help explain to newcomer parents what the school was trying to do?
- Were newsletters sent home to remind and alert parents to ensure that they were not surprised or did not get "stories" out of context?

The principal's conversations and reflections about the school environment and practice also raise the same questions at the macro level. She or he asks a question previously raised: How well prepared are staff members? One may well add—How well prepared are parents and students? Indeed, in some schools a student who has been trained in peer mediation, on overhearing the exchange Mrs. Greenshaw reported, would have intervened to help defuse the conflict.

Not surprisingly, the principal's angst leads her or him to worry about a worst-case scenario. In this instance, the anxiety is also at a personal level about how the district superintendent would react to the way in which the situation is being handled or not handled. This also suggests that the superintendent has not been brought into the loop about the processes and practices of the school. It is usually a better strategy to make the superintendent and trustee aware of a potential problem at the outset and outline the plan of action.

These two incidents could be handled separately without distressing the entire school. At the very least, the two students and their parents should be involved in a discussion, with a minimum outcome of an apology to each other and to the other students in the vicinity at the time of the incident. Although suggested for secondary students, a model with relevance for elementary students is included in *Changing Perspectives: A Resource Guide for Antiracist and Ethnocultural-Equity Education:* "Students discuss the reasons for putdowns, whether based on race, culture, or some other characteristic. Students can use role playing, group discussion, creative writing, etc., to increase their awareness of the issues involved. They should come to realize that the initiator, the recipient of the putdown, and observers who passively accept it are all harmed" (Bidari & Ijaz, 1992).

In the case of Mrs. Ali, the principal needs to find a way to speak with her. The Imam who knows the school could also be invited to the meeting. This would ensure her comfort level, and the Imam could help her better understand the approach of the school.

The questions raised above demonstrate the need for the following:

- In-depth, expert training (including simulations) of staff in schools about antiracist education and ethnocultural equity that would help them explore their own areas of discomfort. It should also assist in ensuring that all problems are not labeled as deriving from intolerance or discrimination.
- Parents, students, and volunteers must be brought into the dialogue, and communications and dialogue must frequently be renewed, especially for the benefit of those new to the school.
- All behaviors of intolerance or discrimination should be addressed immediately.
- Proactive planning is always preferable to reactive scrambling.

❖ EXPLORING THE ISSUES

Assumptions

Brathwaite finds the first exclamations in the case paradoxical. What do the opening words by the students suggest in terms of student learning about intolerance and the principal's assumptions of acceptance of school diversity?

Leadership

Brathwaite asks very pointed questions about the principal's preparation and the communication with parents. How can a member of the administration fully prepare for meetings that concern parents' or guardians' strong opinions on religion?

School Policies

In discussing the school policies, Brathwaite presumes that the principal in this case follows protocol. Brathwaite, however, also poses questions about communication with parents. Why are these steps important in and out of the school itself?

❖ ENGAGING WITH THE COMMENTARIES

School Policies

Why is a holidays-and-heroes approach to creating truly collaborative communities a Band-Aid and temporary solution for resolving deeper issues? Examine Lessow-Hurley's, Miller-Lachmann's, and Dev's concrete examples and reasons for failure of this approach in the case and in schools generally.

Religious Diversity

How would each commentator above comment on the school as a suitable context for applying lessons of tolerance? Compare their insights.

Conflict Resolution

Compare and contrast Brathwaite's four points and Lessow-Hurley's five-point program for addressing the issues of acceptance of religious diversity in schools. Is one preferable to the other? Explain why. Could the reader add to the points?

Multiple Perspectives

Compare and contrast the commentators' views of the principal. Which commentator's view do you accept: enabling or responsible for the breakdown of communication? How might this school community continue to develop into accepting diversity and tolerance?

Connecting Questions

The Connecting Questions located in the introduction highlight themes that are threaded throughout the cases. You may continue your exploration of the issues raised in this case by addressing those connections. For questions pertinent to this case, please see questions 2, 9, and 11.

❖ ADDITIONAL READINGS

Begley, P. (1999). Guiding values for future school leaders. *Orbit, 30*(10), 19–23.

There are 13 articles that address the challenges principals face en route to school improvement. Working with staff, implementing new educational policy, involving parents and community groups, along with an overview of developing leadership on the national level are among the topics presented.

Cohen, E. G. (1986). *Designing group work: Strategies for the heterogeneous classroom.* New York: Teachers College Press.

Designed for many levels, this book examines the challenges of using group work. The authors focus on improving practice and engaging groups collaboratively. Helpful strategies are discussed.

Coles, R. (2000). *Lives of moral leadership.* New York: Random House.

Pulitzer Prize–winning author Robert Coles creates portraits of moral leadership through the narratives of Robert Kennedy, Dietrich Bonhoeffer, Erik Erikson, a Boston bus driver, and teachers in college and in elementary school, among others. Coles explains how one single person can influence an individual's life and change its course. He explores how every person can be engaged in a continual process of personal leadership development.

Delpit, L. (1988). The silenced dialogue: Power and pedagogy in educating other people's children. *Harvard Educational Review, 58*(3), 280–298.

The author looks at meeting the needs of poor and black students. Social justice is at the forefront.

Dow, I. I., & Oakley, W. F. (1992). School effectiveness and leadership. *The Alberta Journal of Educational Research, 38*(1), 33–47.

With a focus on both theory and practice, the book examines the relationship between a principal's style and educational context. Data from questionnaires explain and measure the principal's effectiveness as a leader.

Harper, H. (1997). Difference and diversity in Ontario schooling. *Canadian Journal of Education, 22*(2), 192–206.

The author discusses diversity indepth. She begins with a historical perspective of the production and treatment of human difference in Canadian school policy and practices.

Haynes, F. (1998). *The ethical school.* New York: Routledge.

This very popular book used in most courses on ethics presents case studies that address conflicts that occur routinely in school communities such as issues of dress, censorship, and punishment.

Kouzes, J. M., & Posner, B. (2002). *The leadership challenge.* San Francisco: Jossey-Bass.

The book describes what successful leaders hold in common: challenging the process, sharing a vision, enabling others to act, modeling strategies, and encouragement that is heartfelt and authentic. The book challenges the usual concepts of leadership.

Lee, C. (2003, June/July). Why we need to think race and ethnicity. *Educational Researcher, 32*(5).

Lee's editorial in the journal presents historical and contemporary ways in which cultures differ and are made political footballs for researchers. Her critical stance probes for reasons.

Sergiovanni, T. J. (2000). *The lifeworld of leadership: Creating culture, community and personal meaning in our schools.* San Francisco: Jossey-Bass.

The author explores the link between the character of schools and school improvement. He discusses the levels of interaction that occur in schools: loyalties, compromises, stakeholder needs, upholding standards, and so on. With an aim to develop improved "thoughtfulness" in students, the book examines the virtues associated with good schools and good teaching.

Shapiro, J. P., & Stefkovich, J. A. (2001). *Ethical leadership and decision making in education: Applying theoretical perspectives to complex dilemmas.* Hillsdale, NJ: Lawrence Erlbaum.

This book contains the authors' draw on the ethical paradigms of justice, care, critique, and the teaching profession. It addresses practical, pedagogical, and curricular issues.

Shulman, J., & Mesa-Bains, M. (Eds.). (1993). *Diversity in the classroom: Casebook for teachers and teacher-educators.* San Francisco: FarWest Lab.

The framework of Exploring the Case was adapted from this book.

Trueba, H. T., Au Hu-Pei, K., & Guthrie Pung, G. (Eds.). (1981). *Culture and the bilingual classroom: Studies in classroom ethnography.* Rowley, MA: Newbury House.

This is a collection of 13 papers divided into 2 sections: "General Theoretical and Methodological Issues" and "Microethnic Culture Children in the Classroom." Issues in the classroom concerning cultural diversity, bilingual education, culturally responsive education, validity, and the importance of ethnography for many diverse groups are explored.

2

Is the Teacher's Gender an Issue in a Kindergarten Classroom?

I n this case, a new teacher wonders if the problems he encounters are gender related. The case commentators Ellen Moir, Barbara B. Levin, Kristopher Wells, Jerry Lee Rosiek and Becky M. Atkinson, and Paul Axelrod engage in a case discussion by examining present issues of gender, stereotyping, school, and societal concerns.

❖ THINKING AHEAD

As you read this chapter, reflect on the following questions and issues:

- Consider the knowledge, skills, attitudes, and experience of the teacher. How does he prepare for his new assignment?
- Consider the contextual elements of the school and the class that affect the dilemmas this teacher faces.

The use of "she and he," while it may appear awkward to the reader, is intended to ensure the absence of gender bias.

- What challenges does Hannah pose for this teacher? What conflicts or dilemmas might arise because of the teacher's gender?
- Consider the role of school administration in the kindergarten classroom.

"You are a new teacher to the school. Is this your first year of teaching?" inquires Hannah's mother. I could tell that both she and her daughter were very anxious about the looming start of the school year.

"Yes, I'm very eager to begin teaching. I am from out of town, but I have heard so much about the city and the school community," I respond nervously. "What are Hannah's favorite toys? Does she like puzzles? Well, I look forward to seeing her next week. Thanks for the coffee and cookies."

"Hannah, come out from behind the couch and say good-bye to your teacher," Mrs. Wilkens demands, as Hannah ducks behind her mother's skirt. "Don't worry, all of the children are a little timid at first," I say. "Bye Hannah. See you in school."

I collect the toys that I have brought from the classroom and make my way hurriedly to the front hall. This is my last home visit to the children in my class. Next week, they will begin their entrance into the world of education, and I will make my debut as their kindergarten teacher.

"One more thing before you go," adds Mrs. Wilkens. "My husband and I were discussing how you were going to be Hannah's teacher, and, well, we were expecting a female teacher. And you are a man, fresh out of college. Why would you *want* to teach kindergarten?"

The nerve! My first instinct is to respond sarcastically: *"It's part of my probation, you know, community service."* But I restrain myself and casually remark, "Yes, I am male. And I am professionally trained to educate kindergarten children as well as I am trained to teach the sixth grade. I look forward to meeting the daily challenges 5-year-olds will throw my way. Have a great day. Don't forget to label Hannah's backpack!" I force a smile, turn, and depart.

Why didn't I take that sixth-grade position that I was offered in Hillsdale? Sure, it was an isolated town, but now I'm stuck in the suburbs of Williamstown, teaching kindergarten with parents whose first impression is that since I am a man teaching young children I must have ulterior motives. I am beginning to experience serious reservations regarding my choice of grade.

As I trudge home from that final home visit, troubled by Hannah's mother's probing questions, the words from my principal upon signing my contract resonate in my head: "You are taking a historic journey as the first male teacher in the kindergarten." I guess I was, perhaps, a little too naive to anticipate the struggles that would lie ahead.

Filled with fear and apprehension, I put the final touches on the calendar board in my classroom. How would I respond to the student who gives me a big hug? My eyes wander around the class as I do my final room inspection before the children arrive. Suddenly, I notice a second door in my room. Hey, that's cool. I have my own washroom in my class. Suddenly my delight turns to dread. Oh no! Four- and 5-year-olds are toilet trained, aren't they?

Unfortunately, my imagined fears materialize by the end of September. The children, warming up to me, seek normal childhood affection, be it a hug, touching my leg, holding my hand when we go outside, or wanting to crawl onto my lap for a story. A short time ago, a kindergarten teacher wouldn't think twice about these innocent gestures, but society has changed. Worried about the potential repercussions of these demonstrative childhood behaviors, I deflect every attempt at these shows of affection, each time wondering if I am doing a grave disservice to the children. Am I robbing them of a spontaneous gesture of affection that they need? Affections they would readily receive from a female teacher?

The first snow falls in November, and I eagerly anticipate the fun games we will play outside. The change of season, however, brings with it additional clothing: Gloves. No problem. Hats. A piece of cake. Snow pants? Oh! Oh! A plethora of problems. I wonder if it is possible to put on pants without inadvertently brushing the children's limbs? I remember the first time I heard a child giggle while I was assisting her with her snow pants, and my hand barely grazed her knee. I stopped dead in my tracks. But thankfully, she was laughing at Johnny across the hall. He had put his gloves on backwards.

Fears of false accusations from students and parents trouble my thoughts on a daily basis. I am aware that children have wild imaginations, and I don't want to leave anything that I do open to interpretation. I try to ensure that I am in full view of another adult at all times. Am I so worried about incorrect perceptions that I purposely spill paint on the table before the bell rings just to have the custodian come into the room when I dress the children for home time? He could serve as my witness if any child accuses me of inappropriate acts.

With the Christmas break comes word of a new student. Brad has Down Syndrome and has had minimal toilet training. Funding is not immediately available for a full-time educational assistant so I am expected to change him when he has an accident. I've been told to keep the classroom door open at all times, but what about the washroom door? I wrestle with this issue, as it adds to all of the other worries that I am plagued with because I am a man teaching kindergarten.

My paranoia is getting the best of me, and I was not looking forward to my first interviews with parents. I have already heard the murmurs in the hallway: "He's cute. And sure he'd make a great father. But do you think he is—what kind of man would want to teach small children?" Surprisingly, my fears do not materialize, and I survive the interviews relatively unscathed. In fact, most comments are positive in nature regarding my role as a male in the classroom. Some parents are actually looking forward to having younger siblings register in my class next September. Was I really coping in what was normally seen to be a woman's world?

May 12th. A Monday. It is the annual fundraising tradition at St. Suburb School. Children raise money, and for every donation they receive a ballot to have lunch away from school property with their favorite teacher. Jennifer is elated when I select her name from my class. She is an extroverted child who has shown no problem handling new situations. I suggest we go to The Keg, but, like a typical child, she is eager to get to McDonald's to feast on a Happy Meal, courtesy of me. I tell her mother that we will go on Friday. Casual day means that I will be wearing jeans, just perfect for a lunchtime trip to the local McDonald's.

When Jennifer's mother drops her off early, she repeats incessantly that her daughter is overly excited about having lunch with me. In the eyes of a 5-year-old, she has just won the lottery. Jennifer loudly proclaims that she doesn't want her mother to accompany us to lunch. At 11:30 a.m., we leave for the restaurant.

Jennifer has a love for reading and rambles on nonstop in my car about her favorite story characters. However, her comfort level abruptly changes when we must wait in line to order. Amidst a packed lunchtime crowd, her voice becomes tremulous and she whispers, "I want my Mommy. I want to go home." Her arms start to flail from side to side, and I immediately realize that I have to try to calm her down, order lunch, and get back to school as quickly as possible. In desperation, I use the trustworthy bribe of a toy from a Happy Meal, but to no avail. As we finally sit down, the quiet concerns of an anxious child quickly escalate to hysterical screams, "I WANT MY MOM. I WANT MY DAD." Her cries shake the restaurant as if over the loudspeaker so that all the listening patrons hear her wailing. Defensively, I turn to my suspicious audience and attempt to explain that the sobbing child is my student, and that I am her teacher. But whoops, I am a *male* teacher. I quickly realize that this probably does not look too good. Hurriedly, wrapping up the discarded hamburgers, I decide to return to school as fast as we can exit the restaurant.

But Jennifer refuses to budge. I must carry her, bodily, to my car. It isn't until I pull into the school parking lot that I notice my limbs are no longer shaking. The rest of the school day runs smoothly, and at pickup time, Jennifer's mother and I share a laugh about Jennifer's sudden outburst at McDonald's.

It is 4½ hours later when I am awakened from my daily nap at my apartment (If you have ever taught kindergarten, you'll understand why I needed a nap) by a loud knock at the door upstairs. I had just moved into the basement apartment, so I am slow to my feet in finding my way to the door. I am unsure if upon opening the door, the ticking I hear is from the kitchen clock or from my pounding heart. Three police cruisers are in my driveway, two police at the front door, and two police at the back. I am dumbfounded. Soon, I realize my predicament as the officers explain that an arrest warrant has been issued for an alleged kidnapping.

Apparently, the manager at McDonald's had been watching my car as I left the parking lot, and six people had called the police from the restaurant, and three others had written down my license plate number. When police followed up on the concern from patrons in the restaurant, my license listed my former place of residence—where I no longer lived.

The empty house and the fact that I was last seen dragging a child kicking and screaming into a car quickly raised their alarm. An all-points bulletin was issued for my vehicle and border crossings were alerted. The police were even prepared to release a surveillance video of me to the media in time for the nightly news. It was early evening when I accompanied the officers in the cruiser that day. Once more, my limbs began to tremble uncontrollably.

I kept asking myself one question. If I had been a woman, would the events have unfolded as they did?

❖ EXPLORING THE CASE

A teacher who has taught for 8 years wrote this case.

Identification

Identify the key facts of this case. What factual events are central to understanding the situation? Identify the dilemmas and tensions in this case. Explore the main aspects of each dilemma and tension.

Analysis

Analyze the issue(s) from the viewpoints of the different people in the case. What questions should this teacher ask that require deeper knowledge of teaching principles. How effectively does this teacher cope in and out of his classroom? What educational themes are revealed by the teacher's interactions with the class, and both school and home communities?

Evaluation

Examine critically the teacher's strategies for handling the challenge(s). Does the teacher depicted fulfill, fall short of, or surpass your notion of the role of a teacher?

Alternative Solutions

Were there alternative solutions or strategies available to deal with the dilemma? Generate alternative solutions to the ones presented in the narrative. Take into consideration risks, benefits, and long- and short-term consequences of each proposed action.

Reflection

At the conclusion of the narrative, the teacher ponders the question of his gender as responsible for the unfolding of events in the early stage of his career. Do you agree with his thinking? Has anything been resolved?

Changing Opinions

Consider your thoughts and assumptions at the beginning of the chapter. Who or what has caused you to consider a new way of thinking? How strongly do you still feel about your previous assumptions?

Synthesis

Synthesize your understanding of this case into a statement. What is this a case of?

Case Commentary by Ellen Moir

The life of a beginning teacher is filled with a series of first experiences. As a result, it makes it hard to always anticipate the outcome of one's actions. The traditional "sink or swim" approach to induction leaves beginning teachers on their own to navigate a new role with many complex responsibilities. As a new teacher, embarking on a "historic journey as the first male teacher in the kindergarten," this young man is in need of an experienced, knowledgeable mentor teacher to guide him.

This case is a compelling illustration of how schools and school districts often fail to offer new teachers the job-embedded, ongoing, and structured support they need and deserve as they enter classrooms, regardless of their gender. New teachers come to the classroom from a variety of preparation programs. If they have been fortunate enough to have meaningful and intensive student teaching experiences, they may still, as in this case, lack exposure to the challenges of the grade level they agree to teach. A skilled mentor could have helped him anticipate potential problems and constructively address legitimate concerns about the appropriate physical relationship between male teachers and young students. The mentor could also have helped facilitate clear communication about this issue with students, parents, and his principal.

My work directing a program that has supported more than 12,000 new teachers has convinced me that novice teachers are vulnerable on many levels. Not only are they learning to teach while teaching, but also they are simultaneously forging a new identity from student to teacher. The young teacher's insecurity and uncertainty are understandable but could have been eased had he had a trusted and knowledgeable veteran teacher to honor his fears while helping him move beyond his "paranoia." Without this support, the new teacher is left to fend for himself, questioning both his judgment and the legitimacy of his being a male kindergarten teacher.

Tragically, when a school-sanctioned outing runs awry, the author's greatest fears materialize in full force. As a reader, you can easily identify the sequence of bad decisions that led to the unfortunate and unnecessary encounter with the police. What could have been done to prevent such a fiasco? I suggest that a mentor's ongoing support would have helped this teacher be very clear in advance about professional boundaries and the need to have another adult or child present despite Jennifer's proclamation to the contrary.

The new teacher asks if the outcome would have been the same for a woman. Undoubtedly not, though women must also be guided in how to interact physically with young children and also fear legal consequences stemming from innocent actions. These are difficult considerations for veteran teachers as well as novices. Developing a professional perspective and learning how to create a caring and safe environment for students takes time and guidance. Good intentions do not always result in positive outcomes. Nonetheless, students deserve male role models at every age. Helping new male elementary teachers grapple with the complexity of their role to allow them to succeed is crucial.

Regardless of gender, all new teachers ought to be carefully inducted into the teaching profession. During these critical early years, new teachers are easily overwhelmed by the competing demands of running an effective classroom. When new teachers are left on their own to sink or swim, not only do they leave the profession, but also students receive far less than they deserve. Imagine how different it would have been had a trained mentor been available to forestall this blight on the career of a promising and enthusiastic new teacher.

❖ EXPLORING THE ISSUES

New Teachers

Moir examines the lack of support given to new teachers. How might a mentorship program aid in preparing for new situations, programs, and schools? How has Moir been able to ease new teachers' feelings of insecurity and uncertainty?

Gender Issues

The teacher in the case wonders if outcomes would have been the same for a woman. What do you think? What does Moir suggest is necessary to gain perspective on teaching events?

Teacher Identity

The commentator worries about a teacher's sense of self or even "paranoia" if all good intentions in the classroom do not yield "positive outcomes" or good results. How can teachers develop a "professional perspective" when an "outing runs awry"?

Diversity

Moir comments on the need for all students to have "male role models at every age." How might strategies or knowledge for a male teacher differ at the kindergarten and secondary levels?

Case Commentary by Barbara B. Levin

From my perspective as a teacher-educator for the past 15 years, I think this case asks a very good question: Is the teacher's gender an issue? The easy answer is "Of course gender matters! This was a male kindergarten teacher—very unusual!" However, I also wonder if this case is also about stereotyping. Gender is one way we stereotype people, but we also make uncritical assumptions about people based on age, skin color, accent, occupation, the way they dress, and other rather superficial features. For most of us, it takes getting to know people as individuals to see that our stereotypes are shallow and dangerous manifestations of who people really are. If the people at McDonald's really knew this teacher, they probably would have helped him comfort this child instead of looking at him with suspicion.

Is this a case of gender only, or is it also a case of stereotyping? If I were in this teacher's shoes, I might ask myself some "What if?" questions: What if this child was a boy? What if I was a female? What if I was a female of color? What if I was Caucasian and the child was of color? What if I was a person of color and the child Caucasian? What if I was a much older person? What if I had on the robes of a cleric or wore a military uniform? What if . . . ? What if . . . ? These questions should lead me to think about this case from other perspectives and lead me to ask, "Would the same thing happen to another teacher?" and "What else is this a case of?" (Shulman, 1992, 1996).

This case also says something about our society today and the power of the media. In light of our increasingly instant awareness of child abductions, child molestations by clergy, child pornography, and other forms of child abuse, we have to wonder if everyone observing a distraught child who calls for their mother at McDonald's would call the authorities? Would they have reacted the same way 30 years ago? Would they react the same way in a small town, in the suburbs, or in the city? Are we even more likely to stereotype people as a result of recent media events related to the safety of children? I believe that this crisis did not happen in isolation. Unfortunately, we live in a time that makes us hyperaware of potential threats. Maybe it is a good thing that people were quick to act—not for this teacher, but for the sake of a potential threat to a child. Nevertheless, you have to ask yourself— What would I do if I witnessed the interactions of this child and her teacher? Would I intervene? Ask if I could help? Call the police? Follow the car? Keep my thoughts to myself?

This case raises some "big picture" issues related to teaching, especially those that surround the belief of many people that teaching is women's work. Right or wrong, this stereotype is perpetuated by the numbers, especially in elementary schools, as well as by our cultural assumptions about male and female roles in society. However, I think this case is also about the difficulty of separating gender issues from issues of race, class, and sexuality (Biklen & Pollard, 1993).

❖ EXPLORING THE ISSUES

Stereotyping

On what other bases, besides gender, do people stereotype? How and why can assumptions and models be dangerous in the classroom, as Levin suggests?

Reflection

Are the questions Levin raises that pertain to gender ones that you might have asked if you had observed this scenario? If so, what assumptions were at play to make you react in that prescribed way?

If not, what has caused you to reflect wisely? Did your attitude toward the media play a role in your response?

Case Commentary by Kristopher Wells

At the Center for Research for Teacher Education and Development, we frequently discuss personal, political, and pedagogical issues that arise as we attend to our teaching and research on the landscape of schools. These issues are often based on the moral, ethical, and legal principles that are embedded in professional codes of conduct and standards of teaching practice. These codes and practices are designed to help teachers navigate their way through the daily realities of living and teaching in an increasingly complex world.

The narrative "Is the Teacher's Gender an Issue in a Kindergarten Classroom" raises a series of important questions and tensions that cannot be easily resolved by turning to a set of prescribed guidelines or codes of conduct. In this case study, there are many influential discourses at work that serve to shape and construct the first-year teacher's personal and professional identity. Three of the key discourses presented deal with issues of fear, sexuality, and the body. As educators, we often learn to fear, instead of critique and challenge, many of the unspoken questions or subtle comments that occur in school hallways and staff rooms: "Why would you want to teach kindergarten?" "But do you think he is . . . ?"

These questions, as presented in the case study, serve to cast doubts on the first-year teacher's abilities and motives. These questions also raise the suspicion that as a male elementary teacher he might be gay or, more insidiously, a pedophile. As this young man searches for his teaching identity and voice, he is quickly learning that male elementary teachers are positioned in very particular ways. As you reflect on this case study, I encourage you to explore the discourses at play and consider a few of the following questions:

Discourses of fear: What are the parents afraid of? What is the teacher afraid of? How are these fears similar, yet different? Why are homosexuality and pedophilia constructed as the ultimate fear in schools? How is fear used as a regulatory device in schools? How do silences or absences influence teacher identities? What role does silence play in maintaining fear and control?

Discourses of the body: How is the male teacher's body read in the elementary classroom? What binaries does this reading create? What sanctions are in place for those who transgress these gendered roles? How do these binaries serve to fix and regulate teacher and student identities? How has the feminization of elementary schools—and teachers—served to construct the identity of male teachers?

Discourses of sexuality: How is sexuality constructed in the elementary classroom? How does this construction lead to fixed notions of what it means to be male and female? What effect do these constructions have on student and teacher identities? How are discourses of (hetero)sexuality encoded and inscribed in the daily operations of the classroom and school? In what ways are sexual, emotional, and physical needs and desires present or absent in the classroom and school (Fine, 1988)?

Discourses are not only limited to words or actions, but they are also strongly shaped by silences and absences (Britzman, 1991). When examining discourses, our challenge is to move beyond simplistic binary understandings (i.e., black/white, male/female, mind/body, good/bad, heterosexual/homosexual). Instead, we should attempt to create inclusive and ethical pedagogies that seek to challenge and reshape unquestioned discourses (Boler & Zembylas, 2003). By carefully deconstructing case studies like the one in this chapter, "Is the Teacher's Gender an Issue in a Kindergarten Classroom," perhaps we can begin the challenging work of learning to think about our schools differently. In this way, we are seeking to build the capacity to question, challenge, and critique the structures of education that valorize particular teacher and student identities and marginalize others. When we question the discourses of fear, of the body, of sexuality, we can become catalysts for change that take up and engage new ways of thinking, acting, being, and becoming in our classrooms and communities.

To act differently, we must begin to think differently about our teaching and learning if we are to truly open up and create spaces of hope and languages of possibility where all bodies matter (Butler, 1993). I encourage you to think carefully about the unspoken questions in your school and see where the answers might lead you.

❖ EXPLORING THE ISSUES

Diversity Issues

Wells encourages us to deconstruct discourses of fear, the body, and sexuality as they relate to teaching. Consider and respond to the questions and insights raised. How does this approach of deconstruction encourage a reconstruction of how teachers teach and students learn?

Reflection

Usually simplistic approaches, such as binary understandings, and simple answers ignore underlying issues. What approach does Wells support for tackling the challenges that may not be overt in teaching? How would you apply Wells's suggestion to other societal issues?

Case Commentary by
Jerry Lee Rosiek and Becky M. Atkinson

The answer to the question in the title of this chapter is clear: Yes, gender matters. The question that follows, and that this case study permits us to explore, is this: How does gender matter?

On one level, we can ask whether the fact that the teacher is a man shapes the response of children, parents, teachers, and restaurant workers to his work. The story the teacher tells certainly invites that interpretation. However, it is difficult to discern the exact causes of any specific human response, because human experience is so complex and our ability to know the thoughts and feelings of others is so limited. The author and reader can at best speculate about what is on the minds of the other characters in the story.

On another level, we can ask whether gender identity shapes the experience of the teacher himself. The story above provides a clear answer to this question: yes. As a new male kindergarten teacher, the author finds himself almost obsessively thinking about his gender identity and what it means to others around him. Whether or not anyone else is thinking about his gender, his experience has already been shaped by the gendered cultural discourses that frame the work of teaching.

By "gendered cultural discourses," We mean the taken-for-granted understandings of gender embedded in the language and practices of a given community. These understandings are as real as the bricks and beams that make up the school building. And, as this case study illustrates, these understandings can profoundly influence the work of teaching.

They work this influence in two ways. First, community members internalize the discourses. Consequently, they shape our actions even when no one else is watching us. In this case study, the teacher is constantly monitoring his own behavior even when no one is present to watch him. Second, these discourses are often invisible to the people they influence because they are thought of as "normal" or "natural." The result is that a community will often require a member of a minority population to defend itself against general suspicion, but will not question the source of their suspicion. In this case study, the author observes that no one questions why a woman would want to teach young children, but his decision to teach young children is considered abnormal and interrogated. More dramatically, restaurant workers see a male teacher, not their own assumptions, as the cause for concern.

The ultimate solution to such problems is, of course, challenging and transforming narrow gender roles considered normal in our society. This, however, is unlikely to be achieved soon. Therefore, in the meantime, teachers need to be prepared to work constructively against the grain of narrow gender expectations. This work, I offer, cannot be effectively accomplished alone. Teachers need to learn how to work together to resist the negative effects of oppressive cultural discourses.

It is worth noting that in this case study, the teacher seems to be alone in his struggle with the narrow gender expectations he faced. Rather than ask what he could have done differently, I think the question needs to be asked, "What could his colleagues and administrators have done to support him in this situation?" More generally, how can teachers know when to be an ally to another teacher whose gender, race, class, sexuality, or (dis)ability status is different from their own?

❖   EXPLORING THE ISSUES

Societal Perception

Rosiek and Atkinson examine the variety of ways that gender matters. They address the internalized and invisible ways that biases lodge in our sensibilities. Evaluate the authors' "ultimate solution" to challenging and transforming gender roles. What might you add to their suggestions?

Support for New Teachers

Rosiek and Atkinson comment on the teacher's virtual obsession about thinking about gender identity and how others will perceive him in a traditionally female role as a kindergarten teacher. How does gender affect teachers' personal professional knowledge? Does awareness of gender contribute to new teacher anxiety and "frame the work of teaching"?

Case Commentary by Paul Axelrod

This scenario addresses an issue of utmost importance: personal interactions between teachers and students, and, in particular, the relations between male teachers and young children.

Although the teacher has legitimate concerns about this matter, he appears to be an individual who lacks good judgment and the ability to work comfortably with the students he teaches.

I question, first, why he would be visiting the homes of the children in his kindergarten class. This indicates, inappropriately, that he intends to be a family friend as well as the child's teacher. Home visits on this scale erode the necessary professional distance that teachers should maintain from students and their families. Teachers can demonstrate their accessibility to parents and their genuine interest in the children in their classes in other ways. For example, the teacher could have invited the parent(s) and child to speak to him in the classroom at the beginning of the school year. Only in exceptional circumstances— for example, in the case of immobile parents—and with the knowledge of the vice principal or principal, should the teacher visit the family home. In addition, there may be some small communities and boards where this practice of home visits still has currency, but in all likelihood, this would be rare.

Teachers should certainly avoid any kind of intimate contact with students. Children should not sit on their teachers' laps or engage in prolonged hugs with them. But a certain amount of physical contact— a reassuring arm around the shoulder, for example—is acceptable. Even this level of interaction, however, worries the teacher in the scenario, who lacks insight and perspective on the matter.

The contest, which led to the teacher having lunch with the winning student at McDonald's, was entirely inappropriate and should not have been permitted. At the very least, one of the child's parents should have accompanied them to the restaurant. Even that, however, raises some professional boundary issues. Any such "prizes" ought to have been awarded at the school.

At the restaurant, the teacher handled the student's temper tantrum foolishly and dangerously. Assuming this unlikely situation transpired, the teacher should have called the parent(s) to come to the restaurant or had someone else contact them. He should not have physically handled the child unless she was acting violently or was at risk of harming herself. And even then, it would only be appropriate for the teacher (or any adult) to use restraint, not aggression. He certainly should not have bodily dragged the child from the restaurant, and in calling the police, the manager and patrons of the restaurant acted sensibly.

Finally, one might ask why this teacher felt so isolated and unable to consult his fellow teachers and school authorities. Something is amiss in the organization and culture of the school itself when teachers feel so at sea. There should be channels in the school that allow teachers, especially new ones, to address their concerns without feeling threatened or demeaned.

❖ EXPLORING THE ISSUES

Relationships Between Teachers and Students

Why might Axelrod be critical of the new teacher's preparation for his kindergarten class? Do you agree with Axelrod's statement, "Teachers should certainly avoid any kind of intimate contact with students"? Explain the reason for your answer.

Teacher Behavior

Axelrod questions the teacher's behavior outside of the classroom. What safeguards by the school could prevent a new teacher from encountering similar difficulties?

❖ ENGAGING WITH THE COMMENTARIES

Gender Issues

Moir, Levin, Wells, and Rosiek and Atkinson agree that gender does matter; however, their reasons why it matters and approaches toward eradication of stereotypes differ. Compare and contrast their responses on the topic of stereotyping.

Teacher Effectiveness

Although Moir, Levin, Wells, and Rosiek and Atkinson intellectualize the new teacher's plight, Axelrod states that the teacher "lacks good judgment and the ability to work comfortably with the students he teaches." Do you agree with Axelrod or not? Explain your answer.

New Teacher Support

Compare the suggestions made by all of the commentators for support of new teachers. Which support(s) would most directly affect classroom teaching? Why? Have you followed Wells's line of thinking in responding to this last question?

Student Learning

This case deals with issues that extend beyond the classroom, but will ultimately influence students' acceptance of diversity. How might a teacher prepare her or his students to deal with diversity in and out of the classroom? Do the commentators provide clues?

Connecting Questions

The Connecting Questions located in the introduction highlight themes that are threaded throughout the cases. You may continue your exploration of the issues raised in this case by addressing those connections. For questions pertinent to this case, please see questions 7 and 8.

❖ ADDITIONAL READINGS

Chernin, K. (1998). *The woman who gave birth to her mother: Seven stages of change in women's lives.* New York: Viking.

Kim Chernin offers a new paradigm for women's development. She offers a model for breaking cycles of mothers' stereotypes of blame and forgiveness. Tales from Chernin's clinical practice illustrate this model. This is a good companion piece to the works of Hope Edelman, Mary Pipher, Carol Gilligan, and Mary Catherine Bateson for understanding women's lives.

Cockburn, A. D. (1996). *Teaching under pressure: Looking at primary teachers' stress.* Washington, DC: Falmer, Taylor and Francis.

This book examines the pressures that primary teachers will encounter in their work.

Connelly, M. F., & Clandinin, D. J. (1988). *Teachers as curriculum planners: Narratives of experience.* New York: Teachers College Press.

The authors examine the role of personal professional knowledge in daily teaching practice. Many examples of real-life experience are presented in narratives that are authentic and engaging. This book adds to the impact of qualitative research that goes deeply into understanding teachers' lives and the roles they play in the classroom.

Flanagan, O., & Jackson, K. (1987). Justice, care and gender: The Kohlberg-Gilligan debate revisited. *Ethics, 97*(3), 622–637.

Kohlberg presents the argument that morally good people are reasonable people, acting on principles of justice and fairness. Gilligan looks at how society divides the sexes. She says that men conceive of morality as created by obligations and rights, constituted by the demands of fairness and justice. Women, however, understand moral requirements as emergent from the specific needs of others. The focus here is the contrast of gender stakes.

Gauntlet, M. (2002). *Media, gender and identity: An introduction.* London: Blackwell.

Theories of self, gender, sexuality, and identity are clearly explained, and then connected to current films, TV, and pop music. Within this landscape of complex media messages, there are individuals trying to establish their own identities, to feel comfortable in themselves and as part of society. The author highlights Michel Foucault, queer theory and fluid identities, men's magazines and modern male identities, and women's magazines and female identities today.

Hall, S. (1997). *The work of representation: Cultural representation and signifying practices.* London: Sage.

Stuart Hall discusses issues of identity, gender, and power. Foucault underpins arguments along with concepts of democracy.

Hargreaves, A., & Fullan, M. (1992). *Understanding teacher development.* New York: Teachers College Press.

The 12 chapters in this book focus on teacher development in relation to self-development, reflection, biographies, cultures of teaching, teacher careers, teachers' work, gender identity, and classroom practice.

Hennessy, R. (1993). *Materialist feminism and the politics of discourse.* New York: Routledge.

Hennessy discusses many impasses in materialist feminist work by rethinking the notion of "woman" as discursively constructed. She argues for a theory of discourse as ideology, taking into account the work of Julia Kristeva, Michel Foucault, and Ernesto Laclau.

Shulman, J., & Mesa-Bains, M. (Eds.). (1993). *Diversity in the classroom: Casebook for teachers and teacher-educators.* San Francisco: FarWest Lab.

The framework of Exploring the Case was adapted from this book.

Zembylas, M. (2004). The emotional characteristics of teaching: An ethnographic study of one teacher. *Teaching and Teacher Education, 20*(2), 185.

This article explores the emotional characteristics of an elementary school teacher during a 3-year research project: the role of emotions in teaching, relationships with students, and the political context. Field observations, in-depth interviews, an "emotion diary," and a collection of teaching documents (e.g., lesson plans, philosophy statements, etc.) contribute data. Findings point to the tensions and challenges that teachers experience. Politics and power relations influence the values, discourses, and beliefs of the teacher who was the focus of this study.

3

Working With a
Challenging Student
and His Family

In this case, a teacher reflects on her or his attempts to meet the educational needs of a challenging student. Responding to the unique and changing needs of this learner conjures images of attempts to address a moving target. The divergent learning style of this student also leads to his being a social target for his peers. Case commentators Deborah J. Trumbull, David Booth, Peter McLaren and Nathalia Jaramillo, and David E. Wilson and Joy S. Ritchie along with Janna Dresden examine multifold approaches of concern, empathy, negotiation, and reflection that are prompted by children who do not seem to fit into traditional schooling venues.

The use of "she and he," while it may appear awkward to the reader, is intended to ensure the absence of gender bias.

❖   THINKING AHEAD

As you read this chapter, reflect on the following questions and issues:

- Consider the knowledge, skills, attitudes, and experiences of the teacher.
- What past events and present behavior suggest that Marc is a "divergent learner"?
- List the dilemmas in this case.
- Consider the diverse perspectives of those involved in this case and what each believes are Marc's needs.
- Consider whether or not specific strategies had been put in place to deal with Marc's prior knowledge and observed behavior.

Father: "It's the school's fault!"

It was not the first time that I had heard Mr. Russell blame the school for his son Marc's difficulties. I was sure it was not the school's fault. After all, if it was, that would mean that it was my fault—at least in part, since I was the child's teacher!

Here I was again, facing a parent I dreaded dealing with even in casual conversation because of his hostility. It was the evening of the first term report card interviews by prearranged appointment. I was not sure I could handle this man alone and had accepted the principal's offer to sit in on the session.

How could it be the school's fault? I had worked so diligently to explain to this particular parent that his child had problems that must be faced. I had done my best for his son. I hoped he would want to work with the school to do something to help.

My class that year was shaping up to be as close to heaven as mortal teachers could expect. It was my fifth year of teaching. The class was made up of students I had previously taught, with a few imports who were going to fit in just wonderfully. And Marc, the odd one out. Marc, who, when I asked the class to participate in a paper-tearing activity, immediately took out his scissors. Marc, who, when I told him we were not "doing dinosaurs," brought every dinosaur he could cram into his backpack to school. Marc, who, when reminded that, yes, volcanoes were exciting, but we had already seen the one he made earlier in the year, nevertheless brought in his latest volcano only to be greeted by the less than subtle jeers of his peers. In spite of all these previous incidents, I was confident that I could respond to this "divergent learner."

I felt I had arrived at a very satisfying point in my teaching life. I had a combined class of 25 fourth- and fifth-grade students happy to work in small groups, confident with rubrics, comfortable with peer-self-teacher three-way assessment, who showed promise with project-based learning in the areas of science and social studies. They gathered materials they needed on their own from various storage areas in the room and generally worked independently and interdependently without much fuss. I recognized their individual learning styles, devised activities with awareness of multiple intelligence theory, and provided a variety of teaching and assessment strategies to meet their needs. We were all set for success.

Even Marc was finding some degree of acceptance when he had an opportunity to shine. He could often see and explain unusual solutions to *Find the Intruder* and word games, and the other students even listened to him with interest from time to time. Over the last year, there had been no major conflicts in the classroom. It had helped that I had been team-teaching with a colleague, regrouping our students according to individual needs. We knew these students, and they were beginning to know themselves too.

The schoolyard was a different matter. Unfortunately, Marc was currently experiencing problems there due to his poor social skills. He would not leave others alone. He trailed behind older students, who ignored him. Then, he would try to join younger, more tolerant students, but they, too, would eventually drift away.

Father: "I don't care that he can read better. What are you going to do about the way the other kids pick on him? He gets kept in at recess and then we have to put up with him running all over the place at home."

Present thought: I had fantasized that we would be talking about the signs of progress Marc had shown lately in reading, an area that had always been difficult for him. I thought we had already had quite enough conversations about his social problems. The principal and I exchanged a look. I initiated the conversation, reviewing the old ground about Marc's habit of accusing other kids of conspiring against him. Marc would reiterate that one group would not allow him to spin the roulette wheel in a math game, when often, the other kids were simply following instructions, and it was not Marc's turn yet.

Flashback: The in-class scene replays itself in my mind's eye: "He won't listen. Can't you move him?" Marc's screams pierce the classroom as he sulks purple-faced, fists clenched, body rigid. "Tell the little creep to get out of our way!" "Yeah, I pushed him, but he kept coming up and telling us about his stupid army men!"

Present thought: So many social situations cause Marc difficulty. The principal explains that school policy demands Marc be kept in at recess because he provokes aggressive reactions from the older students. He goes out of his way to intrude on their agreed-upon section of the playground and stands smack in the middle of their games. It saddens me to see us resort to removing Marc from the very social setting he needs practice in handling, but strategies presented through the anger management program and group sessions with the behavior counselor have not yielded much impact on Marc.

Father: "You should be punishing the other kids. I've told Marc he has my permission to fight the other kids. He's pretty good at karate now, you know."

Present thought: It was true. I thought it was essentially not a bad thing for Marc to take karate lessons, as it seemed to help his self-esteem. As if through a thick blanket, I hear the voice of the principal giving the stock answer to Marc's father about violent behavior and the school code.

Father: "Well, you people are gonna hear from me. I'm not putting up with it anymore."

Present thought: Suddenly, I observe Marc's father's hands firmly planted on his thighs, elbows out. His face is quickly turning red.

Father: "You keep telling me Marc has all these problems. He has problems all right. It's the school."

Present thought: I am aware that his hands are now pressing down on the table. He is leaning in toward me. I see him start to rise. I go into panic mode, followed by survival instinct, in a heartbeat.

Flashback: My first principal is telling me never to forget it's their child. Affirm any feelings they have. That's their right, but put the onus back on them. Quick. Say something.

Response to Father: I let him know I understand he must feel very frustrated, that he obviously cares, and that he wants the best for his son. He moves back, sinks into his chair, and looks defeated, almost sheepish. My heart resumes a more normal pace. The conversation gradually takes on a more natural tone. The principal relaxes. Earlier we thought that one of us was about to be hit.

Present thought: I have averted a crisis. But later, I feel unsatisfied. I feel trapped in a kind of professional diplomacy. I really want to tell this man to stop ignoring the signs that are saying, "This child's conflict is going to blow up in our faces one day." I am troubled by Mr. Russell's reluctance to admit there is a problem, troubled by the intensity of Marc's outbursts, troubled by my own deference to parental rights. But then I am also a parent. How would I have reacted in Mr. Russell's place?

Response to Father: Since kindergarten he has played almost exclusively with military toys like tanks and soldiers. What bothers me is not just the nature of the toys, but also the inflexibility of his choice.

I continue on with a few concerns about Mare's physical coordination. He runs in a very stiff-legged way, seemingly on purpose and to please himself somehow. He has trouble putting the beat in his feet to mark time in music, whereas the rest of the class is having no difficulty. I feel obliged to touch on the area of social interactions again, because it is here that his behavior is most volatile. Marc's outlandish statements like "I've flown to Mars in a spaceship" are guaranteed to provoke ridicule from his peers—a reaction which, in turn, infuriates Marc. He seeks attention from adults constantly, to the point where he tells the same stories and asks the same questions repeatedly: "May I go to the washroom?" "Yes." "May I go to the washroom?"

We also examine Marc's academic difficulties. In math, he readily finds relationships between angles in pattern blocks, but confuses addition and subtraction symbols. He varies between fast, accurate responses and erratic ones. He does not often follow procedures either orally or in writing. The quirky way he now insists on writing "ge" instead of "je" puzzles me because I know he used to write the word for "I" in French correctly.

Present thought: Sometimes I wonder if Marc is doing things differently on purpose, just to be different, or if he really doesn't get it. I feel he is increasingly disconnected from me. Ways that were once appealingly eccentric now appear rigidly alien. I have consulted with the principal and the board's behavior counselor. I have kept daily notes on his behavior this year. I have explored the Internet looking for clues as to the nature of the possible dysfunction, discovering references to Asperger's Syndrome, high-functioning autism, and obsessive-compulsive disorder that might provide clues.

I have mentioned my concerns over the course of the last school year to both of his parents. His mother has never shown much interest. She smiles a lot, says very little, and looks as if she is in another world, herself. She seems only to dote on her youngest daughter. Marc's stepfather, Mr. Russell, is usually hostile. Marc is stuck in his behavior patterns. This is not a simple case of immaturity. To make the situation more difficult, there is now a student in the same class whom I refer to in the privacy of my own mind as a predator. I found out at the beginning of the year that Marc has been the target, his "prey" in kindergarten, and the two of them have been separated ever since. Now, there is no option but to place them in the same classroom. The old relationship barely camouflaged by a veneer of civility is returning. If the old rivalry resumes, it would surely fuel the accusations that we are not safeguarding Marc.

It seems I have not been able to change anything. Despite all of my concerns, Marc's father refuses to acknowledge the possibility that his son might need a diagnosis or support for his situation. He states that he sees no reason to discuss the subject further with the family doctor or any kind of specialist. He threatens that he will just move Marc to a different school. And, in fact, he does just that.

Reflection: Other students have moved on, and they have faded from memory. This student still haunts me. After events such as the Columbine school shooting tragedy, it is not hard for me to picture Marc striking back one day. He knows he is different from others. He is forever stuck in behaviors that create conflict. He made little or no progress in social skills. He believed others were out to get him, and he always seemed fascinated by weapons. He dwelled in a fantasy-land. All his "symptoms" were significant to me. I always felt caught between deference to parental rights and concern for the child. It is tempting to try to find out how he is doing, but I am not sure I want to know.

❖   EXPLORING THE CASE

A curriculum coordinator, recalling an experience in the fifth year of teaching, wrote this case.

Identification

Identify the key facts of this case. What factual events are central to understanding this situation? Identify the dilemmas and tensions in this case. Explore the main aspects of each dilemma and tension.

Analysis

Analyze the issue(s) from the viewpoints of the different people in the case. Based on the teacher's interactions with Marc, his parents, and the teacher's colleagues, what educational issues are suggested?

Evaluation

Examine critically the teacher's strategies for handling the challenge(s) with the student, his parents, and school administration. Does the teacher depicted fulfill, fall short of, or surpass your notion of the role of a teacher?

Alternative Solutions

Were there alternative solutions or strategies available to deal with the dilemma? Generate alternative solutions to the ones presented in the narrative. Take into consideration risks, benefits, and long- and short-term consequences of each proposed action.

Reflection

Even years after the incident, the teacher is still troubled by Marc's story. Why is the teacher's concluding reflection poignant? Has anything been resolved?

Changing Opinions

Consider your thoughts and assumptions at the beginning of the chapter. Who or what has caused you to consider a new way of thinking? How strongly do you still feel about your previous assumptions?

Synthesis

Synthesize your understanding of this case into a statement. What is this a case of?

Case Commentary by Deborah J. Trumbull

I found this case haunting. The story of Marc and his difficulties was indeed moving. Too many accounts of teaching gloss over the powerful emotions associated with practice—fear, anger, frustration, and deep impatience. This case brings these emotions to life. If our emotions are not engaged by this case, we are not paying attention. This case shows us the extent to which pupils become part of a teacher's life and the impressions they leave on it. Not all memories of former pupils are endearing. The case also illustrates the way former and present experiences and images weave themselves into inter-actions. The teacher was not just interacting with the stepfather in one conference, but with earlier images and experiences, and future concerns.

The idea of target permeates this case. Haven't we all, as teachers, wanted to target the causes for a pupil's difficulties, looked for the diagnoses or classifications or home factors that would explain why this particular boy behaves in these peculiar ways. This wish for a tar-get seems based on an assumption that once we know the cause(s), we can design a successful treatment. Others wish to target, too. The step-father targets the school as the source of Marc's difficulties, and acts accordingly.

There are other images of target. Marc's behaviors make him a target for other students' exasperation. More ominously, Marc is in danger of becoming a target for another boy the author sees as a predator. There are many targets that move around in this case as we are moved by it.

The author describes Marc with carefully observed details, details to which good teachers learn to attend but details easy to overlook in the rush of daily life. This case is valuable for the exemplar it provides for close study of a pupil. The author uses general (and usually impov-erished) terms such as "poor social skills" or "self-esteem" to orient us, but these terms are richly supplemented with details about Marc's actions and interactions. These details provide us a glimpse of the hard-to-understand actions of this boy. The author gives us a look into Marc's home conditions. Some descriptions of the stepfather mirror descriptions of Marc. As I read this case the first time, I found it easy to target Marc's family as the cause of his difficulties; easy to say Marc's problems were the fault of his mother and stepfather. The author wor-ries about capitulating to the stepfather's concerns at the conference. Did this happen?

There are other factors at play in Marc's difficulties. The case cap-tures the complex network of social interactions that operate in schools and the ways in which selves are embodied and enacted in the ordi-nary interchanges of the day. The author, for example, is honest about her or his unwillingness to believe the school is to blame for Marc's problems because of an awareness that she or he embodies the school to the pupils, so the school's failure would be a personal failure. And this teacher has tried hard. She or he describes other elements in the contexts of the school—the "agreed-upon sections of the playground" claimed by older students, the students who refer to him as "the little creep," the time for sharing in the classroom that Marc abuses. Marc seems not to be able to read the rules operating in any of these contexts.

Just as it is easy to wish to target the causes of Marc's odd behaviors, it is easy to wish for a hero story, a story in which this exceptional teacher had been able to provide what Marc needed to improve. Indeed, Marc had been improving in his reading, not an insignificant gain, but one ignored by his stepfather. But this is not a hero story. It is a story of heroic efforts. We learn about the steps a concerned teacher can take and the realities with which this teacher dealt. I found myself wondering how I would feel about a student as difficult as Marc, and then wondered how I handled those students with whom I do not seem able to make a difference, those who consistently fail to see and negotiate the interrelations around them or who target me as the source of their difficulties. How do these situations make me feel? How do I deal with my emotions? How do I accept my failures with some students?

❖ EXPLORING THE ISSUES

Student Behavior

What past events and present behavior suggest that Marc is a "divergent learner" or an "at-risk" learner? How does Trumbull suggest that teachers think about and attend to the needs of difficult students in class? How should teachers think about their own progress or difficulties with troublesome students?

Trumbull suggests that past experience and assumptions might target a teacher's attitude toward a student for better or worse. Was this true for Marc and his teacher's steps for helping him?

Programming

Trumbull examines what "good" teachers should do in difficult cases. Do you agree with her approach, and what might you add?

Schools in Society

Trumbull says that the teacher thinks "she or he embodies the school to the pupils." Why would a teacher want to separate her or his persona from that of the school's? Who is responsible when a child fails at school?

Case Commentary by David Booth

All of the teachers that I have met in my years in education have encountered children like Marc in their classrooms. And his father. We carry those memories of those children at risk forever, and often they act as change agents for our teaching. As we meet new children with similar problems, we scan those past recollections to redesign our responses from the always-looming shadows in our teaching psyches. We need to learn from our unsuccessful episodes with children and families as we try to invent new teaching selves, just as when we view a videotape record of who we used to be, and shudder, even tremble, at our past teaching personas and behaviors.

Rather than forgetting these children or being afraid of meeting them in the future, we need to reuse these memory icons, as the author of the case study has done, to help locate us in the present, to support our new professional knowledge of helping these children and parents inside the school community. It was especially comforting to hear the author connect her or his parenting self to the issues she or he was confronting in the classroom as a teacher, to recognize the pain and frustration of a parent over a child's unhappiness in school. That ability to distance personal "teacher response" deepened understanding of those involved in the meeting, and let the teacher regain her or his balance and clarify the focus. However, the first principal's first words still echo in my ears: Never forget it's their child.

Often the parents are presenting their own needs and fears during the parent-teacher interview, and they may value this particular forum for venting their frustration and unhappiness. Children move to and fro every weekday—from home to classroom to home and homework. How we integrate these dual worlds is one of the central complexities of raising children, and the teeter-totter of childhood quickly becomes unbalanced if one party feels the other is somehow neglecting the requisite assistance that children need, especially children at risk.

In spite of our best efforts, we are sometimes unable to offer enough supportive strategies to a child in difficulty to ensure a successful school life. And it may be that some children will need other environments, other structures, in order to progress. But to paraphrase the psychoanalyst D. W. Winnicott, we have to be "the good enough teacher," and for me, therein lies the struggle. I need to know that I did all that I could at that time in those circumstances with that particular child. By remembering that experience, I look at every new child differently. I have the opportunity to grow wiser because of that special child.

As a teacher, I read and take courses and talk to other professionals, with Marc as a benchmark. Knowing what I couldn't do, didn't do, and might now do, is how I grow professionally. Next time, perhaps, I will prepare differently for the meeting with the parent: I will review the child's portfolio of work, highlighting examples of her or his progress; I will create an action plan for school and home that works toward the child's social growth; I will find a booklet or an article (or an outside agency) that offers help for the parent; I will interview the child in order to have her or his own words to point toward change; I will have a practice interview with the principal to smooth out the wrinkles in my own approach; and after the interview, I will debrief with a school leader to move toward a professional response to the situation. And if the child leaves, I will follow up with a supportive note to the family, wishing them success in finding a more effective placement for the child they love.

These case studies that every teacher carries forever are not records of failure to disturb our sleep. Instead, they are signposts, computer icons to click on, that signal future possibilities in interacting with children and parents. Schools are integral aspects of a family's community. And those families come in all kinds of configurations, with all types of needs and wants. I am still pleased that most children have satisfying and nurturing school lives, and that most parents recognize the inherent values of the schools where their children spend most of childhood.

The "felt imperative" to help every child in our care is a good one for every teacher to experience; perhaps it has to be tempered with our professional sense of having done everything we could at that time for that child, strengthened by the knowledge that the experience of knowing Marc and his father will nudge us toward new understandings in our relationships with the children and their parents, in the place called school.

❖ EXPLORING THE ISSUES

Parental Relationships

Booth examines the fact that Mr. Russell and the rest of Marc's family have different perceptions about Marc and his learning behavior.

What differing sets of values have provoked the unpleasant confrontations for the participants? Booth says that Marc and his father may have nudged us to a new place of understanding. How can that place be created?

Booth ponders the worlds of schooling and home. Consider how parents respond to their children's unhappiness when those worlds collide. How might the teacher have improved communication with the family?

Reflection

Booth suggests that cycles of reflection are helpful in thinking about events that plague teachers. How do "signposts" such as Marc aid in teachers' professional growth? What positive outcome does Booth foresee from narratives such as Marc's?

Case Commentary by Peter McLaren and Nathalia Jaramillo

Novice and senior teachers alike routinely enter the classroom with preconceived notions of how their students should act, of how learning should take place, of what are deemed "successful" teaching strategies. Preconceptions are constituted by, among other things, personal history, the ideology of the dominant class, social relations and class location, cultural and societal values, and lived experiences. In "Working With a Challenging Student and His Family," we are presented with a scenario of a seasoned teacher who has "arrived at a very satisfying point" in her or his life. A thorough look into the author's description of professional satisfaction accentuates the importance placed on student's docile and formative reactions to rules, procedures, and routines. Marc, the moving target, represents the "odd man out"—the student most teachers dread for his perceived unruly and truculent behavior.

The case author analyzed the "Marc" problem from the perspective that she or he has done everything possible to accommodate the child's behavior both in and out of the classroom. According to the author, conferences with the principal and behavior counselor resulted in no observable outcomes and have therefore satisfied the teacher's responsibilities—it is ultimately "Marc's" problem. The unit of analysis encompasses the family and the author's interactions with a seemingly hostile parent that she or he dreads confronting during conferences. The family is notably resistant and blinded by "Marc's problem," which, in turn, obstructs the level of collaboration between the school and family. In conclusion, the author resorts to the fatal Columbine massacre metaphor; Marc will travel through the educational pipeline shadowed by social maladjustment and accompanied by a lack of family intervention. As the author states at the closing, "He is forever stuck in behaviors that create conflict."

When teachers serving diverse populations of learners fantasize about the academic strides their students make in reading, writing, and math while at the same time clinging to the notion that some students are beyond behavioral redemption, they are exhibiting the same fatalistic attitude as the students that they fear. Although the author highlighted several points of insight—such as Marc's constant desire for attention and acceptance—little was done to maximize on those points of departure. Marc's overindulgence in military artifacts pointed to an opportunity to engage the class in a critical discourse around symbolic violence and aggression. Perhaps the author may have utilized the information provided by Marc and built upon his interests to create an environment where he could challenge his own behavior. The teacher could accomplish this while engaging the entire class in a critical dialogue on the topic of conflict and social acceptance. It is the responsibility of critical educators to contextualize learning and connect it to all students' lived experience and to do this not in an ideological vacuum of presumed neutrality, but by approaching the concept of student behavior dialectically, as an ensemble of social relations linked to race, class, gender, sexual orientation, and subjectivity and agency.

Although Marc may not have interacted well with peers on the playground throughout the entire year, it does not cast him into a pit of emotional entropy for the remainder of his life. A critical perspective is hopeful and transformative—which may have allowed the author to establish meaningful objectives not only for Marc, but also for her- or himself and for the other students in the class. This is not to suggest that change would have been immediate or would have occurred at all, but it is intended to stress the importance of constructing teaching and learning dialectically.

"Working With a Challenging Student and His Family" depicts a caring—yet frustrated—teacher jarred by a "nonnormative" student and family. There are multiple ways of critically examining and responding to this scenario. The key point we wish to emphasize is that educators need to be empowered critically to develop a working understanding of how student behavior has been constructed by the interaction of multiple forces and social relations and how those forces and relations can be challenged and transformed through focusing on the determinants of behavior, not the symptoms. The challenge of the critical educator is to accomplish this without silencing student voice. To be voiceless is to be powerless. The voices of students can—and often should—be critically challenged, but they can never be silenced or denied, or rendered irredeemable.

❖ EXPLORING THE ISSUES

Programming

Consider why the school and the teacher have arrived at the attitude that "it is ultimately Marc's problem?" McLaren and Jaramillo extend a scenario that would draw on Marc's interests as opportunities for fostering responsibility in improved learning and social acceptance. Are there possible intersections between school and Marc himself for transforming the situation? What role might students play so that they are not silenced and rendered powerless?

Teacher Self-Image

If a teacher assumes that all the "right things" are done, and yet there is no development, particularly social development as in Marc's case, how might teachers deal with their frustration and then resume work with unbiased views toward the student? According to the commentators, how should a teacher stand away from personal feelings and think critically?

Student Behavior

The commentators exhort the readers to look deeper and more critically for reasons, not just the symptoms of student behavior that is "nonnormative." How can dialectics and discourses on teaching and learning foster that critical evaluation?

Case Commentary by David E. Wilson and Joy S. Ritchie

This case enacts the very usefulness of case narratives themselves for readers and for writers. It immediately invoked in us memories of students we've each had over the years who presented themselves in our classrooms and our lives in ways that troubled us then and still trouble us now. This text invites us to author our own texts and engage in a kind of reflection that would allow us to probe more deeply our experiences with and responses to those troublesome students.

Fortunately, "Working With a Challenging Student and His Family" enacts a reflective stance that is instructive; the author shows us one way of being more analytical about our teaching. Through writing, she or he dramatizes the encounter, and then draws back from that moment and from and present perspective, that reexamines it. The author attempts to carefully reconstruct various perspectives: the action and thought at that time, flashbacks to prior moments, an analysis from the present, and possibilities for the future. The author's use of narrative and drama allows her or him to recapture or construct the complexity of the situation—its context, language, and emotions. Rather than a one-dimensional, impersonal, or pseudo-objective description, this case is more infused with the kinds of complexities and tensions teachers face in any given encounter with a parent, child, or administrator.

In reading this, we were reminded of Ann Berthoff's double-entry journal, a reflective method that allows a writer to document an experience or observation and then return to reexamine and re-narrate that experience (Berthoff, 1982). This process permits the writer to be both participant and spectator, to be in the world and to step back from the world, gaining distance, perspective, and understanding. This resembles a strategy we have used with pre-service and in-service teachers in which we've asked them to consider a moment that—like the author's experience with Marc and his father—continues to haunt them. Reconstructing that experience is itself a reflective move; then the written text provides another opportunity for reflection, either by the author alone or in concert with peers.

In "Working With a Challenging Student and His Family," further construction of the narrative might allow the author an opportunity to begin to see and understand the rich, complex human ecosystems in which Marc, his father, the teacher, and the principal lived. Such a process may allow educators to better understand the rich complexities we face while not necessarily leading us to a "solution" or fix. Although this may seem somehow incomplete or even frustrating, we believe we are in far better positions when we can name the complexities we face, as the author of this narrative does. With this speculative stance, Marc's teacher may be better prepared in her or his present role to negotiate the challenges posed by the troublesome students and parents educators will no doubt continue to encounter.

❖ EXPLORING THE ISSUES

Teacher Self-Confidence

Explain how the commentators' reference to Berthoff's "double-entry" journal approach of both participant and spectator might provide insight for teachers working with challenging students. How does reflection and sharing dilemmas enable us to reach and receive new perspectives on a situation?

Parental Relationships

Wilson and Ritchie discuss the purpose of reconstructing narratives. How might rewriting the narrative open up understanding of new perspectives and suggest a new story for Marc?

Case Commentary by Janna Dresden

As I read the first page or two of the case, my initial reaction was to be rather critical of the teacher. I wondered why she or he objected when Marc insisted on bringing his dinosaurs to school—was his interest only acceptable in the context of a school-sanctioned topic? But then, as the case writer began to describe Marc in more detail, my attitude changed. I could hear the screams of the child, and see his clenched fists and purple face. And I could feel the frustration of the teacher as she or he dealt with inanely repeated questions, preposterous comments about flights to Mars, and the complaints of his peers.

This case makes it very clear that detailed descriptions of behavior convey more information and have a greater impact than conclusions or analysis of that behavior. My attitude became more understanding when the picture became more vivid. When I began to relate this teacher's experiences to my own, it became much more difficult to sit in judgment of her or him. We have all been there—we have all worked with difficult children and with difficult parents and it is never easy.

As I read through this case, however, I was reminded that working with parents, like working with children, is not about accomplishing a specific goal, but about sharing a journey. In many ways this cliché is an even more apt description of our work with parents than it is of our classroom teaching. From this perspective, each meeting with parents can be viewed as a step on that journey rather than as yet another futile attempt to get the parent to see things our way.

The case writer describes how she or he told the father that she or he knew he must be frustrated and that he only wanted the best for his son. These types of comments, which affirm parents' feelings, can be extremely helpful, but they should also be viewed as a beginning. The purpose of such comments is not to short-circuit a confrontation, but to serve as a foundation for a meaningful and trusting relationship.

Near the end of the case, the writer poses some very poignant questions: "I wonder if Marc is doing things differently on purpose, just to be different, or if he really doesn't get it." I wonder if she or he shared these questions with Marc's parents. In my work with parents, I have found that voicing exactly those kinds of questions can often be the link we need. When I admit that I am confused or bewildered, parents will often (not always) confess that they have similar concerns.

But having said all of this, I must close by pointing out that many of the families we serve have problems that are beyond our capabilities as teachers. And it seems that the children and families with the greatest problems are the most likely to move from setting to setting. We work to establish trusting relationships and then, often, just as we begin to see some progress, they leave. And we are left knowing that all we can do is our best, knowing full well that trying to meet the needs of these families is quite literally like trying to hit "a moving target."

❖ EXPLORING THE ISSUES

Student Behavior

Dresden describes Marc as a complicated child. Feelings of empathy but also annoyance trouble Dresden. Evaluate her proposition to think of a process for children like Marc as a "journey."

Schools in Society

Dresden sadly concludes "that many of the families we serve have problems that are beyond our capabilities as teachers." Is this statement a result of frustration, insight into teacher limitations, or a comment on the inability of schools to deal with societal issues?

❖ ENGAGING WITH THE COMMENTARIES

Support and Resources

This case provides a variety of time shifts as well as a source of deep reflection for teachers who encounter tense situations. Booth, Wilson and Ritchie, and Dresden all present practical strategies to help teachers respond to students like Marc whose needs continue to change just like a moving target. What other supports, resources, and reinforcements would help teachers reflect in similar situations?

Schools in Society

All commentators point to several "dual worlds" in this case. Identify those worlds that compose Marc's interior and exterior environments. Compare and contrast McLaren and Jaramillo's and Wilson and Ritchie's suggestions about how to deal with the inner worlds of the student and the teacher.

Assessment

When students fail, whose responsibility is it? How would each commentator answer this question? How is failure measured? Have both Marc and the teacher failed?

Connecting Questions

The Connecting Questions located in the introduction highlight themes that are threaded throughout the cases. You may continue your exploration of the issues raised in this case by addressing those connections. For questions pertinent to this case, please see questions 6 and 7.

❖ ADDITIONAL READINGS

Cartledge, G., & Johnson, C. T. (1996). Inclusive classrooms for students with emotional and behavioral disorders: Critical variables. *Theory Into Practice, 35*(1), 51–57.

The writers discuss issues related to the social integration of students with emotional and behavioral disorders with a focus on mainstreaming and the education of the disabled. The social integration and development of all students may be impeded by failure to proactively teach social skills, especially to students who are at risk and who have behavioral disorders. Critical teacher, student, and program variables that affect and aid successful social integration are discussed.

DeGeorge, K. L. (1998). Friendship and stories: Using children's literature to teach friendship skills to children with learning disabilities. *Intervention in School and Clinic, 33*(3), 157–162.

Using children's literature in the classroom enhances teaching strategies for children with learning disabilities, providing valuable skills for making and maintaining friendships. Friendships result from using children's literature: steps to follow, practice in context, and reflection or analysis of lesson and skills. A practice lesson illustrates this strategy, while enabling students to relate to feelings in the story. Activities of modeling and guided practice are described.

Garbarino, J., & Stott, F. M. (2004). *What children can tell us: Eliciting, interpreting, and evaluating critical information from children.* San Francisco: Jossey-Bass.

This book will aid adults in listening more carefully to children and asking relevant questions. The focus is on abuse and other stressful situations that affect children in a variety of settings.

McCombs, B. L., & Pope, J. E. (1994). *Motivating hard to reach students.* Washington, DC: American Psychological Association.

The authors work with students who have developed negative attitudes toward themselves and school. The authors present strategies and theories for improving classroom management. The book showcases ways teachers can improve relationships by working with students' motivation. There is a focus on classroom context and working toward learning goals. The book has activities and guidelines that describe how to individualize programs for the development of self-determination and academic risk taking.

Napier, E. (1995). *Integrating students with special needs: Effective strategies to provide the most enabling education for all students.* Vancouver, BC: Educational Service.

This book focuses on critical issues facing every school district. With a view to provide an appropriate enabling education that accommodates all students, the book offers practical strategies and ideas for creating systemic changes in school districts. The aim is to provide opportunities for students. The authors maintain that adaptation and accommodation by the school system are necessary factors for successful results.

Newman, J. (1987). Learning to teach by uncovering our assumptions. *Language Arts, 64*(7), 727–737.

Newman presents the notion that research is messy. It is a quest that often leads the searcher into new areas and reveals truths previously unknown. Newman's focus includes the use of critical incidents to discover teachers' current beliefs about assumptions that underpin practice.

Reif, S., & Heimburge, J. (2002). *How to reach & teach all students in the inclusive classroom: Ready-to-use strategies lessons & activities teaching students with diverse learning needs.* San Francisco: Jossey-Bass.

This is a useful resource with strategies, lessons, and activities for helping teachers work with student with special needs. There is a focus on learning styles, ability levels, skills, and behaviors in inclusive classrooms.

Shulman, J., & Mesa-Bains, M. (Eds.). (1993). *Diversity in the classroom: Casebook for teachers and teacher-educators.* San Francisco: FarWest Lab.

The framework of Exploring the Case was adapted from this book.

Spaulding, S. (1994). Four steps to effective parent conferences. *Learning, 23*(3), 36–38.

Spaulding outlines four steps to enable teachers to make parents educational partners to support and strengthen students' academic, social, and emotional well-being. There are worksheets.

4

Negotiating Different Styles When Two Teachers Share a Class

I n this case, two teachers who share a classroom have differing approaches to instruction and classroom management. Commentators Rita Silverman, Ron Wideman, and Cheryl J. Craig discuss conflicting teaching styles, classroom management, and the role of administration, power shifts, and the need for cooperation and collaboration among educational partners.

❖ THINKING AHEAD

As you read this chapter, reflect on the following questions and issues:

- Consider the two teachers in this case and their teaching experiences.
- How do the afternoon and morning programs differ?

The use of "she and he," while it may appear awkward to the reader, is intended to ensure the absence of gender bias.

- Consider how the students in both contexts behave.
- What decisions have been made that affect the learning environments described in the case?
- What are the dilemmas in this case?
- What steps to remedy the situation are taken by the teacher who relates the case?
- Why does the administration become involved?

"But Mrs. Tebbetts lets us do this!"

Argh! How tired I was of hearing these words! My teaching partner and I hold very different expectations of the children we share, and it shows. Hanging on to my patience, I wait until the students are seated again before continuing my instructions to the class.

There are 27 students in my fifth-grade class, and I am certain that most of them will end up making their living as lawyers. I have never seen a group so adept at arguing any position.

"Please write in pencil, so you can correct your mistakes," I instruct.

"But I prefer to write in pen. I have a whole set of pens that my parents bought me," Julia bellows from the back of the room.

"All of your chair's legs need to be on the floor," I remind Sal.

"He's not going to fall," Josie informs me.

"Yeah, and it's more comfortable like this," another lawyer and his friend retort.

"Backpacks need to be in the lockers, not on the floor."

"She might need to get something out of it later," Jonathan reprimands me.

"Hitting is not allowed in this classroom."

"I'm allowed to defend myself. I know my rights!" Frances barks back.

No instruction passes unchallenged.

They come to me each afternoon, following a morning of freedom and frolic in which assignments are few and A-pluses are plentiful. Finding the energy and attention to learn a second language requires effort that many students feel they don't need to expend. Why should they work hard, struggling to learn in the afternoon, when they have nothing but fun in the morning, and marks are handed out like candy?

A good question! Why should learning be work? There ought to be fun involved! That is my attitude, too. I have always put serious and thoughtful effort into planning lessons and activities that balance the need for fun with the expectation for learning.

However, the fifth-grade program is a heavy one, and it is difficult under the best of circumstances to cram everything into a half day. The program is divided into halves: Language Arts, Science, Physical Education, and Music in English; and Language Arts, Social Studies, Math, and Art in French for all the junior-level French Immersion students in the school. Recognizing the rigorous nature of the program, the administration has decreed that the French half of the day will be in the morning when the students are fresh, well rested, and ready to learn. It sounded like a good plan. Unfortunately, it hasn't worked out that way for my class because my English partner, Mrs. Tebbetts, is a half-time teacher who only works mornings. Too bad for me.

Mrs. Tebbetts is a very pleasant woman who is passionate about instilling self-esteem in her students. No one is ever wrong in her class. No one is ever corrected. Students do what they like, and, with minimal effort, achieve better than perfect marks. I often wonder how it is possible to come away with 1,200 bonus marks on a 100-mark assignment. Amazing! Truly amazing!

Although the mysteries of her teaching methods elude me, some might argue that Mrs. Tebbetts has established a sustainable learning environment for some students in their first language. However, I feel that this approach is untenable for learning a second language. My experience has taught me that students must put significant effort into acquiring a second language along with ongoing support from their teacher. They need to concentrate on developing a basic vocabulary, manipulating the structure of language, and extending their ability to communicate in their new language. So, although the students may be eager to persist in the same laissez-faire vein as established in the morning, this teacher is not.

Very quickly, I become "the heavy," and the refrain of "Mrs. Tebbetts lets us!" booms in my ears. What I had believed to be universal classroom understandings, like listening to the person who is speaking and completing your best work on time, turn into class battlegrounds.

Wave after inexhaustible wave of student lawyers join the fray against the common foe who, for the first time in 8 years of teaching, is I. I, who have never experienced any trouble building rapport with my students, am now identified as "the mean one." I, who have never had difficulty with communication between home and school, suddenly have parents demanding to know why their children are only experiencing trouble in *my* class. Incredibly, every single behavior problem that has ever disturbed my sleep coalesces in several of my students. I begin to dread crossing the threshold into my own classroom.

At home, at night, I worry the problem like a dog with a bone. What to do? What to do? I am caught in a dilemma. In part, I tend to agree with my students. Why should learning be work? Shouldn't all learning be motivated by curiosity and a desire to know? But where is that curiosity, and how do I stimulate them when they are unwilling to ask questions, or even listen to the ones I am asking? How do we arrive at the point of searching when the children even refuse to discuss what we need to search for?

What to do? Solve the problem. Make expectations clear. What does listening look like? Sound like? Feel like? Make contracts with the kids; use cooperative learning techniques; hold class meetings; try humor; *bribe them!* I continue to look for the way out of this teaching conundrum. I try a myriad of solutions—all with limited success.

Meanwhile, I figure my teaching partner and I have some talking to do. Maybe if both of us could move a little, just a little, toward the class management style of the other, we could ease some of the tensions in the class. Maybe . . . I could hope. With the best of intentions, I begin to outline the situation, as I see it, to Mrs. Tebbetts.

"I'm so sorry you're having a rough time, dear. Maybe they're just tired in the afternoon. They're angels for me in the morning!" she declares, unloading the entire burden on my shoulders and smoothly gliding away.

Each attempt I make to discuss the effects of our disparate teaching styles on the kids invariably receives the same response. She is pleasant, but she is iron.

Inevitably, the problems grow to entwine the administration. The vice principal is a young, dynamic woman who exhibits a great rapport with both students and staff. She is very knowledgeable and adept at answering parents' questions, parents who want to know why their children are receiving only average grades in French when they are so obviously geniuses in English. They telephone, listing their litany of complaints: It isn't fair. It doesn't make sense. Is the program too hard? Is Sally, Tommy, or Samantha not suited for French Immersion? Or is the French teacher just being too tough on their child?

To diagnose and remedy the situation, the vice principal allots quite a bit of time talking with me to gather background information. She spends several mornings and afternoons observing the class. When she has completed her observations, and with both Mrs. Tebbetts and myself present, the vice principal discusses at length with the class the expectations for learning.

Finally, I feel valued and somewhat vindicated by the administration's approach to both the class and the problem. The vice principal confirms that I am not the only source of the problem. This solution appeases me, and I am optimistic enough to try again for positive change. With a feeling of relief, I say so.

Mrs. Tebbetts sighs, smiles, and says, "They're never a problem for me, dear."

❖ EXPLORING THE CASE

An elementary school teacher with 18 years of experience wrote this case.

Identification

Identify the key facts of this case. What events are central to understanding this situation? Identify the dilemmas and tensions in this case. Explore the main aspects of each dilemma and tension.

Analysis

Analyze the issue(s) from the viewpoints of the different people in the case. Discuss the writer's attempts and frustrations in attempting to work with the morning teacher. Why do parental relationships become strained? What educational themes are revealed by the teachers' inability to communicate?

Evaluation

Examine critically the teachers' strategies for handling the challenge(s) in class and with one another. Does the teacher depicted fulfill, fall short of, or surpass your notion of the role of a teacher?

Alternative Solutions

Were there alternative solutions or strategies available to deal with the dilemmas? Generate alternative solutions to the ones presented in the narrative. Take into consideration risks, benefits, and long- and short-term consequences of each proposed action.

Reflection

Why might the teacher-writer feel vindicated at the story's end until Mrs. Tebbetts makes her final response? Has anything been resolved?

Changing Opinions

Consider your thoughts and assumptions at the beginning of the chapter. Who or what has caused you to consider a new way of thinking? How strongly do you still feel about your previous assumptions?

Synthesis

Synthesize your understanding of this case into a statement. What is this a case of?

Case Commentary by Rita Silverman

The teacher/protagonist in "Negotiating Different Styles When Two Teachers Share a Class" offers the reader a familiar scenario. The villain, Mrs. Tebbetts, is setting up our "hero." While Mrs. Tebbetts may not be your typical villain (no black hat or nasty temperament here), her behaviors (setting no boundaries, giving many grades of A-plus) and her attitude ("They're angels for me.") mark her as the "bad guy," while our protagonist is the teacher of lofty ideals and high standards.

It's too simplistic a scenario and one that prospective teachers should be wary of. What is really going on in this case? In the words of Lee Shulman, "What is this a case of?" We have to begin to analyze this case by digging beneath the surface to look more deeply than our protagonist has. An obvious place to begin is the students' responses to the teacher's instructions. The students' arguments and challenges suggest that this teacher has failed to gain the students' cooperation. The teacher attributes the students' attitude to Mrs. Tebbetts's laxity. But we need to ask what our hero did to establish the norms of behavior in this classroom *in the beginning of the year.* The teacher reports that she or he tried *solutions* to the problem that included a variety of classroom management techniques. A deeper analysis would suggest that the teacher didn't start early enough. Classroom management research informs us that those teachers who employ effective classroom management techniques early in the school year face fewer management problems. Weinstein and Mignano (2003) summarize this research when they write, "Most problems of disorder can be avoided if teachers use good *preventative* [my emphasis] management strategies" (p. 10). The analysis here could respond to some retrospective questions: "What might our hero have done at the beginning of the year to ensure the students' cooperation? What procedures and routines should have been established? What is the best way to establish community with fifth-grade students?"

Then, we need to try to understand how this teacher is teaching. The teacher seems ambivalent about the question of whether learning (and teaching) should be work. It seems that part of her or his ambivalence stems from Mrs. Tebbetts's teaching style, a style our hero describes as "laissez-faire." Once again, this teacher is attributing her or his problems outside her- or himself, not reflecting on her or his own teaching as the potential source of the problem. Teaching that is learner-centered, active, and engaging is not synonymous with laissez-faire instruction. Rather, it is demanding on the learners and the teacher, both rigorous and motivating.

Hidi and Harackiewicz (2000) suggest that when students are not excited to learn, teachers must increase their efforts to create classrooms that tap students' interests and involve them in learning. So, for this part of the analysis, we need to establish how this teacher has been teaching and what then might be done to develop more learner-centered instruction.

Finally, this case begs for a solution different from the one that is offered. As with the identification of the problems, the teacher looked outside her- or himself for answers, and they came from the vice principal. An in-depth analysis of the case should help prospective teachers to see the benefit of teachers reflecting on their own practice and accepting the responsibility for classroom events. New teachers should eschew seeking to lay blame outside themselves.

❖ EXPLORING THE ISSUES

Reflection

Silverman quotes Lee Shulman's probing question, "What is this a case of?" Silverman suggests a step-by-step analysis and questions that should be asked in order to pierce the outwardly "simplistic" scenario. Consider her line of questions. Have they deepened your understanding of the issues and what this is a case of? What does Silverman suggest that the teacher do to improve practice?

Classroom Management

Silverman raises the issues of lackluster instruction and disruptive student behavior. Do you concur with her assertion that the writer-teacher's classroom management problems exist because she or he did not "establish the norms of behavior in this classroom" early enough? Are lackluster instruction and student behavior related? If so, how?

Teaching Styles

According to Silverman, "Teaching that is learner-centered, active, and engaging is not synonymous with laissez-faire instruction." Compare and contrast the ways in which the two teachers' teaching styles engage the students. Does the case support Silverman's assertions? Consider if and how the morning teacher's teaching style would engage any students (beyond this case) in a way that the afternoon teacher's does not.

Case Commentary by Ron Wideman

These two are not "teaching partners." Partnership involves working together toward mutual goals. Instead, the two seem locked in the age-old isolation that plagues the teaching profession—isolation that interferes with professional growth.

It is only through the eyes of the afternoon teacher that we know Mrs. Tebbetts as a laissez-faire, love-the-children type whose program is not challenging. On the other hand, we know the afternoon teacher only by self-portrait as the hard-done-by defender of academic and behavioral standards. Mrs. Tebbetts's disdain for the afternoon teacher is implied: "They're never a problem for me, dear." How can you work with someone who is not able to win the hearts and minds of children?

Have these teachers ever observed each other's teaching and discussed each other's programs to try to understand and learn from one another? It seems unlikely. The situation militates against the development of a collegial relationship. The one works in the morning and the other, perhaps, only in the afternoon: no time for classroom visits, no time to share goals and methods, no time to co-plan program. Like ships passing in the night, they only sense each other's presence and distrust each other's intentions.

The students they share know the "good cop," "bad cop" roles. They know how to use critical thinking to put the bad cop on the defensive and keep her or him there.

The values of the two teachers seem at odds. The one focuses on standards, effort, and compliance, the other on relationships, independent thinking, and enjoyment of learning. They strive to maintain their individual professional integrity. Yet underneath, they seem to share a deeply rooted commitment to the well-being of students. Perhaps this is common ground for possible partnership down the road.

How do you begin to build collegial relationship? The afternoon teacher's attempts to initiate conversation have been to try to change Mrs. Tebbetts—not a good basis for professional dialogue. But Mrs. Tebbetts sees no reason to change.

The administrator's solution of talking to the students does nothing to bridge the gulf between the two teachers. Instead, there is a need to involve all staff in schoolwide program planning, implementation, and evaluation so that teaching partnership can become a reality.

If partnership with Mrs. Tebbetts is not possible, the afternoon teacher's alternative is to "own" the problem her- or himself. After all, it is she or he who is unhappy with the results of her or his teaching, not Mrs. Tebbetts. By blaming Mrs. Tebbetts, she or he leaves her- or himself unable to remedy the situation. To gain needed leverage, therefore, the afternoon teacher must find the courage to define the problem differently, so that it focuses on her or his own practice— "What am I doing or not doing?"—and to develop and test possible solutions. In doing so, she or he would benefit from partnering with another French Immersion teacher who shares her or his values, is committed to solving a similar problem (e.g., How can I engage my students in the work of becoming fluent in a second language?), and who will provide honest and supportive feedback.

There is a long history of improving professional practice through problem-based investigation that is described in the literature on learning projects, reflective practice, and action research. These approaches to professional development honor teacher professionalism and recognize that teachers are at the heart of school improvement. School improvement, after all, involves learning by teachers, and learning is an individual activity, driven by personally felt needs and fueled by opportunities to think, to act, to talk, and to listen.

❖ EXPLORING THE ISSUES

Working With Colleagues

What suggestions does Wideman make toward resolving teaching tensions between the two teachers? Do you think there is "common ground" for these two in the future? If yes, why? If not, are there compromises that could occur? Generate responses to Wideman's questions: "How do you begin to build collegial relationships?" and consider "Who will ultimately suffer if tensions cannot be resolved?"

Classroom Management

Wideman discusses the different approaches each teacher takes with the class. How important are values in structuring classroom dynamics?

Case Commentary by Cheryl J. Craig

The dilemmas presented in "Negotiating Different Styles When Two Teachers Share a Class" beautifully demonstrates how complicated classroom life can be when instruction takes place in two languages and involves two teachers—an English-language teacher in the morning and a French-language teacher in the afternoon. These classroom complexities become further intensified when the teaching story the morning English teacher lives and tells spills over to profoundly shape the stories the fifth-grade students live and tell, and ultimately their pedagogical and personal relationships with their afternoon French teacher, the author of the case.

Clearly, this story of experience lifts the veil on the anonymous afternoon teacher's perspective of the bilingual and presumably bicultural/multicultural situation. But other perspectives besides those of Mrs. Tebbetts remain available. What is known are passing glimpses of their actions, inactions, and reactions sifted through the teller's version of the tale.

In the afternoon French teacher's view, Mrs. Tebbetts sets a "laissez-faire" rhythm to the students' school day, tolerates behaviors that would be less than acceptable by other people's standards (most specifically her or his own), and hands out grades "like candy." In short, Mrs. Tebbetts appears to live the "Pygmalion in the classroom" philosophy—to the extreme.

Mrs. Tebbetts's unyielding stance not only establishes the margins and sets the tone for how the fifth-grade students interact with her, but also with her team partner who, by happenstance, teaches later in the day. In this way, the afternoon French teacher finds her- or himself embroiled in a plotline that is foreign to her or him. Becoming "the heavy"—her or his students' enemy—she or he engages in constant fire with a growing number of student "lawyers" as the classroom sadly dissolves into a "battleground" whose threshold she or he "dread[s] crossing."

Thankfully, through personal reflection and the writing of the case, the afternoon French teacher interrupts the destructive story line. By recognizing and naming the "teaching conundrum," she or he makes it a topic of robust inquiry. All sorts of insightful wonders and ponders emerge. Not only do question marks begin to mark her or his thinking; they also start to punctuate her or his prose. A "myriad of solutions" are attempted, albeit with "limited success." Even the teacher's good humor becomes restored.

Recognizing that no pat answers exist for dilemmas, she or he leaves the readers with the keen sense that she or he is better equipped to move forward—even if her or his teaching partner remains unchanged. Through her or his framing and reframing of the problem, the French teacher's personal perspective has subtly shifted. The possibility of more productive and informed future relationships with students and team partners seems imminent.

But the French teacher's public presentation of the case accomplishes much more. It spurs those of us who vicariously experience it to entertain questions we might not have otherwise done. I, for example, feel compelled to think hard about how cultural and linguistic traditions influence how different teachers approach curriculum and students. I wonder whether Mrs. Tebbetts's and the French instructor's teacher preparation programs were different and whether the two teachers are representative of different generations of teacher development.

I ponder why teachers' relationships, particularly in team teaching situations, are so taken for granted—even by experienced teachers themselves. I am troubled about why administrative interventions and judgments so easily become authoritative and the extent to which teachers' self-talk is influenced by their principals' positions on issues. I toss around the idea of hidden contracts executed and acted on by teachers, students, parents, and administrators.

I imagine parents who enact different parenting styles in uncompromising ways and the consequences of their lack of flexibility on their children. I question why parents and administrators only become actively involved in school situations when the smooth veneers of their perceived realities become disturbed. I even view my teaching career longitudinally and recall similar situations I have known. And I dwell on the notion of complexity itself and desire to know more—not only about the French teacher's predicament, but also about other teachers' puzzles and my own. In short, the anonymous author's storied account becomes my "reflective prompt." In sum, I revisit—in a fresh way—what Doris Lessing had to say about learning: "That is what learning is. You suddenly understand something you've understood all your life, but in a new way."

❖ EXPLORING THE ISSUES

Teacher Isolation

Craig focuses her narrative on our ability to create our lives into stories. She comments that the afternoon French teacher "interrupts the destructive story line." How can teachers rewrite their lives into positive teaching stories?

Power Struggles

Toward the end of Craig's commentary, she ponders the role of authority by administration and teachers who invite and allow that authority to influence or guide decision making. What does Craig suggest instead of following that traditional route? Evaluate the short-term and long-term effects of her proposal.

Teacher Identity

Craig suggests that this story is not of the teller's making; rather she is embroiled in Mrs. Tebbetts's narrative in which she or he would like to be "the hero." How do the complexities of sharing a class prevent a teacher from being master of his or her own stories?

❖ ENGAGING WITH THE COMMENTARIES

Creating Conducive Learning Contexts

Both Craig and Silverman discuss the attempts made to remedy the uncooperative behavior of the teachers. However, the commentators have contrasting insights about the actions taken by the teachers. Compare those views and consider why Silverman appears to be negative, whereas Craig is positive in her comments regarding the French teacher's actions.

Theory and Practice

Wideman, Craig, and Silverman find that the story devolves into a "good cop, bad cop" scenario. Compare the commentators' suggestions to go more deeply into the narrative. Is one approach more helpful than the others? How can a teacher ensure that her or his theories actually work in practice?

Reflection

If only looking outward, as the commentators suggest, is not particularly effective in solving teaching problems, where should a teacher look and why? Compare the directions that Wideman, Craig, and Silverman suggest for beginning to diagnose and remedy the writer-teacher's problem.

Classroom Management

Wideman and Silverman make practical suggestions for improving professional practice. Howard Gardner (1999) has written a study of multiple intelligences in which he examines the variety of ways that children learn. How would all of these suggestions aid in this situation? Based on the commentaries, what resources or suggestions might help teachers who team teach.

Connecting Questions

The Connecting Questions located in the introduction highlight themes that are threaded throughout the cases. You may continue your exploration of the issues raised in this case by addressing those connections. For questions pertinent to this case, please see questions 3, 7, and 11.

❖ ADDITIONAL READINGS

Acker, S. (1999). *The realities of teachers' work.* New York: Cassell.
   This text follows the fortunes of the teachers of Hillview Primary School over 10 years. From the perspective of a primary or elementary school teacher in an urban school, the author suggests how teachers can prepare for the future. She describes the school, the children, the school's resources, and its ethos. The book explores the preponderance of female teachers and a teaching culture that stresses caring and coping. While examining school as a part of the wider community, the author looks

at changes in teachers' careers over time and the effects of educational reform.

Bagin, D., & Gallagher, D. (2004). *The school and community relations*. San Francisco: Jossey-Bass.

This book will aid school officials in improving communication with their staff and their communities, resulting in better school quality and student learning. The text is practical as it explains "how" to foster effective relations among educational partners, staff, and so on. The research has been field-tested.

Darling-Hammond, L. (1998). Teacher learning that supports student learning. *Educational Leadership, 55*, 6–11.

This discussion examines new strategies for training student teachers that address the need for programs to support learning for the teachers. More than conventional readings and pedagogy, practical experience, collaboration among teachers, student evaluation, and the sharing of experiences are necessary.

Friend, M., & Cook, L. (1992). *Interactions: Collaboration skills for school professionals*. Toronto, ON: Copp Clark Pitman.

This book provides a look at how teams of school professionals effectively work together with classroom teachers, special education teachers, and counselors for students with special needs. It addresses collaboration as a style, stressing the need for accompanying knowledge and skills to guide practice. Future teachers learn collaboration skills with school professionals and families of students who are often placed in general classroom settings.

Jenlink, P., & Kinnucan-Welsh, K. (2001). Case stories of facilitating professional development. *Teaching and Teacher Education, 17*, 705–724.

This article discusses the benefits of working collaboratively and the supportive cultures that result when groups of teachers meet on a regular basis to discuss their teaching dilemmas.

Martin, J., & Sugarman, J. (1993). Models of classroom management: Principles, applications and critical perspectives. In J. Anghileri (Ed.), *Principles and practices in arithmetic teaching: Innovative approaches for the primary classroom* (2nd ed.). Calgary, AB: Detselig Open University Press.

This book culls works from a number of authors to present their perspectives on the principles of arithmetic, classroom practices, and the development of research. Discussion of curriculum and differing approaches in England and elsewhere are examined.

Mazur, J., & Lynch, M. D. (1989). Differential impact of administrative, organizational and personality factors on teacher burnout. *Teaching and Teacher Education, 5,* 335–337.

The authors examine relationships among principals' leadership styles, school organization, and the personalities of teachers. Special attention is paid to teacher burnout. A total of 200 high school teachers were included in this survey.

Merleau-Ponty, M. (1989). *Phenomenology of perception.* London: Routledge.

Merleau-Ponty's arguments grow from the lived experience of a person. He focuses on the body not as geometrical, but as having dimensions of spatiality and an orientation toward a possible world. He looks at "body image" in gesture, speech, and sexuality as modes of expression that accrue meaning in dynamic relations. He compares and rejects varying conceptions of perception. He suggests that the body is not one object among many, but instead it is our way to belong to the world.

Shulman, J., & Mesa-Bains, M. (Eds.). (1993). *Diversity in the classroom: Casebook for teachers and teacher-educators.* San Francisco: FarWest Lab.

The framework of Exploring the Case was adapted from this book.

5

Managing Conflict When Working With Educational Partners

I n this case, a teacher rediscovers that Annie, her student with special needs, is the reason for her continued efforts in teaching. The case commentators, Becky Wai-Ling Packard, Nancy L. Hutchinson, and Anne Jordan examine issues of trust and the conflicts that surround the effective teaching and assessment of Annie.

❖ THINKING AHEAD

As you read this chapter, reflect on the following questions and issues:

- Consider the knowledge, skills, attitudes, and experience of the teacher.
- Consider Annie and her special needs. What supports have been put in place for Annie at home and at school?

The use of "she and he," while it may appear awkward to the reader, is intended to ensure the absence of gender bias.

- Consider the contextual elements influence the dilemmas.
- What role does the private tutoring company play in the case?
- Consider the diverse needs and perspectives of the people in this story. Why might tensions arise when dealing with Annie's mother?

"How is this possible? How are you teaching Annie to add three-digit numbers when she's having difficulty understanding the concept of adding? Does she even understand what adding means?"

The questions just fly out of my mouth. I can't understand how a private company that provides evaluation services is better able to make these kinds of promises for educational improvements when my student, Annie, isn't demonstrating this knowledge at school. Although I am new to the school, I have observed Annie on many occasions prior to this intense parent meeting that is presently taking place. What I have recorded in her classroom, and what the tutoring company claims she can do, are two very different things.

"She can do the work" is the response.

The meeting ends without a consensus. My principal, Mr. Miller, reassures me that we are going to continue doing that with which we are comfortable.

"Annie obviously hasn't generalized in class what she has learned with the private company," Mr. Miller explains.

A few months before this meeting, Mr. Miller had called to offer me this position. I felt excited about changing schools. I had requested a transfer from my former school and hoped that I would get a special education position. I had been working in special education for a few years, and I felt that I was ready for a new school environment and was looking forward to working with a different group of students. I anticipated that it would be a lot of work to change schools, but I felt I was ready for the challenge.

My new school is in the suburbs and located in a multicultural community. The school is highly populated, with approximately 900 students, many with special needs. Most are integrated into regular classrooms. As a special education teacher, I have the option to work with a child within his or her own classroom, or withdraw that student and concentrate on a specific skill. This decision depends on the needs of the student.

Annie, who has been diagnosed with a developmental disability, is my greatest concern. She is a curious, happy girl, famous for her huge smile. She is nonverbal and functions academically at the early primary level. Due to safety issues, she receives full-time support from an educational assistant in her fifth-grade classroom. I see her for 30 minutes every day. My goal in September is to get inside Annie's brain and understand how she learns. With my knowledge of students with high needs, I am confident that I can achieve this objective by the end of September.

At the beginning of the school year, Annie's classroom teacher, Mrs. Hilton, informs me that Annie's learning is supported by a private company at home for 3 hours a week. This private company works specifically with students with developmental disabilities.

Part of my role as a special education teacher is to provide a liaison with outside agencies and other support services that are linked to my students. I've done it before, and I am actually looking forward to meeting Annie's tutor. Perhaps this person will be able to give the school some useful suggestions that we can adapt to Annie's Individualized Education Plan (IEP).

After meeting with members of the company and Annie's parents for the first time, I begin to question everything I do with Annie. Maybe they're right and I'm wrong. Maybe I'm missing something. Second guesses flood my mind all through the first term. The excitement of being in a new school with new students is quickly deflated, leaving me confused, exhausted, and discouraged.

During the second term of school, I meet again with Annie's mother. At this point, I am feeling apprehensive. At the beginning of the year, I believed I would be successful in developing parental trust: It would be a given. They would just have to see how dedicated, knowledgeable, and caring I am, and I, exuding concern and confidence, would gain their trust. I quickly realize this hasn't happened the way I had planned it. This part of the process is consuming much more time and energy than I had expected. I walk into the school the morning of the meeting, my shoulders drooping, my feet dragging on the floor, dreading the coming battle. My colleagues try to lift my spirits, but to no avail. I know that I must meet with Annie's tutor and Annie's mother, and I will leave the meeting, feeling even more confused.

Annie's mother is the first to enter the room. She has a big smile on her face. In a gentle voice, she greets us. I quickly remember my first impression of Annie's mother: easygoing, approachable, and polite. She takes a seat in the office. Mrs. Hilton and I greet the mother. Annie's mother informs us that the owner of the company and Annie's tutor will be joining us as well. Mrs. Hilton comments on how much progress Annie has made since the beginning of September. Annie's mother agrees. We comment on how Annie is beginning to interact more with her peers, she's much more compliant, and she is even beginning to use some spontaneous language to communicate.

At that moment, the owner of the company and the tutor arrive. The owner is the first to stride into the office. She makes direct eye contact with me. She has a very serious look on her face. The tutor follows closely behind. The two women take the seats on either side of Annie's mother. I am so nervous that I imagine I am in a scene from a courthouse rather than a school meeting.

I introduce myself to the owner of the company and offer my hand. She shakes my hand and pairs it with an awkward smile. I invite the group into the principal's office. The principal and the classroom teacher join me. I take a deep breath and begin reviewing Annie's updated IEP.

As we review the IEP, the tutor tells me what goals they have been reviewing at home. I am happy to hear that both of us are working on developing Annie's receptive and expressive vocabulary. These are in alignment both at home and at school. The tutor then says, "We have also been working on developing reading comprehension."

Reading comprehension? Those words intrigue me. Out of curiosity, I ask her to elaborate on the reading comprehension. "What kinds of activities do you do with Annie?" I ask. After a few seconds, she confidently responds, "Annie and I write a sentence together on a sentence strip, we cut it up, and Annie puts it back together."

I'm stunned. I wonder what the purpose of this activity is for Annie? How will this activity assess Annie's reading comprehension? How can Annie "write" a sentence? This does not make any sense to me.

I have to comment: "Annie has a strong visual memory. That activity sounds like it's assessing her visual memory, not her reading comprehension."

No one responds. There's an awkward silence. The owner of the company begins to change the subject, but then decides to widen the scope of the conversation: "Why doesn't Annie have her own computer at school? What is the school doing to improve her social skills outside at recess?"

Annie's mother takes over: "We taught Annie this math in the second grade. Annie is beyond this. Why doesn't she work on the same math that her tutor completes with her? Don't you understand that this math is too easy for Annie?"

The room is silent. Mr. Miller looks over at me. Mrs. Hilton buries herself in her notes. I am fighting this battle on my own. For each question, I am able to produce strategies that have been working well at school. For the comment about the math, I ignore it. I picture Annie sitting at her desk while she is completing the math. No, the math isn't too easy for Annie.

I feel some relief because I am able to answer a few questions. But I am left feeling that we do not share a common understanding of Annie's learning. My self-doubt sets in once more. Am I a good teacher? Maybe I shouldn't be in special education. I wonder if there's a regular classroom position available next year.

The meeting ends abruptly. Finally, the tension in the air dissipates. It is quite clear that we are not going to agree today. Annie's mom obviously will continue to put her faith and trust in the tutoring company and not in the school. My heavy heart sinks even further when I think that I have not been successful in gaining her trust. I feel as though I have lost the battle.

After the meeting ends, we decide that, at the school level, we are going to continue with the program that we have set up for Annie. We've seen an impressive amount of progress because of the current educational program, and that's what counts.

After some reflection, I can't help but wonder—is it even disagreement among stakeholders? Would I ever gain the parents' support when we do not see Annie's learning in the same way? Do we even share a common understanding of Annie's needs and abilities? Are we seeing Annie for who she is? Is the tutoring company telling the parents what they want to hear? What is in Annie's best interest?

A few days later, I walk into Annie's fifth-grade classroom for my scheduled time to work with her. She looks up from her desk. Her eyes immediately widen, and she gives me her famous smile—her big, toothy grin. At that exact moment, I realize that it is her smile that has helped me so many times when I was up to my ears in paperwork or filled with self-doubt. Her smile reminds me of the reason why I entered teaching in the first place—to help children learn and grow.

As I smile back at Annie, I hope that I have done just that.

❖ EXPLORING THE CASE

An elementary special education teacher with 5 years of experience wrote this case.

Identification

Identify the key facts of this case. What events are central to understanding this situation? Identify the dilemmas and tensions in this case. Explore the main aspects of each dilemma and tension.

Analysis

Analyze the issue(s) from the viewpoints of the different people in the case. How do the interactions between the teacher and the tutoring company, the teacher and the parent, the teacher and colleagues, and finally, the teacher and her- or himself create tensions for the teacher? What role does Annie play in all of these discussions?

Evaluation

Examine critically the teacher's strategies for handling the challenge(s) with Annie's mother, the tutoring company, and Annie. Does the teacher depicted fulfill, fall short of, or surpass your notion of the role of a teacher?

Alternative Solutions

Were there alternative solutions or strategies available to deal with the dilemmas? Generate alternative solutions to the ones presented in the narrative. Take into consideration risks, benefits, and long- and short-term consequences of each proposed action.

Reflection

Although the teacher appears to be able to deal with the conflict at the story's conclusion, does her or his concluding reflection provide a satisfying ending? Why is the student, Annie, herself a way for the teacher to refocus her or his thinking on working with students with special needs? Has anything been resolved?

Changing Opinions

Consider your thoughts and assumptions at the beginning of the chapter. Who or what has caused you to consider a new way of thinking? How strongly do you still feel about your previous assumptions?

Synthesis

Synthesize your understanding of this case into a statement. What is this a case of?

Case Commentary by Becky Wai-Ling Packard

Students learn and develop across multiple contexts, including the home and school. Thus, facilitating communication between home and school is an important aspect of supporting student learning. However, each party must act on the information gained from communication—not only must the home act in response to the school. This case highlights the difficulty school-based educators can face when engaging in negotiations with the home in the effort to engage in a bidirectional model of change.

The author provides a special education teacher's perspective on her or his work with a student at school named Annie. Specifically, we learn of this teacher's encounter with agents from the home, who include the parent and the staff from a tutoring company hired by the family. Because the student develops and learns in multiple contexts, the student's potential may be perceived differently in each context. In other words, identity, learning, and potential may not be stable entities, but rather are influenced by context. What a student appears capable of in one context may change when placed in another context. What is "true" of a student, then, may depend on context. Although obvious in some sense, this notion can be difficult to conceive when an educator only has the opportunity to see a student in one context. This is illustrated when the author writes, with some sense of astonishment, "What I have recorded in her classroom, and what the tutoring company claims she can do, are two very different things." The terms used by the author are important. She or he uses "recorded," implying objectivity, to describe her or his own actions, and "claims," suggesting perception, to describe the actions of the home-based agents. Perhaps too often, the teacher's perspective is taken as fact, and one is left to wonder why the teacher appears to be in the position of underestimating the student's potential.

Moreover, the teacher interprets the alternative perspective provided by the home context as a challenge to her or his authority that makes her or him feel that she or he is not "trusted" by the home. A teacher could think that believing a student is performing better at home with the tutoring company means that she or he, as the teacher, is not doing everything possible to support the student's learning at school. Although surely unintentional, this possibility appears to be devastating to the teacher's perception of her- or himself as an effective teacher.

The author writes, "After meeting with the company and Annie's parents for the first time, I begin to question everything I do with Annie. Maybe they're right and I'm wrong. Maybe I'm missing something. Second guesses flood my mind all through the first term." Thus, the teacher may feel she or he has to choose between believing the home account, which would mean she or he is a "bad" teacher, and denying the home account, which would mean that she or he has done everything right. A teacher, however, can resist entering into a paradigm that leads her or him to making a choice, as neither choice leads to supporting the student or sustaining her or his development as a teacher.

Instead, a teacher could conceive of new information from the home context as a gift rather than evidence of her or his own ineffectiveness, and view points of disagreement as places to begin conversations rather than a battleground where she or he must strive to appear "right." If we can operate out of a "teacher as learner" framework, we can begin to see multiple possibilities of where to go next. Adopting this framework wholeheartedly is difficult, especially for teachers, but necessary. Openness to learning may be what makes individuals truly great teachers. And perhaps this quality can help lead to greater trust among parties.

Finally, over the long run, one must also consider what factors sustain teachers through this challenging, albeit rewarding, profession, especially when the students, families, or schools do not readily provide gracious, instant feedback as to the worth of their investments. For the teacher in this case, a few smiles from her student Annie appeared to be enough to sustain her or him on a given day. But one can consider alternative scenarios with students who differ from Annie and what incentives there are for teachers to engage in rigorous self-examination, continued reinvestment in their own learning, creative problem solving with students, and complicated negotiations across contexts.

❖ EXPLORING THE ISSUES

Trust Relationships

Packard suggests that a main focus for this teacher is her or his perceived inability to gain parental trust. How important is this goal? Describe how teachers might attain this.

Power Struggles

The commentator considers how the teacher in this case feels that her or his authority is being threatened and/or challenged. How does this influence her or his actions (both positively and negatively) in the meeting and in the classroom? When stressful meetings occur, how can a teacher deal with the residual effects on her or his identity?

Assessments for Students With Special Needs

Why is the context critical in assessing the ability of students with special needs to learn?

Teacher Choices

Examine the paradigm choice that the commentator presents in the second-to-last paragraph of this commentary. Do you support the framework she proposes to avoid either "bad" choice?

Case Commentary by Nancy L. Hutchinson

This case brings us face-to-face with some of the most important dilemmas faced by teachers in publicly funded education systems. Parents know their children well, having been their children's first and most enduring teachers. Teachers must respect and work collaboratively with the parents of their students. However, parents of exceptional children often have little experience of their children's participation in the academic and social contexts of the classroom and of the school. What parents see in the very familiar, very supportive, and, in this case, probably very predictable context of home—and of private tutoring—may not represent what the child can do or is willing to do at school.

Private tutors can spend long periods of time, under ideal conditions, working with children on small tasks drawn from the curriculum, sometimes in quite decontextualized ways. With repetition and predictability, exceptional children, such as those with developmental disabilities, may develop quite accomplished responses to specific tasks. In many cases, private tutors have frequent and close contact with parents and much more opportunity to develop friendly and trusting relationships with them than with teachers. Because continued payment for services may depend on the exceptional student making documented progress, the choice of tasks in tutoring can vary greatly from the curriculum-based sequence usually adopted in schools.

Teachers are acutely aware of the professional and ethical guidelines that they adopt when they enter the profession. In my experience, teachers worry a great deal both about disappointing and about misleading the parents of exceptional children. Teachers know that they must neither overstate the accomplishments of these learners nor contribute to parents' unrealistic expectations. At the same time, they must be encouraging and help the student to believe that meeting the next goal is possible. Sometimes the small learning and curriculum gains that buoy special education teachers and their exceptional students, made in the context of active, noisy, child-filled schools, are not sufficient to meet parents' high expectations. Such teachers face a moral dilemma.

While the teacher in this case must question her or his own teaching and collect reliable evidence of the child's progress at school and in private tutoring, she or he must also offer opportunities for the parent and tutor to observe the child learning at school. When everyone has the same data, a future meeting could profitably explore the importance of context to the learning and assessment of a student like Annie. With the common understandings that could be developed with such an approach, progress toward shared goals and consistent planning for Annie at home and school might be more possible.

This case reminds us that to meet the ethical demands of their profession, teachers must be scrupulously honest with parents and avoid fueling unrealistic hopes while providing encouragement and the best possible education for the exceptional students in their charge. A tall order, to be sure!

❖ EXPLORING THE ISSUES

Working With Students With Special Needs

Hutchinson considers the contextual elements that affect the dilemma faced by the teacher. Explain how differing situations may alter performance. How might a student like Annie be assessed and how does a teacher know that the assessment and tools selected are reliable? If skills can only be performed in individual contexts, then have they been learned?

Teacher Identity

Why does Hutchinson suggest that student performance influences a teacher's self-confidence? Should a teacher evaluate her- or himself based on a student's level of success?

Trust Relationships

Hutchinson in her conclusion refers to the ethical dilemmas that teachers will face. Examine the moral dilemmas she presents (referred to in paragraph 3) and discuss how teachers must balance needs and make decisions that are honest.

Case Commentary by Anne Jordan

This case is a good example of how poor communication can destroy the best efforts and intentions of educators. The meeting between the private tutoring company owner, the private tutor, the author, Annie's mother, classroom teacher, and the principal could have been the key to establishing successful collaboration on behalf of Annie.

Instead, it starts with confusion among the participants about the purpose of the meeting, then degenerates into opposing "camps" and a bid for each camp to score points against the other. The meeting is later described by the author as a "battle." The principal has to take much of the responsibility for the breakdown in collaboration. He or his designated team leader should coordinate the meeting to arrive at a consensus about Annie's needs and clarity about the roles of each participant at the meeting and beyond. The point of no return occurs in the meeting when the author challenges the owner about what is essentially a semantic question: What is meant by the term "reading comprehension." In the silence that follows the challenge, each group retrenches to a position of blaming the other for failing to understand Annie's needs.

This meeting could have resulted in a different outcome. But before considering how, some questions need to be answered. First, why was the meeting called and who called it? Was the school holding an IEP review, and, if so, what is contained in the IEP? Why was the author so insecure and confused about her or his role and responsibilities in the meeting?

Let's assume that this was an IEP review meeting, called by the school with the intention of collaborating with the tutoring company and Annie's parents to develop a suitable plan for Annie. Let's also assume that the participants have been asked to bring their records about Annie's current achievements, such as assessment data and samples of work. Mr. Miller should begin the meeting by establishing the purpose of the meeting (e.g., to find out how Annie is progressing and to collaborate in developing the IEP). He should then ask each participant to describe how he or she sees Annie's current strengths, progress, and needs. Participants would be encouraged to illustrate their perspectives from the materials they brought.

The next step would be for the group to discuss what were the priorities for revising Annie's placement in a special education program, known in Canada as an Identification, Placement, and Review Committee (IPRC), including the expectations for the next term and the balance of the school year. A discussion of the evaluation criteria would complete the proceedings ("If this plan is working, what will Annie be doing differently that we will all be able to see when we next meet?").

An astute team leader would demonstrate skills in leading a collaborative team process: making people comfortable, acknowledging achievements, listening for agreement, and, if necessary, intervening by reminding participants that they hold a common interest in meeting Annie's needs. The leader would close the meeting with a summary of what had been accomplished and the tasks to which the group had agreed, and by asking how well the group felt the meeting had gone.

❖ EXPLORING THE ISSUES

Communication

Working with parental and community groups can be challenging. Jordan points out that the poor communication among all involved parties adds to the challenge. When parties disagree on the best plan of action, what other steps might be taken to facilitate solutions?

Leadership

Jordan speculates on who called the meeting and why. What role might the principal have played to ease tensions and work toward a more positive outcome?

❖ ENGAGING WITH THE COMMENTARIES

Assessment

Consider the teacher's assessment of Annie's academic performance versus that of Annie's parents and tutor. Wai-Ling Packard and Hutchinson point out that contextual elements may influence learning. Compare and contrast these two commentaries.

Students With Special Needs

Dealing with students with special needs can be stressful. How can a teacher know if content, teaching approaches, and student development all align? How can teachers ensure that they have met the needs of their students?

Collaboration

Hutchinson focuses on ethical issues, whereas Jordan takes a very practical stance. How would Hutchinson's ethical consideration affect implementing Jordan's suggestions?

Teacher Identity

The commentators write about the upsetting impact the meeting with Annie's team had on the teacher. How do Packard and Hutchinson suggest the teacher find ways to cope and preserve sense of self?

Connecting Questions

The Connecting Questions located in the introduction highlight themes that are threaded throughout the cases. You may continue your exploration of the issues raised in this case by addressing those connections. For questions pertinent to this case, please see questions 6, 7, and 10.

❖ ADDITIONAL READINGS

Alberta Education, Special Education Branches. (1996). *Partners during changing times: An information booklet for parents of children with special needs.* Edmonton, AB: Author.

This is a guide for parents of children of disabilities. There are four parts: responsibilities and resources for parents; assessments and planning for exceptional children, supports, and resources; dispute resolution and appeals; and funding. Appendixes include helpful tips.

Boesel Dunn, K., & Boesel Dunn, A. (1993). *Trouble with school: A family story about learning disabilities.* Bethesda, MD: Woodbine House.

Based on a true-life experience, one family's narrative reveals the stress when a child is diagnosed with a learning disability and the family learns to cope and adjust.

Cohen, E. G. (1994). *Designing group work: Strategies for the heterogeneous classroom* (2nd ed.). New York: Teachers College Press.

The focus here is group work at any grade level. The authors suggest that group work alleviates challenges that teachers face. Strategies, perspective on group dynamics, and creative team building examples are presented.

Friend, M., & Cook, L. (1992). *Interactions: Collaboration skills for school professionals.* Toronto, ON: Copp Clark Pitman.

This book provides a look at how teams of school professionals effectively work together to provide a range of services for classroom teachers, special education teachers, and counselors for students with special needs. It addresses collaboration as a style, stressing the need for accompanying knowledge and skills to guide practice. Future teachers may learn how to collaborate with school professionals and families of students who are often placed in general classroom settings.

Hargreaves, A. (1995). *Changing teachers, changing times: Teachers' work and culture in the postmodern age.* New York: Teachers College Press.

This book features a discussion by Hargreaves on modernity, postmodernism, postmodernity, and a view toward teachers' roles against a materialistic, functionalist view of history and social change.

Kilbourn, B. (1990). *Constructive feedback: Learning the art.* Toronto, ON: Ontario Institute for Studies in Education Press.

The 13 stages in this case study inquiry provide a model that features a teacher and his colleagues. In order to foster professional development, two teachers engage in (1) Beginning the Process, (2) Feedback

Overload, (3) Different Perspectives on Success, (4) Being Explicit in the Process, and so on, until they reach (13) Stress of the Process.

Loughran, J. J. (2002, January/February). Effective reflective practice: In search of meaning in learning about teaching. *Journal of Teacher Education, 53*(1), 33–43.

Reflective practice is useful and informing to practice. It is important, however, to identify the nature of reflection to provoke ways of questioning taken-for-granted assumptions and noting diverse points of view. By examining teacher practice and the relationship between time, experience, and expectations of learning through reflection, Loughran explains how reflection can influence professional knowledge.

Shulman, J., & Mesa-Bains, M. (Eds.). (1993). *Diversity in the classroom: Casebook for teachers and teacher-educators.* San Francisco: FarWest Lab.

The framework of Exploring the Case was adapted from this book.

6

A Student Teacher Faces the Challenges of the Classroom

I n this case, when a teacher is away, a teacher candidate gains insight into students, colleagues, and herself. At the moment of acquiring this self-knowledge, the school bell rings and interrupts her from transferring this insight into immediate action. The case commentators Tom Russell, William J. Hunter, D. Jean Clandinin, and Janet L. Miller, along with two new teachers, examine the challenges that new teachers experience, namely, classroom management, lack of support, power struggles, and crises of identity. When gender issues confound the situation, teacher assumptions must be reexamined.

❖ THINKING AHEAD

As you read this chapter, reflect on the following questions and issues:

The use of "she and he," while it may appear awkward to the reader, is intended to ensure the absence of gender bias.

- Consider the teacher candidate's experience, skills, and knowledge. Examine the teacher candidate's preconceptions about the students, classroom management, and school community even before she encounters the principal dilemmas in the case.
- Consider the many contextual elements of the classroom that play a role in framing this case.
- Consider the teacher's ability to deal with classroom disruptions.
- What are the dilemmas that confront this neophyte? Are the problems that occur caused by teacher inexperience?

"I'll be away tomorrow, so you'll be working with a substitute teacher for the day," Mr. Harris, my mentor teacher, an experienced teacher with the ability to calmly manage even the most unconventional classes, informs me. As a teacher candidate, I am not as excited as my students are to spend the day with a substitute teacher. I have several burning questions that cannot be answered at this moment: "Who will the substitute teacher be? Will the class be manageable? How bad can they really be?" I am in the middle of my placement in a seventh-grade integrated learning disabled homeroom that has been designated, by the teachers, as the school's worst class. On a normal day, there are two regular teachers, an educational assistant, and I, the teacher candidate, in the class. I know that the students are aware of their negative reputation. In addition, the constant supervision by four adults, resembling police officers on a stakeout, is a constant reminder of their difference. With all of the attention that these students receive on a daily basis, a substitute teacher represents an opportunity to act out without suffering severe consequences. I actually feel tremendous excitement because I will be able to teach the class as if it is my own, and the substitute can sit back and watch. Tomorrow this class will be mine. I will be in charge.

The next day, when I meet the substitute teacher, a young female like myself, she introduces herself and very pleasantly remarks, "I'm not the type of substitute teacher who just sits back and does nothing, but I will try not to interfere with any of your plans." She seems very honest and friendly, but I am more concerned about the upcoming day, and I am ready to begin. The morning consists of geography and history classes as well as French. The French class is a much-needed prep for me. I find that it is difficult to begin the geography class due to the students' inability to focus. One child, Dennis, refuses to do any work. This is his regular behavior, and, as well, there is constant pervasive chatter that continues to irritate me. Miraculously, I am able to quiet down the class to deliver a brief lesson about the economy. The class even cooperates enough to hear the subsequent explanations of the textbook assignment. Now my confidence mounts, and I begin to think that this class is not as bad as their reputation with the other teachers that has been reported. I execute the history class lesson in the similarly successful method that I have established earlier, although amidst gossipy chatter, but I still can't envisage this class without four attentive adults in the room.

The school is an ethnically diverse kindergarten-to-eighth-grade inner-city school. In addition, most classes have as many as five English as a Second Language (ESL) students. This also presents its own challenge. Boy, am I ever relieved that the morning is over, and that I have completed two entire lessons. Hooray for me! I am definitely beginning to understand the stress and irritation that is predominant in teaching. More important, I am enjoying the challenge and am pleased with the present outcome.

After lunch, I am anticipating the students' increased energy because I have been warned of the bizarre mood swings that occur after the lunch hour. It was not long ago that I was the perpetrator of such hyperactive behavior! During the afternoon, the seventh- and eighth-grade students rotate from classroom to classroom, and I will be teaching guidance along with the very friendly substitute teacher. My lesson involves a survey and a small debate about issues of gender equity in the sports world. My first class is my homeroom class, with whom I have already established a rapport. I am preparing for a noisy class in which a lot of discussion will occur. For some reason unknown to me, I am finding it extremely difficult to take full command of the class. I am able to distribute the surveys, but the attentive behavior is slowly dissipating. Dennis is having a scientific debate with Steven across the room about whether or not a human brain will explode on Mars, a group of five girls is giggling, and nonstop conversations are relentlessly escalating in volume.

Earlier in the term, I had established a successful method that quieted the class, and now I am ready to use it. I ask the class for their attention and wait while keeping an eye on the clock. The students know that I mean business, and that I am not afraid to keep them late after school to complete any parts of the lesson that they have prevented me from presenting due to the incessant noise.

I am not quite sure of the substitute teacher's opinion of my teaching and classroom management methods, but I soon learn that she is not willing to wait for silence. She interjects, "You are all in the eighth grade and I think it's about time that you started acting like it! I can't believe how rude you all are!" She is obviously appalled by their lack of respect for me, but I also experience disrespect from her for the abrupt interruption of my silencing method. Her plea is successful for a moment. Then the noise returns. Insecurity briefly races through me: She must think that I'm an incompetent teacher, but she'll see that this method works with these students. Confidently, I continue with my classroom management strategy.

Finally, the substitute teacher, unable to control her irritation, storms next door to grab the class's special education teacher in desperation. This teacher is a large male who is feared by many students, both male and female.

At this moment I am not sure whether my face is red and burning or pale and cold; however, I know that I am both angry and in awe of the situation. I can't seem to understand the act of desperation that has just occurred. Why did she have to go and get him? I thought I had everything controlled. My authority—whatever authority remains—has been squashed. I am very embarrassed. I can't believe she decided that two young female teachers needed to be saved by a strong male figure. This is a far cry from my lesson on gender equity and the positive model I have attempted to establish as a strong, confident, and "in control" female: *we can hold our own ground.* Immediately, upon entering the classroom, the male teacher uses his powerful and domineering voice. He demands answers from the students: "What is going on in here? Why can't you cooperate with Ms. Elvin and Ms. Wright?"

Garit, one of the students who immigrated over 8 years ago, forcefully raises his hand and confidently answers the questions: "Sir, I feel that it's just much easier to respect male teachers than female teachers!"

My jaw drops. I think to myself, did I just hear that correctly? I thought that throughout the past 2 months I had created a community in the classroom that respected and valued both male and female students. I couldn't help but wonder, "Is this how my students see me?" Am I a powerless female when compared with dominant male teachers? I certainly think not!

I notice that I am frozen in my shoes in front of the class, unable to respond, and unsure of exactly how to approach the situation. How can I take action without challenging this student's belief, which may reflect deep cultural roots? How do I prevent other students from agreeing with Garit's point of view? Then the bell rings, but somehow, at this moment I do not feel that I am saved by the bell but rather interrupted.

❖ EXPLORING THE CASE

A pre-service teaching candidate wrote this case.

Identification

Identify the key facts of this case. What factual events are central to understanding this situation? Identify the dilemmas and tensions in this case. Explore the main aspects of each dilemma and tension. Consider the dilemma from the various perspectives of the individuals involved in the case.

Analysis

Analyze the issue(s) from the viewpoints of the different people in the case. Analyze the situation by examining the benefits and risks of the teacher candidate's actions. How might the teacher plan for the next class after being "saved by the bell"?

Evaluation

Examine critically the teacher's strategies for handling the challenge(s). Does the teacher depicted fulfill, fall short of, or surpass your notion of the role of a teacher?

Alternative Solutions

Were there alternative solutions or strategies available to deal with the dilemma? Generate alternative solutions to the ones presented in the narrative. Take into consideration risks, benefits, and long- and short-term consequences of each proposed action.

Reflection

Does the teacher's concluding reflection provide a satisfying ending? What does her reference to being "saved by the bell" suggest?

Changing Opinions

Consider your thoughts and assumptions at the beginning of the chapter. Who or what has caused you to consider a new way of thinking? How strongly do you still feel about your previous assumptions?

Synthesis

Synthesize your understanding of this case into a statement. What is this a case of?

Case Commentary by Tom Russell

After 25 years in pre-service teacher education, I sometimes think (foolishly) that I have seen and heard everything. The case in this chapter, "A Student Teacher Faces the Challenges of the Classroom," raises many familiar issues. Practicum assignments will always be the most significant feature of the pre-service experience. One of the inevitable tensions of the practicum involves the teacher, who remains the "real teacher" no matter how long the "student teacher" stays and no matter how much the students love, hate, or merely tolerate the arrival of another person at the front of their classroom. On the surface, this case highlights the early teaching concerns familiar to all teacher candidates: Can I plan a lesson? Can I control the students?

Inevitably, a case omits far more than it includes, and this one is no exception. As the teacher candidate eagerly anticipates being in charge and having ownership of the class, we are also told that the class normally has four adults "resembling police officers on a stakeout." With this ominous image, we are not surprised that "there is constant pervasive chatter," but we should pay close attention to the author's account. When used in a teacher's account of a lesson, part of me weeps at words such as "deliver" and "execute." Terms like these have crept into our professional vocabulary from other areas of society, yet they are so far removed from the teacher-student relationship that new and old teachers alike strive for in their work. These words signal to me that we are reading an account of an individual whose first year of teaching will be intensely focused on discovering herself as a teacher and on deciding what type of teacher she really wants to be. These are discoveries and decisions that cannot be taken as a teacher candidate but are central to the first year of teaching.

One of the best teachers I know was a student in my own pre-service classes just a few years ago. While working with his first teacher candidate, he resolved never to interrupt that person's teaching unless he was asked to; if he were asked, he would respond fully and resolve the situation into which he had been invited. Being interrupted by another teacher with more authority is every teacher candidate's nightmare.

Although this interruption is the case's critical incident, this case is not about the substitute teacher. We can do little more than share the author's disappointment and anger.

Issues such as gender equity are complex beyond words. It seems puzzling that the author had been in this classroom for 2 months and yet was so very eager to feel personal ownership in the teacher's absence. Creating a classroom community that respects gender equity is a tall order for anyone. Teachers with full responsibility would see gender equity as an issue that requires patience, persistence, and skill. This case highlights the complexity of the pre-service practicum and reminds us of the constraints inherent in the practicum's emotionally charged experiences.

❖ EXPLORING THE ISSUES

New Teachers

Russell, speaking from his experience of 25 years, considers that what is most significant in the education of new teachers is practicum assignments. What early teaching concerns does this case highlight for new teachers?

Collaboration

Russell says, "Creating a classroom community that respects gender equity is a tall order for anyone." How might faculties of education or school communities work with schools to address that issue?

Power Struggles

Why does Russell feel that disrupting a new teacher when she or he is teaching is harmful? How can suggestions for improvements be made in a nonthreatening and supportive manner?

Self-Knowledge

Although Russell expresses surprise that the teacher candidate—after only 2 months—felt responsibility for the deeply rooted issues of gender discrimination, he himself acknowledges that teachers continue to learn and be surprised (see the opening line). How do "surprises" or sudden revelations create opportunities for fresh insights? Conversely, how can teachers ensure that they do not "take for granted" their own and student responses to routines in education?

Case Commentary by William J. Hunter

I was intrigued by what the last statement in this case study says about the case itself or at least about the author's view of the case. The fact that this case was written by a teacher candidate (nice job, teacher candidate) makes me even more intrigued. If we take the allusion to boxing seriously, "saved by the bell" (in the last line of the case) might connote one of two things: Either it is the end of the final round and the teacher candidate in the story has been spared from a knockout, or it is an earlier round and she has been given a reprieve in her corner and will come back to "fight" again. The final sentence suggests it is the latter, but the school bell provides a longer reprieve, so I'd like to offer some suggestions about what the corner team should be doing before the teacher candidate goes back in the ring.

My first response to this case was to draft advice or questions to all the characters in the teacher candidate's "corner." For example, to the trainer (mentor teacher) I wanted to say this: "You know the success of this venture really depends on you. Part of her difficulty right now is that she really didn't seem to have enough preparation for this event—I mean the fact that she had only one day's notice." And to the "cut" person (the university's faculty associate), I wanted to say, "You know the success of this venture really depends on you. You have to get in there and help the teacher candidate heal. She took a beating in this last round and her confidence is shaken. Remind her of her skills and get her to listen to the trainer."

I wanted to get across one major point: There is a lot of shared responsibility in any student teaching placement and, for each of the people involved, it is fair to say, "You know the success of this venture really depends on you." But the central character here is the teacher candidate. She needs to look hard at her own performance and ask herself questions like the following:

- Why do I think the class is my sole responsibility? What do I think the substitute teacher's role is? How am I taking advantage of the in-classroom support?

- Why am I saying I would continue with "my classroom management strategy," but not saying what that strategy entails?
- Why do I seem to have so much confidence in a single method? Should I be considering other "punches"?
- Is a lecture format really the way I want to work with learning-disabled kids? Why am I focusing so much of their attention on a textbook if reading is one of their difficulties?
- Why would a student who has been in the school system for 8 years suddenly express a concern about learning from a female teacher? Is this really the issue?
- If it really is the issue, why am I taking this as a personal issue when I know that it is a function of Garit's traditional culture? Did I park my respect for diversity somewhere? Can I find ways to help Garit see that I respect him, but that I have an obligation to help him prepare for a life where women have equality in the workforce (at least theoretically)?

The teacher candidate in the story is overly concerned with "control," but that is normal. She does not yet see that the most effective control is a consequence of good material and constructive learning environments. She has been in this placement for 2 months but she describes the class (which is evidently quite diverse in a variety of ways) as if they were all the same and her "methods" of teaching and classroom management assume a "one-size-fits-all" world.

If the bell was a temporary reprieve, the teacher candidate has a chance to come back. Her odds will improve if she and everyone on her team understand: "The success of this venture really depends on you."

❖ EXPLORING THE ISSUES

Metaphors

With a focus on metaphors, Hunter connects with one of the main themes in this case. Does thinking in metaphors add to your understanding of the issues? If so, how?

New Teachers

Evaluate the six questions that Hunter suggests the teacher candidate should ask herself. How useful and practical is this list? Which point or points would be most helpful in guiding new teachers? Explain your reasons for your choices.

Case Commentary by D. Jean Clandinin

In the Center for Research for Teacher Education and Development at the University of Alberta, we frequently talk about teacher identities and what it means to live and tell a story of oneself as a teacher. Because I take a narrative view of teaching, research, and teacher education, I see a teacher's identity as storied, as evolving, as fluid, as multiple, as composed over the temporal span of a teacher's life. Michael Connelly and I wrote about teacher identity as stories to live by, as storied lives on storied landscapes (Connelly & Clandinin, 1999).

In reading the case, "A Student Teacher Faces the Challenges of the Classroom," I thought about the storied life the teacher candidate was in the midst of composing for herself on that school landscape. She was in the midst of composing not only a gendered story of herself, a story of herself as a woman teacher, but also stories of herself as someone committed to social justice, as someone with subject matter knowledge, as someone committed to being attentive to student needs. These stories were shaping her story to live by, at least as she told of herself in this case.

She does not attend closely to the storied landscape on which she finds herself. However, the institutional plotline of what it means to be a teacher candidate shapes this landscape. Others, it seems, know this story: the substitute teacher, the special education teacher, and the students. The student teacher hopes she can live a different story of who she is as teacher by quietly assuming a different part in the story of school. She finds, however, she is trapped into the plotline that lives on this landscape. When there is a tension in the classroom, everyone moves into the part they are to play in the story of teacher candidate. The substitute teacher goes for help, the special education teacher comes in and enacts his part, and that is to make sure the students behave for the student teacher. The unexpected part of the case is when the male student raises the issue of the place of women in his story of school. There is much to consider in the student's comment, but issues of honoring diversity and what that might mean in our classrooms is not my main focus in this brief set of comments.

I want to attend to how we might begin to shift the story of which teacher candidates are in the story of school. Shifting this story is indeed difficult and requires that we work together—university faculty, cooperating teachers, teacher candidates, and students—if we are to shift the story of school. In one partnership program in which

I engaged (Clandinin, Davies, Hogan, & Kennard, 1993), we worked to reimagine how we might live and tell a new story of teacher education, one that positions teacher candidates as people already living and telling a story of who they are becoming as teachers, not as "not yet teachers" who are positioned in a story of "not yet experts." In "A Student Teacher Faces the Challenges of the Classroom," the teacher candidate has a sense of "being interrupted" in her attempts to compose a new story of teacher education, a story she was trying to compose without involving others in the conversation.

❖ EXPLORING THE ISSUES

Identity Issues

Clandinin's work in education has focused on the personal professional nature of teachers' work and how teachers create and think about their "storied landscapes." How might teacher candidates decide how to compose stories for themselves and their students?

Power Struggles

When tensions occur, Clandinin speculates that people take on a variety of roles. How do the roles the substitute teacher, the special education teacher, and the students assume alter the context and the teacher's sense of herself as teacher?

Equity

Clandinin says that the unexpected part of the story occurs when Garit raises his hand and speaks his thoughts out loud. Although the teacher in the case thought that the students had assimilated the lesson on gender equity in sports, she now realizes they had not. How are teachers able to ascertain the effectiveness of a lesson?

Identity Issues

Clandinin's concept of a teacher's identity is one that has many facets. It is organic and continues to grow. Examine the growth of the teacher in the narrative and how she might continue to develop her story as a teacher, particularly having been faced with the challenges in this "landscape."

Case Commentary by Janet L. Miller

On the surface, this case presents a scenario that most pre-service teacher candidates—and practicing teachers—fear: an unruly class whose members' noncompliant behaviors lead to another teacher being called into the room to establish "order." But there's something more here lurking beneath what the teacher candidate in this scenario initially frames as "classroom management dilemmas." Intertwined throughout this case are social and cultural constructions of gendered interactions, expectations, and assumptions that ultimately influence and construct "appropriate" teacher and student identities, roles, and behaviors.

The teacher candidate, a young woman, welcomes the chance to have the day to herself as the "real teacher" when her mentor teacher, a male, must miss a day of school. Working with an already labeled "worst class in the school" integrated learning-disabled group, the teacher candidate gains confidence as she successfully moves her students through the first half of the school day. But she is wary of the "bizarre behaviors" that are often said to characterize these students after their lunchtime break. The teacher candidate is also a bit wary of the substitute teacher, a young woman not too much older than herself, who seems willing to let the teacher candidate enact her planned lessons, but who also establishes herself as a substitute teacher who doesn't just sit back and watch. Given the "policing" that these students receive from four adults assigned to help with the class on a daily basis, both the teacher candidate and the substitute teacher apparently feel pressure to "maintain control" of the class. The emphasis, for both teachers, is on establishing their "authority" with these students (and with one another).

By constructing the details of this case around such issues, rather than around an analysis of ways in which positions of authority are predicated on a hierarchical and often patriarchal order, the teacher candidate is surprised by the rapid turn of events that undermines her supposedly already developed stance of authority and control in this classroom. For it is the young female substitute teacher who interrupts the teacher candidate's attempts to "manage" the unruly class and thus undermines the teacher candidate's precarious position of authority. This interruption further complicates the gender dynamics and constructions that characterize this case. By running to the male special education teacher next door and asking him to reestablish order, the substitute teacher not only replicates a gendered dynamic of male superiority but also re-inscribes a hierarchical relationship between herself and the teacher candidate. The final and perhaps most devastating repetition of gendered constructions of male and female identity is one male student's declaration that he always finds it easier to respect a male teacher than a female one.

What might educators, both pre-service and in-service, do to challenge classroom practices and curricula that insist on predictable, controllable, and normative (or, in this classroom, nonnormative) identities for both teachers and students? In particular, how might we explore examples of typical school discourses and practices that produce, through reiteration, social and cultural constructions of gender identity? Because teachers and teacher-educators are under pressure, in this unrelenting era of standardization of educational practices, to conform their self-representations to particular and predetermined identity frames, such as the "good" teacher, their identities at the same time run the risk of hardening into rigid, polarized, constitutive gender categories— the "strong and in-control male teacher" or the "weak and dependent female teacher." The teacher candidate clearly wished to avoid such duplication of gendered identities with her students, and yet ironically is re-inscribed as that which she hoped to disrupt. How to engage both her students and herself in rethinking and reworking normalized conceptions of what and who are possible remains one of the most important and most difficult challenges that this teaching candidate—or any educator—will ever face.

❖ EXPLORING THE ISSUES

Classroom Management

Miller exposes the issues that underpin problems of classroom management. In particular, she addresses the "social and cultural constructions of gendered interactions . . . that ultimately influence and construct 'appropriate' teacher and student identities, roles, and behaviors." Identify the "gendered" dynamics that might arise in classes and interfere with effective classroom management in this case.

Reflection

Consider how Miller's final paragraph also offers probes to examine how teachers should think about the duplication and standardizing of educational practices. Are there benefits for new teachers to follow this particular path? Explain your thinking.

Diversity Issues

Miller suggests that often there are cultural issues that arise and surprise us. The teacher candidate is concerned about challenging Garit's beliefs. How might a teacher respect cultural, gender, and individual differences, yet deal with the multicultural issues that arise? How would you address the issues differently at the elementary and secondary levels?

Societal Biases

Although the teacher candidate wished to avoid polarized concepts of "gender identity," the events in the classroom demonstrated otherwise. Respond to Miller's question: How do we engage students and ourselves in rethinking and reworking "normalized conceptions"?

❖ NEW TEACHER REFLECTIONS

While reading the case, my first opinion formed when the teacher candidate was trying to implement her classroom management technique and was interrupted by the substitute teacher. I feel that if more discussion of how the day might unfold had occurred, between the pre-service teacher and the substitute teacher, many of the events could have been avoided.

The pre-service teacher should have been confident in speaking with the substitute teacher and described the overall context/behavior of the class before the actual school day started. Her classroom management techniques could have been thoroughly explained and classroom rules fully discussed before the day unraveled. I feel that I can relate to the pre-service teacher in that although you are an "authority" figure in the classroom, you're not quite sure of your boundaries. Possibly, these kinds of situations could be avoided if more discussion at the start of the practicum between the pre-service and the classroom teacher had taken place. The issues of confidence for pre-service teachers continue to arise, but I don't think that this pre-service teacher lacked confidence, solely experience, which as we know, or anticipate, will only come with time.

If I were to write about the possible agenda for the next day, I would hope that the pre-service teacher would find a chance or the opportunity to revisit the situation and talk with the students and take advantage of the "teachable moment." The pre-service teacher has had a very valuable day of learning. She should consider this experience in light of the possibilities of self-growth and reflection.

These comments were written by a first-year teacher.

My reaction to the case in "A Student Teacher Faces the Challenges of the Classroom" is one of relief. I remember what it is like to be a pre-service teacher, a substitute teacher, and maybe, more important, an eighth-grade student. I believe that in this case, the pre-service teacher adhered to her ethical standards as a "teacher." I think her areas of growth could be greater collaboration with colleagues and development of more self-confidence. If these are her areas of growth—that's pretty good! There really are no mistakes here, but rather opportunities for learning.

A teacher with 18 months of experience wrote this comment.

❖ ENGAGING WITH THE COMMENTARIES

Power Struggles

Miller and Clandinin address power struggles and the need for social justice: Miller looks at schools and society, whereas Clandinin's remarks center on the individual. Compare their insights and suggest redress for dealing with these issues on personal and global levels.

New Teachers

Miller and Russell both discuss the special issues that concern new teachers and the need to become the "real" teacher. Compare these commentators' conjectures on the topic. How do Clandinin and Hunter suggest avenues for transition and improved self-knowledge?

Reflections

Compare the responses of the new teachers to the case. Which commentator has expressed similar views? Consider the new teachers' reflections on authority and self-confidence. Do those thoughts mirror ones you have had?

Connecting Questions

The Connecting Questions located in the introduction highlight themes that are threaded throughout the cases. You may continue your exploration of the issues raised in this case by addressing those connections. For questions pertinent to this case, please see questions 1, 5, and 8.

❖ ADDITIONAL READINGS

Biddle, B. J., Good, T., & Goodson, I. (1997). *International handbook of teachers and teaching*. Dordrecht, The Netherlands: Kluwer.

This handbook provides chapters, written by leading authorities, that review both the major traditions of work and the newest perspectives, concepts, insights, and research-based knowledge concerned with teachers and teaching. Many of the chapters discuss developments that are international in scope. Many chapters review contemporary problems faced by educators and the challenges posed by "reform" schools and school systems.

Carter, K., & Koehler, V. R. (1987). The process and content of initial year of teaching programs. In G. A. Griffin & S. Mills (Eds.), *The first years of teaching: Background papers and a proposal.* Chicago: University of Illinois.

This guide for beginning teachers explains how to grow professionally, develop relationships with students and peers, motivate students, and manage a diverse classroom while designing, delivering, and evaluating instruction.

Hammerness, K., Darling-Hammond, L., & Shulman, L. (2002). Toward expert thinking: How curriculum case writing prompts the development of theory based professional knowledge in student teachers. *Teaching Education, 13*(2), 220–245.

Working with pre-service candidates, the authors identify themes that elucidate John Dewey's thinking about reflection that includes notions of diversity, open-mindedness, and responsibility, which are helpful for developing teacher thinking.

Mills, G. (2003). *Action research: A guide for the teacher researcher.* Upper Saddle River, NJ: Pearson Education.

From the author's own experience working with teachers and principals, this book provides a step-by-step outline of how to "do" action research—backed by theory and research. Mills guides future educators through the action research process via concrete illustrations and online resources, positioning class-based research as a fundamental component of teaching, alongside curriculum development, assessment, and classroom management.

Posner, G. (1993). *Field experience: A guide to reflective teaching* (3rd ed.). New York: Longman.
This practical book examines types, concerns, personal goals, planning, and instruction for teachers, including a fieldwork portfolio. Chapters relate to customizing school, community, curriculum, and student needs.

Shulman, J. (1987). From veteran parent to novice teacher: A case study of a student teacher. *Teaching and Teacher Education, 3*(1), 13–28.
Shulman's excellent work on cases focuses on the authentic voices of the participants. Her use of the case methodology invites readers to make connections with their own practice, reflect on their assumptions, revise, and plan for classroom improvements.

Shulman, J., & Mesa-Bains, M. (Eds.). (1993). *Diversity in the classroom: Casebook for teachers and teacher-educators*. San Francisco: FarWest Lab.
The framework of Exploring the Case was adapted from this book.

7

Engaging in Action
Research in the Classroom

I n this case, a teacher reflects on the effect that an action research
project has had on a class. Commentators Robert E. Stake, Stefinee
Pinnegar, Andrea K. Whittaker, and the teacher author offer insights
into the meaning of this case that range from discussions on the classroom as a site for application of theory to student behavior and the
negotiation of power relationships. When contradictions between
theory and practice in the classroom exist, teachers are faced with
exploring the reasons why their attempts have been less than perfect.

❖ THINKING AHEAD

As you read this chapter, reflect on the following questions and issues:

- Consider the skills, attitudes, experience, and knowledge of the
  teacher. How are students encouraged to actively develop their
  own knowledge?

The use of "she and he," while it may appear awkward to the reader, is intended
to ensure the absence of gender bias.

- Consider the context.
- What are the pressure points in the case?
- There appear to be several stories with their own dilemmas in this case. Identify the stories and the dilemmas at the heart of each.

From the hall, for the unknowing, all is going well. There is peaceful quiet, a silence that presents itself as a controlled positive energy. It feels as if the school is how it should be. Indeed, we should be whispering. Teachers are teaching. Students are listening, working, and learning. Suddenly a different reality disturbs the solitude.

Everyone jumps as they hear a crashing kick, a door flying open, a loud frustrated voice booming, "I am never coming back to this stupid school again!" And finally, the last door, the outside door, slams shut. Debbie has left the school, angry, frustrated, out of control.

I am just coming around the corner when this curious scene plays out. Unfortunately for me, Debbie is a student in my seventh-grade class. My stomach sinks.

At the beginning of the year, I had decided to extend a previous study that had originated as an action research project. At the outset, the purpose of the study had been to improve student initiative and independent learning in seventh-grade students, but it had evolved into an initiative to build self-advocacy skills. I had worked for almost 2 years on this project, and it underpinned everything I did in my classroom. I believed developing these skills would be two-sided. One side would enable me to be an effective teacher, and the other side would allow my students to develop skills that they would need as they moved up and into high school. I had set out a plan to motivate my students to take charge of themselves to improve their learning and achievement. I wanted to facilitate their development of self-advocacy skills so that their specific needs could be met or, at the very least, accommodated.

At first, my students could not believe that they might have a voice that directed their own education. Surprisingly, they were hesitant to try. Debbie's derogatory attitude spoke for the group: "Why bother? We're only kids. No one will listen. No one takes us seriously. It's not worth it."

But I persevered. Slowly but surely, they began to grow. My students started to believe in themselves. They were realizing their potential and saw that they were responsible for their own changes. Students were completing homework, using time wisely, and asking for help. Taking responsibility for his own learning, one student asked if he could work on his creative writing during art. Managing classroom activities was an educator's dream, and it showed. Other teachers began to compliment my class on their positive attitudes, their ability to listen, and their settled demeanor in class. It was an ego boost for me, and I would always share the compliments with the class, who shone in the well-deserved praise.

My students were becoming their own "learning specialists," and I believed that we were moving forward as planned. I was even more convinced of our success when a reticent once-cynical Debbie offered this view: "My goals were to get rid of my attitude, come in for extra help, be a good student, and pass. I have begun to reach my goals. I now think positive [sic] about myself. I set my alarm at night to come in for extra help, and I study. I think my strengths are my ability to change, and find solutions." I was thrilled.

Shelly was my "critical friend." She was another teacher in my school involved in action research. We worked independently on different research topics, but formed a team to help each other through the process and the pitfalls. Thankfully, our friendship deepened over time, and we celebrated our successes, no matter how trivial. We were privy to all aspects of each other's work. We provided constant support and feedback to one another. This collaboration constituted an integral component of my action research.

On this particular day, I was to be out of class for an hour at a computer training session. I had left a simple hands-on activity, building 3-D objects using nets. It was a key component of our geometry unit, and my students enjoyed this type of activity. It required very little direction and would provide a simple activity while I was away. With these considerations in mind, I had purposely saved this assignment for that day. To ensure a successful and profitable morning for my class, I had spoken directly to the substitute teacher at recess, explained the activity, and assured her that I had a *fabulous* class, and that she would most definitely enjoy her time in my room. In fact, I do recall almost bragging that I had an excellent class. I don't believe that I was stretching the truth even a little, but my prediction could not have been further from the truth. I created a positive scenario, but not because I believed that the teacher would be unable to handle the group; I have a certain empathy for substitute teachers because of a haunting experience that occurred before I even graduated as a teacher candidate.

It could have been yesterday. A cool misty morning, I arrive at the school early and offer to help outside on yards. Already, there are a few kids on the wet grass, playing. I'm unsure because I can feel them ignoring me, yet staring and glaring simultaneously at me. I pretend to ignore the negative affronts. Eventually, one lone boy approaches. He challenges me with a surly tone and a rough look: "Are you our substitute teacher?" I reply that I am the new teacher candidate assigned to Mrs. Smith. I mistake his look for disappointment, but not for long. His simple reply is slow to come, but it sends a chill through me: "That's too bad, because if you were, we were going to make you leave crying. Ha! That's what we did to our last substitute." He smirks and strides away.

His words never left me. I felt their aftereffects years later, when I became a substitute teacher. I have become quite well aware of all the substitute teacher roadblocks that impart a feeling of failure and frustration. You are supposedly in charge, yet the routines, rules, assignments, and expectations all belong to someone else. It feels surreal to be a placeholder for the *real* teacher and so, to this day, I strive to create and maintain a different standard of respect and productivity in my classes when a substitute teacher must come in and take over classes. I want that person to feel in charge because I have left work that is well thought out, and a class that will participate.

Therefore, on this fateful morning, with my stomach sinking, I return to my class. The students could not wait to tattle that they had endured terrible distress in my absence. At lunch, I sought out the substitute teacher. Now it was her turn to express her views on the subject. Both sides were telling the same story, but, interestingly, from their own perspectives, and neither side seemed to appreciate the other's version. All of our work with self-advocacy for naught! I kept needling myself, repeatedly asking myself, were the students moving ahead doing all these great things, following our plan, growing? I really thought they were. How could it be that Debbie, who had been bragging about her hard work, her changed attitude, her solutions, had been reduced to her previous ways so quickly?

I was confused. Hadn't my students been evolving into self-advocates, or had I only fostered their dependence? Was it my fault? Had I been the center of control? Was I only the ringmaster, and without me, were my students unable to perform their tricks?

Feelings of great disappointment and failure washed over me. I was filled with self-doubt. I questioned the entire action research project, thinking that it might just be a sham, a self-serving tool for myself.

I hoped Shelly was not too busy. I needed a friend.

❖ EXPLORING THE CASE

An elementary school teacher with 10 years of experience wrote this case.

Identification

Identify the key facts of this case. What factual events are central to understanding this situation? Identify the dilemmas and tensions in this case. Explore the main aspects of each dilemma and tension.

Analysis

Analyze the issue(s) from the viewpoints of the different people in the case. Why is action research so important to this teacher? Explain the teacher's frustration when she or he returns to class.

Evaluation

Examine critically the teacher's strategies for handling the challenge(s). Does the teacher depicted fulfill, fall short of, or surpass your notion of the role of a teacher?

Alternative Solutions

Were there alternative solutions or strategies available to deal with the dilemmas? Generate alternative solutions to the ones presented in the narrative. Take into consideration risks, benefits, and long- and short-term consequences of each proposed action.

Reflection

Although the teacher needs to speak with her or his "critical friend" and appears disappointed, do you think her or his attempts to implement action research failed? Has anything been resolved?

Changing Opinions

Consider your thoughts and assumptions at the beginning of the chapter. Who or what has caused you to consider a new way of thinking? How strongly do you still feel about your previous assumptions?

Synthesis

Synthesize your understanding of this case into a statement. What is this a case of?

Case Commentary by Robert E. Stake

"Engaging in Action Research in the Classroom" is a marvelous reverie, heartfelt and compelling. I am greatly pleased when a teacher doing action research finds a way to express her- or himself so well.

Both of her or his issues deserve the reader's attention. Yes, the substitute teacher situation is completely out of whack in many places. But that is beyond the author's action/reach and not really that for which she or he pleads our enlistment.

A teacher with 10 years of experience should be something of an authority, respected for wisdom others on all sides do not have. Across the land, there is a grand conspiracy to embarrass the schools for leaving so many youth problems unfixed.

And part of it is to raise doubt that education can be left in any large part to the wisdom of teachers. So curricular guidelines and standards and tests are beefed up to subordinate the teacher.

Well, many teachers do not do some of their work very well. And some of those who do things that twitch my pride (as a fellow teacher) do things that some parents, community, leaders, and district officials don't understand and don't like such as teaching self-reflection and assertiveness.

It should not be expected that any other person will define education or democracy or youth well-being the way any teacher does. And action research and case study are partly here to help us tease out the other meanings, the other realities.

So here we have a plea for colleagueship, elegant in its omissions and presumptions of universalities. As a research case, it makes the point that children and classes differ, but it doesn't make the point that what we value in life changes with the situation.

As a teaching case, it works, for me at least. It makes me think. It isn't important what it was that drove Debbie out the door. It is important to figure out how we can live with different aspirations for teaching, and how it's much better with us than without us.

❖ EXPLORING THE ISSUES

Reflection

Stake appears philosophical about the role teachers can play in the classroom. In this case, he points to the teachers' wisdom. How does that "special wisdom" affect students in the classroom?

Teacher Authority

Stake suggests that we must look for reasons for how we might live with "different aspirations for teaching." Discuss whether teachers should be directors or catalysts in student education.

Teacher Self-Confidence

Stake's own "reverie" addresses larger areas of education and democracy. How does he see the place of the teacher in the larger scheme of society?

Reflection

Stake is drawn in by the reverie of this story that is "heartfelt and compelling." What are the benefits of using authentic voices that narrate their own stories to teach about practice?

Case Commentary by Stefinee Pinnegar

When I read this narrative, my mind is filled with questions. First, I wonder about Debbie. I wonder if this is indeed the last time she'll be back to this "stupid school." I wonder what it meant to Debbie to leave. I wonder if this leaving is evidence of the teacher's success or failure. I wonder about the other students. I wonder whether Debbie was the flashpoint or the leader in the event. I wonder how the students experienced the substitute teacher and what Debbie's leaving meant to them. I wonder what the students learned about self-advocacy and taking responsibility for learning. I wonder about the living contradictions experienced by the teacher and what these contradictions evidenced in the somatic reactions to the event as well as the recalled event, the conflicting perspectives on the incident itself and the confusion the teacher felt. I wonder about this teacher's conception of action research and what it means to be an action researcher.

Action research is for me about living contradictions and the creation of living educational theory. Action research is not so much about arriving but about learning about teaching from the bends in the road along the way (McNiff, Lomax, & Whitehead, 2003). Events like this are the nodal moments of action research (Bullough & Pinnegar, 2001). They are the experiences that promise rich learning, new thinking, and teacher development. From events like this and the action researcher's careful reconsideration of teaching in response, assertions for action and understanding of classrooms grows. In such moments, the action researcher experiences him- or herself as a living contradiction. What is made evident in experience is a contradiction between our idealized image of who we are and what the experience reveals to us we are. After an experience such as this, I would imagine the action researcher asking, "What do I mean by self-advocacy?" "Why does Debbie's action make me a failure when I am promoting taking responsibility for learning and the development of self-advocacy?" "What evidence about my teaching does the action of my students give me?" "What does this event reveal to me about the next steps I need to take to develop students' and my own responsibility for learning?" "Do I completely understand Debbie's, the other students', and the substitute teacher's perspectives on this incident?" "What new lenses would be helpful in thinking through the experience as well as my deep emotional response to it?" "What does it mean for a teacher to be 'in charge' in a classroom based in student responsibility for learning?" "What does my response as an action researcher and teacher reveal about how I understand teaching and learning? Are those understandings revealed in this event and my response to it the living educational theory that I as an educator want to construct?"

In the end, I wonder what the teacher learned about her- or himself as a teacher, about her or his school, about Debbie, about the other students, and about action research.

❖ EXPLORING THE ISSUES

School as a Testing Ground

Pinnegar's first paragraph presents the questions she would like to ask about the story. Were they the same ones you would have liked answered? What contradictions cause her to reflect on the teacher's foray into action research?

Student Behavior

The teacher believed that the students had reached a learning plateau in becoming self-sufficient learners (self-advocates, too). However, Pinnegar highlights what role action research should or can play as "experiences" and "events." How can the failure of an "idealized image of who we are" teach teachers more than success?

Teacher Self-Confidence

Pinnegar identifies the schism between our idealized sense of who we are "and what we must come to accept about ourselves." What does this experience with action research reveal to the teacher? How might teachers become more objective when "failures" occur, and how might they restore a point of balance?

Case Commentary by Andrea K. Whittaker

In this case, the image of the ringmaster taming (Was I only the ring-master . . . ? p. 128) or directing behavior is the teacher author's worst fear. Despite the time and reputed success of her action research focused on building students' capacity to work independently and to "take charge of themselves" through self-advocacy, the author's students fall into traditional young adolescent behavior—terrorizing a substitute teacher.

The case represents issues of power and control and the ways in which young adolescents perceive power and control playing out in their classroom. Young adolescents are struggling to develop independence, autonomy, and their own sense of power or self-advocacy outside the control of adults (parents and teachers alike). Throughout the action research project, this teacher seems to have engaged the class in developing some agreed-on norms for the class and for individuals' rights and responsibilities as contributing class members. These norms (either implicitly or explicitly stated) focus the distribution of power and self-control within individuals in the classroom rather than solely within the teacher. Together with their teacher, students learned ways to direct their own behavior and make good decisions about tasks and social interactions. Their teacher was not a ringmaster taming them through sanctions and rewards but rather a co-constructor of a shared social, cognitive, and affective culture for learning in which they were powerful, self-controlling individuals who work well with others.

Such shared cultures are often developed in classrooms where students are supported in activity settings that acknowledge and build upon what Tharp, Estrada, Dalton, and Yamauchi (2000) have termed "the great cycle of social sorting." The teacher in this case seems to have developed a culture of distributed power and control through social interactions in joint productive activity. Enter the substitute teacher who has not participated in this culture and is unfamiliar with its norms (lacks intersubjectivity) and without the affinity shared among students and teacher. The substitute teacher is the proverbial lamb entering the lion's den. For the students, who have developed all their skills in a relational context, this suspicious stranger, by the author's own account, brings a historical reputation (based on students' past experience) as one who must be controlled or will become the controller. The author recalls her or his experience as a substitute teacher and how students threatened to make her or him cry! Students can indeed be cruel to substitute teachers, and even the most well behaving students often cannot resist the temptation to torment the substitute. Why? Because she or he is from outside the culture they have established.

What could this teacher have done to extend the students' skills of independence, interdependence, and self-advocacy to avoid the disaster and disappointment experienced with the substitute teacher? Acknowledging with students the norms they have developed, as a class, is a good beginning. Perhaps their ways of working together were merely implicit and assumed by students as the way of working with THEIR TEACHER and not necessarily generalizable beyond the current context. Prior to the arrival of the substitute, teacher and students can articulate the norms and make them explicit enough so that students can teach the substitute teacher how their classroom operates. This teaching role for the students empowers them immediately with the substitute teacher who will learn from students the expectations for students and teachers alike. Likewise, the regular teacher must also prepare the substitute teacher for what to expect from students as they teach about their classroom. Rather than saying, "I have a fabulous class" and that the substitute would "enjoy her time" with them, the teacher prepares the substitute teacher for how the students will include him or her in their culture of distributed control and power. With such an approach, the ensuing power struggle may be avoided and the students' self-advocacy skills will be maintained. The substitute is no longer the lamb entering the lion's den absent their trainer, but an anticipated newcomer welcomed into a community of self-directed, collaborative, and powerful learners.

❖ EXPLORING THE ISSUES

Power Struggles

Whittaker suggests the shift in power is due to adolescent behavior as students develop independence and autonomy of their own. Do you agree with this evaluation of what occurs in the classroom, or does the explanation hide the real reasons for disruption, particularly in this case? Explain your answer.

Student Behavior

Whittaker analyzes how the teacher has invested her- or himself in student learning with ways to facilitate student growth. Rather than a "ringmaster" (see the third to last paragraph), Whittaker suggests the teacher was a "co-instructor" in a shared culture. Does Whittaker's interpretation of the shift in student behavior explain or invalidate her insight? What might have been missing in the teacher's preparation with the substitute teacher that would have made a difference?

❖ AUTHOR REFLECTION

Debbie is once again in my room as I now teach eighth grade. She had requested that she be in my class again. Debbie is settling down and doing well. She is growing into an interesting young woman. Her insights about life are, likewise, interesting, too. I enjoy talking with her and the contributions that she makes during class discussions. I am still dedicated to promoting self-advocacy. Currently, we have been reading *The 7 Habits of Highly Effective Teens* by Sean Covey. Debbie came to me and said, "He says a lot of the things I've already read in another book." She suggested that I might like to read that book and added that she has put it aside for me. She told me she would bring it to school, and I'm still waiting, but it feels like hope. I look forward to meeting her one day as an adult and asking her about the path she has traveled.

❖ EXPLORING THE ISSUES

Reflection

What does the teacher's reflection reveal about the teacher's sense of accomplishment or failure with her or his action research inquiry years earlier? What lesson can other teachers learn from this reflection? Consider Whittaker's suggestion here that there are periods of maturation in all students' lives.

❖ ENGAGING WITH THE COMMENTARIES

Inquiry

Pinnegar poses many probing questions throughout her commentary. List them. How do the other commentators answer or address those questions?

Reflection

All of the commentators, with the exception of Dr. Whittaker, focus for the most part on the class—and not the substitute teacher, whom Whittaker refers to as the "proverbial lamb entering the lion's den." Interestingly, the regular teacher recalls her or his own sad memories of days as a substitute teacher. Why do you think that Stake and Pinnegar have not chosen to focus on the issue of substitute teachers? Why would the writer's memory as a substitute teacher her- or himself have played a role in the teacher's telling of her or his case?

Action Research

In action research, a teacher will identify a problem, research it, propose solutions, enact them, study the results, and discover more problems that prompt further and deeper investigations, all in the examination of "the theory of practice." Compare Pinnegar's and Whittaker's commentaries that analyze practice through concrete examples to generate new questions for inquiry.

Connecting Questions

The Connecting Questions located in the introduction highlight themes that are threaded throughout the cases. You may continue your exploration of the issues raised in this case by addressing those connections. For questions pertinent to this case, please see questions 4 and 10.

❖ ADDITIONAL READINGS

Bosner, G. (1987). Addressing the problem of elsewhereness: A case for action research in schools. In D. Goswami & P. Stillman (Eds.), *Reclaiming the classroom: Teacher research as an agency for change* (pp. 4–13). Portsmouth, NH: Boynton/Cook.

The focus here is that all English teachers should be involved in ongoing research in the classroom.

Cochran-Smith, M., & Lyttle, S. L. (1999). Relationships of knowledge and practice: Teacher learning communities. In A. Iran-Nejad & P. D. Pearson (Eds.), *Review of research in education, 24*, 249–305. Washington, DC: American Educational Research Association.

The authors point out the difference of what "knowing more" and "teaching better" mean in terms of change efforts. There are distinctions explained among "knowledge-for-practice," "knowledge-in-practice," and "knowledge-of-practice." The chapter considers various change initiatives related to teacher learning. The writers explain that in spite of some strategies sounding similar, they are, in fact, quite different, affecting quite distinctly the everyday lives of students and teachers.

Connelly, F. M., & Clandinin, D. J. (2000). *Narrative inquiry.* New York: Teachers College Press.

Narrative inquiry can be central to gathering the human dimension in research because it captures more than statistics and numbers. In this text, Connelly and Clandinin discuss how narrative exploration can be used in educational and social science research. Their useful book offers new and practical ideas for conducting fieldwork, composing field notes, and conveying research results. The authors use many stories and examples to illustrate their process.

Kroll, L., Cossey, R., Donahue, D., Galquera, T., LaBoskey, V., Richert, A. E., & Tucher, P. (2004). *Teaching as principled practice: Managing complexity for social justice.* Thousand Oaks, CA: Sage.

This book, complete with questions, is guided by four principles: morality; teaching as an act of inquiry and reflection; learning as developmental and constructive process; and teaching as a collegial and political activity. The authors give examples that aid in clarifying their principles and are applicable to action research. The text is a catalyst to insights, reflections, and meaningful discussions.

McNiff, J., Lomax, P., & Whitehead, J. (1996). *You and your action research project.* London: Routledge.

Referring to the relationship between values and research, this book offers practical advice as well as grounding in a scholarly manner. Information is arranged in stages to support action inquiry, while outlining the necessity of rigor, self-reflection, and the development of individual theory in action research. The range here is comprehensive. The style and organization are accessible with examples to foster deeper understanding.

Mills, G. (2003). *Action research: A guide for the teacher researcher.* Upper Saddle River, NJ: Pearson Education.

From the author's own experience working with teachers and principals, this book provides a step-by-step outline of how to "do" action research—backed by theory and research. Mills guides future educators through the action research process via concrete illustrations and online resources, positioning class-based research as a fundamental component of teaching, alongside curriculum development, assessment, and classroom management.

Shulman, J., & Colbert, J. (Eds.). (1988). *The intern teacher casesbook.* San Francisco: WestEd.

Shulman and Colbert present a collection of cases that focus on a variety of topics pertinent to practice and possible sources of action research projects from "classroom trouble" and "nontraditional activities" to "passion of teaching." The introduction of these topics along with reactions to the cases along with an annotated bibliography make this a very useable text.

Shulman, J., & Mesa-Bains, M. (Eds.). (1993). *Diversity in the classroom: Casebook for teachers and teacher-educators.* San Francisco: FarWest Lab.

The framework of Exploring the Case was adapted from this book.

Talbert, J. E., & McLaughlin, M. W. (1993). Understanding teaching in context. In D. K. Cohen, M. W. McLaughlin, & J. E. Talbert (Eds.),

Teaching for understanding: Challenges for policy and practice (pp. 167–206). San Francisco: Jossey-Bass.

The authors, who are leading experts in teaching and policy research, provide examples of what teaching for understanding entails. They describe how to foster, sustain, and support the knowledge, capacity, and professional beliefs essential for teachers. They dispute the "teach and test" approach in favor of meaningful reflection on classroom life and relationships with students. They diagnose elements in schools that are prohibitive or enhancing.

Westheimer, J., & Kahne, J. (2003, September). Teaching democracy: What schools need to do. *Phi Delta Kappan, 85*(1).

In studying 10 educational programs that purport to develop democratic citizens, the authors say that civic commitments, capacities, and connections aid in promoting thinking about democracy in schools. They critique the constant testing and messages of curriculum reform, lauding Elliot Eisner's approach to learning that extends beyond the classroom to life.

8

Evaluating a Teacher's Classroom Management Strategy

In this case, an evaluator questions a classroom teacher's instructional management strategies when she applies for a permanent teaching credential. Case commentators Elizabeth Campbell, Iain Munro, Frances Squire, and Jay Martin reveal the underpinnings of tensions between the teacher and the evaluator in this case, noting conflicts that expose the vulnerability of a new teacher, who is experiencing isolation in her early years of teaching. The commentators all recommend supportive networks to ease the transition into the unexpected surprises that ingénues will face in their early years.

❖ THINKING AHEAD

As you read this chapter, reflect on the following questions and issues:

The use of "she and he," while it may appear awkward to the reader, is intended to ensure the absence of gender bias.

- Consider the teacher's skills and knowledge in the classroom.
- What special problems occur because of contextual elements?
- Does inexperience cause the teacher to demonstrate too much flexibility?
- Has positive class behavior been encouraged?
- Consider the diverse perspectives of participants described in this case.

"Do you really think that you can interest 'techies' (boys with a passion for technology) in art?" the principal asks me. I have just signed my first probationary contract, and I am beaming, towering over this man who resembles a drill sergeant, brush cut and all, who stands maybe 5 feet tall. With the arrogance of youth, I ramble on, energetically: "I'll show them Salvador Dali's *Premonition of Civil War*. Do you know it, Mr. Prentice?" Mr. Prentice's patronizing smile and near inability to hold back laughter encourages me to plow on. "It's an oil painting of a body tearing itself apart. Techies will just adore it." At the same time, believing that I can conquer all students by knowing how to enter into their worlds, I have an uneasy feeling that encouraging any kind of violence, whether metaphorical or not, may not be such a good idea.

The school is located in the city core, yet close to industrial sites. The kids hang out on the street corners or wander off into the barren fields, to drink and carouse. There are no sports facilities for roller or figure skating, no tennis courts, not even a basketball hoop nearby. We know drugs and guns are easily available. Southern secondary holds a reputation for explosive fights and confrontations with the authorities. We check lockers from time to time, rarely disappointed in our search for beer cans, knives, or other kinds of contraband. It's rather a tough place to begin my career, but there is a strong feeling of energy. The teachers here seem to have a camaraderie that suggests to me that the school has a special culture of its own, and that the staff must believe that they can make a difference in the students' lives. I'm apprehensive, but excited.

One year later I am still at Southern secondary, preparing for an evaluation that will, no doubt, grant me my permanent credential. Since I am allowed to choose my best class, I decide to dazzle the evaluator with my ninth-grade techies. Not always easy, these adolescents, nonetheless, are following the mandated curriculum. There are some flare-ups during class when someone mysteriously shoves someone else, or when artwork is mysteriously knocked off tabletops, but I am vigilant, on the lookout for bullying, too. However, when rowdy boys, all hormones and hair gel, gather in any one place there is always the possibility of trouble.

I carefully plan my lessons, consciously deciding that I will instruct for no more than 10 minutes. Since the boys insist on music, I've permitted a boom box, but no Walkman in the class—at least, not when I am teaching. The choice of music is theirs, but then I don't really hear the words to the songs because the noise blares so loudly. I constantly have to adjust the volume as I move from student to student, offering suggestions and making sure they are fully aware that I am in their midst. I want them to feel that I share their space, and I want to provide a deterrent to any possible misbehaving. Sometimes, I consider I may be just a paper tiger, but for the most part, my classes are popular, and I rarely have had complaints, except for the noise level. I reflect that is why art classes are always in school basements, because the administration has determined that "those arts types" are either messy slobs or belong on another planet. Being removed from the academics affords me privacy, and I don't really mind the jibes about being "artsy-fartsy."

I ruminate about the evaluation. At first, I select my senior art class since every student has requested art, rather than having had no choice in the selection, as the ninth-grade techies who have to take the art credit for their Technological Studies. Except for one student in that senior group who thinks art is an easy credit and who goes out of his way to let me know he is *killing himself* in my class to get a high mark, the atmosphere is contemplative and peaceful. The students are doing exactly what they should. In this class, one student has decided to apply to art college, and another, the *only* one in the entire school, has decided to go on to university, and—believe it or not—to pursue a fine arts degree! I am pleased although I realize that I may have played only a very small part in his decision.

We have a strong art department. The head of Art is young, but unlike me, she began her teaching with a fierce confident manner and after years of making monolithic pieces of sculpture. She is even married to a videographer, and she thinks like an artist. Not surprisingly, Charlene has put together a rigorous and vigorous program that is growing year after year.

Still contemplating which class to showcase, my heart is with the raw excitement in that ninth-grade class with which I've worked so hard. So, I choose it for my evaluation, surmising how impressed the evaluator will be.

As Mr. Jackson enters the room, I sense he is a self-contained presence, even a bit prissy, a man in a green suit who holds himself separate, not touching desks or chairs as he carefully circumvents objects and weaves a path among the slovenly-dressed students who chew gum, toss balls and hackey-sacs to one another, or drape their restless bodies nonchalantly over tables and stools. Indeed, they are a messy lot. He has silently communicated to me that there is a very bad smell in the room—or perhaps that he would have preferred to be in the company of prep school boys who are pouring over Greek or Latin classics.

"Hey sir, how ya doing?" they mock. He makes no eye contact. Maybe I am imagining his response or being, as usual, overly sensitive.

Stupidly, I am not daunted and welcome him with a big sloppy grin. I won't turn down the music or alter my lesson plan. He should see my boys as they really are. Besides, I have outlined on the sheets that I will turn over to him at the end of class, my lesson, step-by-step plans, rubrics, and assignments for the month.

When I contemplate my lessons, I think of what will appeal to these fellows, and I do know machines fascinate them. All take machine shop. I have slides of Leonardo da Vinci's helicopters and bridges, even miniature pulleys and motors that show the running and operation of parts.

I take a deep breath and plunge into my lesson. It is like magic. The boys have circled closer to the slides and to me, gawking with their mouths open, entranced. They ask questions. I give them historical information and provide answers. I instruct them: "Today, you will become Leonardo and plan on paper your own inventions."

The silence has dissipated. They nod and jostle one another back to their seats, one or two trip and fall on the floor, and they laugh as I separate their entwined big-footed legs. They are consumed in noisy, happy artwork. Some of it even looks pretty good. Hands go up immediately, "Miss, Miss, come and see . . ."

I do my usual tour, relieved that my scrutiny has ended. I look toward Mr. Jackson, and I realize he has been glued to his chair at the back of the class—the entire time. He is writing furiously. He closes his book, suddenly rises, does not acknowledge my existence in any way, and departs. Oh well, I tell myself, he must be on to Sue's class on the second floor. She teaches English.

I think I am pretty insightful and knew from my student teaching days which classes were successful. Some I would leave in tears, mentally castigating myself and flinging myself at the first person

I saw to ask for assistance: "What went wrong? How can I get those kids to pay attention to me?" I replay every detail in that ninth-grade class. Really, the kids were interested. They went to work. There were no overturned jars of paint—just two kids on the floor. I'm satisfied that even an experienced teacher couldn't have created a better learning environment.

But before I can even exit the room, Charlene meets me. She is babbling nonstop, "unorganized . . . messy . . . didn't communicate tasks . . . unfocused . . . pictures at strange angles . . . inappropriate music . . ."

Who is Charlene talking about? And why is she telling me all this? I stop her diatribe. "Charlene, who are you talking about? Is it Sue? Didn't Mr. Jackson like her class? What was his problem?"

"You!" she blurts out. I am in shock. I am incredulous. I just taught the most perfect class in my life to the toughest group in the school. What does this mean?

Tears flood my eyes. They drip down my nose, my chin, and my neck, and soak my shirt. They threaten to wash away the school and my world.

"Mr. Prentice wants to see you immediately." Once I've started crying, I cannot stop. So, embarrassed, nose dripping and red-eyed, I somehow make my way to the principal's office.

I know Mr. Prentice values Charlene's opinion. He is always increasing the budget for art supplies. I see them chatting in the staff room. As I wait for him, I realize that I have only conversed with him three times in the 2 years I've taught at the school—once on that hiring day and another time when I first wore pants to school. He had said, "If you intend to dress like a man, make sure your fly is all the way up." There was one other time. It was my grandfather's 80th birthday in Green Acres' Home. I had asked to be excused from Parents' Night. Mr. Prentice had said he was sorry, but I could not even leave early. I guess I understood.

I wonder now what Mr. Prentice really thinks about me. I have noticed the vice principal, John Drake, a former athlete, watches the staff. I wonder if he reports to Mr. Prentice. He peers through the glass corridors in the halls into my senior art class sometimes. When I catch his eye, he moves off, never acknowledging the intrusion, or that I have observed him.

Today, Mr. Prentice moves from behind his desk and sits beside me. I think he even takes my hand. He tries to reassure me, telling me that he has faith in me and that Mr. Jackson is an old friend, so he will come back tomorrow and give me a second chance. "Besides," he says and winks at Charlene, "Your Art head says you are a good teacher, Pam." Is this the first time I have ever heard him use my name?

"But what should I do?" I whimper, barely audibe. I hate myself when I cry. "It really was a great class, Mr. Prentice," I plead, wanting to convince him, seeking and needing his approval. Again he looks at me with that quizzical smile I first saw when I mentioned Salvador Dali. In spite of my turmoil, part of me stands outside of my ridiculous emotional self and speculates. Does he think I have no perspective on myself and that I am delusional? Was it really a bad art class? Maybe he even regrets hiring me. He commands Charlene, "Make sure those pictures on her walls are straight."

The following day Mr. Jackson reappears, same green suit, same route through the tumult, same chair. I teach the class, subdued, voice shaking. The kids sense something is amiss. They keep turning around in their seats and look first at Mr. Jackson, then at me, quizzically, then back at him, and then toward me. Perhaps they think it is a new game they can play. For me, each head twist broadcasts my doom. The music is hardly audible, but no one plays with the dial. I think the kids are caught in a trance. They seem stunned, fixed to their seats. Jackson has us in his power. I feel like a beaten dog. He does not take his eyes off me. I cannot meet his. I am afraid I will begin to weep again. Halfway through the hour, he rises, sharply inclines his head, and gives a curt nod and leaves.

❖ EXPLORING THE CASE

A secondary school teacher with more than 20 years of experience wrote this case.

Identification

Identify the key facts of this case. What factual events are central to understanding this situation? Identify the dilemmas and tensions in this case. Explore the main aspects of each dilemma and tension.

Analysis

Analyze the issue(s) from the viewpoints of the different people in the case. Describe how the teacher applies her skills and knowledge in the classroom. Does a messy classroom indicate that no learning is occurring? If not, what evidence is there that students are actually engaged in learning? By examining the teacher's relationships with the students, staff, and administration, what educational themes can be deduced?

Evaluation

Examine critically the teacher's strategies for handling the challenge(s). Does the teacher depicted fulfill, fall short of, or surpass your notion of the role of a teacher?

Alternative Solutions

Were there alternative solutions or strategies available to deal with the teacher's dilemma? Generate alternative solutions to the ones presented in the narrative. Take into consideration risks, benefits, and long- and short-term consequences of each proposed action.

Reflection

How does Mr. Jackson's curt leave-taking affect the teacher? How does she react? Has anything been resolved for the teacher?

Changing Opinions

Consider your thoughts and assumptions at the beginning of the chapter. Who or what has caused you to consider a new way of thinking? How strongly do you still feel about your previous assumptions?

Synthesis

Synthesize your understanding of this case into a statement. What is this a case of?

Case Commentary by Elizabeth Campbell

If the essence of a professional is partly explained through individual discretion, informed judgment, and confidence in one's competence and dedication to serve the best interests of those for whom she or he is responsible, then this case sets back the spirit of teacher professionalism more than 50 years. In my account of professional ethics in teaching (Campbell, 2003), I argue that teachers should be marked as professionals not only for their technical skill, mastery of subject matter, or pedagogical success, but also "by the wisdom and humanity they reflect in the day-to-day realities, dilemmas, and challenges of assuming responsibility for other people's children." I further urge teachers to take hold of themselves in the name of professional self-determination. It is for this reason that I find Pam's school culture so very discouraging as a legacy of organizational cronyism and for its assumption that the teacher is merely a helpless victim of administrators.

Of course, teachers are accountable to others within the educational system. Professional discretion does not mean irresponsible individualism. However, this does not seem to be descriptive of Pam's practice. Let's consider what she is doing in the classroom. She follows the set curriculum; she carefully plans her lessons and reflects continuously on her practice; she prepares thoroughly for the evaluation by providing extensive lesson plans, rubrics, and monthly assignments; she clearly adapts her instruction to the unique needs of her students; she engages them both collectively and individually in the learning process; she exhibits professional knowledge that does not appear to be in dispute; and she does all this from a perspective of warmth and respect for her students. However, there is little evidence in this case to suggest that, as a beginning teacher, Pam is in any way supported by those most able to collaborate with her in ways that enhance professional learning and growth.

Theoretically, Pam, alone or with colleagues, needs to raise concerns about this evaluation process with the administration. In reality, however, how can she do this when the "appropriate people" are so central to the problem—a patronizing principal, an evaluator whose evaluation of her seems remote from professional standards in both substance and style, a gifted but ineffectual department head whose timidity is only slightly more veiled than Pam's, a vice principal whose leadership approach includes lurking and spying, and an apparently silent teaching staff?

Despite this, I am reluctant to suggest that Pam should acquiesce without objection to this situation and thereby reinforce the teacher as "helpless victim" image. Surely, professionalism resides, to a great extent, in the capacity of individual teachers to assert their legitimate authority as responsible professionals.

❖ EXPLORING THE ISSUES

New Teacher Support

Campbell's focus on ethics draws on the responsibility of the collective to support new teachers so that they do not experience isolation. How and why does Campbell exhort teachers to support their colleagues? What would be the benefits of a collaborative approach?

Classroom Management

In order to be accountable, Campbell lists how the teacher fulfills classroom management and preparation responsibilities. Yet Campbell also speaks of Pam as a victim. How might a new teacher avoid becoming a "helpless victim"?

Case Commentary by Iain Munro

Pam is demonstrably passionate about the impact that art can make on her students. From the very beginning, there is nothing condescending in her relationship with her "techies," and nothing in her approach with these boys shows that Pam is anything but keenly committed to her students. Furthermore, Pam has intuitively infused Gardner's (1999) multiple intelligence theories into her program, as well as her implied belief that great art informs our souls. Pam loves art and believes that art belongs to us all. How many of us would not be profoundly moved by the horrific images in Dali's *Premonition of Civil War* or by the stark transformative power of a Goya firing squad. For Canadians, the strong and sublime north of Tom Thomson, the lonely winter landscapes of Jean-Paul Lemieux, and the searing poignancy of the mourning specters on Vimy Ridge all conspire to inform our common psyche—including that of ninth-grade techies. If I were a principal, Pam is exactly the kind of young teacher I would treasure on my staff.

Unfortunately, this is not a happy story. We are introduced to the brusque and insensitive Principal Prentice, who appears smugly comfortable in his ignorance of the art curriculum. He clearly prefers the confident and creative young department head, Charlene, who runs a tidy and organized program and causes him no problems. The evaluator,

Mr. Jackson, whose "body language" suggests a clear distain for the educational attributes and potential of Pam's ninth-grade Technology class, really has no idea what he is observing. Instead of seeing lively, excited, and good-humored learners, Jackson sees only misdirection, messiness, and general anarchy. It is indeed ironic that Pam, who does not "measure up" in the eyes of Mr. Jackson, clearly demonstrates that she effectively fulfills—often superbly—her responsibilities as an educator. This "disconnect" can only be explained by the fact that Mr. Jackson represents different education standards of a bygone and unlamented era. His replicative educational philosophy is mostly concerned with narrow, uncreative strategies for classroom management. And one suspects his main goal for the ninth-grade techies is to prepare them for lives of pliant service on industrial assembly lines. That's why the best part of Pam's story comes at the very end. Here we may have witnessed the magical moment of the collective conversion of her satisfied active students—who were happy enough just to be able to use a pumped-up boom box in the classroom—into a caring community of learners who now truly realize just how good their teacher is. At the moment of Mr. Jackson's abrupt and rude departure, they had become hers.

Pam's short case study evokes one of life's great paradoxes. Although she now feels "like a beaten dog," Pam has really experienced an epiphany that she will certainly carry with her for continuous reflection, for the rest of her life. Indeed, every professional career can be seen as myriad episodes of "action research," where one learns that the truest moments of discovery are often those times of apparent "failure," to which the application of thoughtful reflection magically helps us become better and wiser than before.

However, no young teacher, no matter how confident and committed, can forever sustain professional growth without continuing collegial support and goodwill. Pam was let down by her own administrators. Principal Prentice wants to hear nothing unpleasant coming from the basement and Vice Principal Drake helps to ensure this through his zealous surveillance activities. Most disappointing, however, is the lack of support from department head Charlene. Charlene, who apparently thinks Pam is a "good teacher," nonetheless did not prepare her for the evaluator's first visit. Nor did she seem to provide much counsel and support for Pam afterwards. Charlene's lack of courage or willingness to stand up to the principal and defend the work of her young colleague indicates an abrogation of one of her main duties—to provide effective mentorship to junior members of her department.

Let me guess the rest of Pam's story (an optimistic version). The door closes behind Mr. Jackson. The period is not yet complete. Pam turns to the chalkboard, vainly trying to focus on the remaining minutes before the period's end when she finally can be alone in her quiet despair. Her eyes fill with tears. But lanky, silent Bill speaks first. Yes Bill, who usually uses Pam's class to sleep off a previous night's carousing, speaks first. "Miss, don't worry about him. We think you're great. You're the best teacher we have. You're the only one that thinks we're any good." And then after a pause Adam chimes in: "Hey, we're your gang." Pam turns to the class. They all nod and smile vigorously.

In the midst of this fire of disapproval, Pam had found a safe, cool place. Out of the ashes wrought by imperious judgement, Pam had truly "connected." They indeed were hers.

❖ EXPLORING THE ISSUES

Teacher Self-Confidence

Munro praises Pam's instructional style, highlighting her passion and her teaching style, reminiscent of Howard Gardner's (1999) multiple intelligences strategies. How does her way to work with the class contrast with Mr. Jackson's ideas, which represent the "standards of a bygone" era? When two such opposing forces collide, what attempts should be made to resolve conflicts?

Reflection

Munro is sensitive to Pam's narrative of a teacher new to teaching. How helpful would Munro's suggestion be of writing a new ending or looking toward the future to provide perspective for teachers' growing self-awareness?

Case Commentary by Frances Squire

Thirty yellow ducks carefully crafted from construction paper, all cut from the same pattern yet each one unique. One has green feathers, another red rubber boots, all marching across the blackboard of my first first-grade classroom. It's 1964 and the Art supervisor is not amused. The ducks were to be identical. My ducks were not!

Reading the case "Evaluating a Teacher's Classroom Management Strategy," I thought back to those yellow ducks and how the notion of "teacher as technician," the maker of identical yellow ducks, is embedded in this case. The novice art teacher who narrates the case is not a technician. She is, however, passionate about her creative ideas for teaching art to techies, intuitively understanding her students' interests. She *models the curiosity, enthusiasm, and joy of learning* from the Ontario College of Teachers' Standards of Practice (2000) and adapts the curriculum to capture the attention of this class of challenging ninth-grade boys. She wants the students to know that she shares their space. There will be no lines of identical yellow ducks in this classroom.

But what does her evaluator think? There is no room, from the evaluator's perspective, for her vision of teaching that embraces *commitment to students and student learning*, no room for innovative assignments that *connect learning to students' life experiences*—also words from the standards (2000). The evaluator and the teacher seem to have dramatically different expectations of what a good art teacher should be.

One way to think about "expectations" may be to consider them as stories whose plotlines we have imagined in a certain prescribed way. When events do not follow our anticipated and mentally rehearsed scenarios, dissonance occurs. Our newest teachers often carry such projected stories of teaching derived from personal experience, pre-service training, or mythical images of teachers created by the media. The tensions between the personal self and the wider social context of teaching can be powerful turning points or debilitating experiences. Looking at the case through this lens, I thought about

- The trusting expectations of the students who work only with a boom box blaring.
- The powerful expectation of invincibility that the novice art teacher can conquer all students by getting into their world.
- The expectation that she will "dazzle" the evaluator with her ninth-grade boys' response to a creative lesson on Leonardo da Vinci.
- The institutional unspoken expectations of the evaluator, the man in the green suit who holds himself separate, who never discusses the intent of the isolated observation exercise with the teacher.
- The department head's expectation that her newest colleague will not let her rigorous program down.

- The principal's sudden interest in his new art teacher, his expectations that she will act appropriately as a "good" teacher for his old friend, Mr. Jackson, who has given her a second chance.

Finally, we are faced with the new teacher's shattered expectations as the lesson that she had considered a wonderful learning experience is pulled apart, her disbelief and sorrow that she has to play the game to satisfy Mr. Jackson. Her words of disillusionment in closing carry a frightening expectation of fitting in, of compromise and conformity: "Jackson has us in his power. I feel like a beaten dog." Her perception of the teacher appraisal process is far removed from the positive professional learning opportunity it could have been. She learns the difficult lesson that her teaching practice is shaped not only by her professional knowledge of art and lesson planning. It is also defined by where she teaches, whom she teaches, and, unfortunately in this case, the rigid expectations of her evaluator. Her preconceived story has unfolded in unexpected ways.

Powerful cases like this one provide a bridge between theoretical documents and the reality of life in classrooms. This is, however, a story that could and indeed should be told, recognized, and understood from multiple perspectives. How would the story read if the evaluator was the narrator? What additional information would be revealed to help us understand his role? What details of plot or dialogue would the principal or the students choose to leave in or take out? How would the department head see her role? It is likely that each character in the story views the incident differently from her or his vantage point. (Each character would no doubt have a strong opinion about rows of identical yellow ducks!) Such diverse accounts would, I believe, provide a rich catalyst for discussion.

❖ EXPLORING THE ISSUES

Teaching Strategies

Squire ponders what the evaluator's notion of education is. She wonders about his own stories of teaching and what lessons he has learned or not learned from them. Squire's reflection provides a list of six points. Read Squire's list and evaluate the expectations and interests that she proposes for helping new teachers.

Teacher Self-Confidence

Squire identifies the "shattered expectations" teachers experience when lessons are pulled apart. How can teachers prevent their work from being shaped by others? From where might they draw support, particularly if their ideas are not conventional ones?

Case Commentary by Jay Martin

What we call "understanding" can be understood in several ways, so that mis-"understanding" can easily arise. In the case of "Evaluating a Teacher's Classroom Management Strategy," Pam and Mr. Jackson, as she represents this, arrive at different kinds of understanding and therefore badly misunderstand each other.

Pam's theory of understanding is centered on the process of inter-active empathy: Different experiences meet and merge into a new entity. Her aim is to teach her students by "enter[ing] into their worlds." She wants them to be "fully aware that I am in their midst." She yearns to have them tell " . . . that I share their space." Then, she will be able to engage them where they are; and she assumes that in turn she will be able to attract the empathy of students, so that they will enter into her world, bringing them from their limited experience into her world of richer and fuller appreciation.

During her first exciting year as a teacher, she has come to assume that the students are her allies, as she is theirs, while the "academic" administrators are her enemies; for them she has no empathy. By intro-ducing her students to the "special culture" of art, she will "make a dif-ference" in their lives, creating a counterbalance to their otherwise "barren" environment. This will occur through what I call the "interac-tive thread," as separate students and teachers are transformed into new beings by reciprocity.

For her, this transformation seems to occur. She wants to " . . . think like an artist," and indeed she does. The class she presents is "magic," a piece of performance art. She is a "tiger," not an academic "paper tiger." Her "heart" is filled with the "raw excitement" of creation.

By contrast, as she portrays them, the administrators conceive "understanding" as an orderly process of the transmission and accu-mulation of knowledge, a purposeful integration rather than the delib-erate disintegration represented in the Dali painting. Fully interactive with her students, she sees the school authorities as her opponents, never wondering, empathetically, what they are thinking or feeling. She believes that Mr. Prentice "resembles a drill sergeant," patronizingly believing that artists are "messy slobs or belong on another planet." Her apparently irrelevant remark that Prentice is "maybe 5 feet tall" relevantly reveals that she regards him as beneath her notice.

He is not likely to know anything of Dali. Drake, the vice principal, is "intrusive." Mr. Jackson, her evaluator, is "self-contained . . . and prissy"; she sees him in traditionally feminine terms, while she wears the pants in the school. She is anti-empathetic toward him, projecting that he "silently communicated that there is a very bad smell in the room." She projects, too, that he would prefer to hear recitations in Latin and Greek. She wants to force him to "see my boys as they really are." She dashes and darts among students, while he sits in the rear, "glued to his chair."

The result is a going misalliance. Pam berates her own unexamined theory of "understanding" to an imperial, single-minded principle, leaving no room for the kind of "understanding" intrinsic in the aims of the administrators. In her view, only her students understand her, as she them. There is little perception on her part that if she could extend the same sort of empathy to the Prentices and Jacksons of education, she can achieve a heuristic balance. And so, what began as an effort at understanding Pam's capacity as a teacher seems to have ended in hostility, bitter tears, confusion, despair, and complete mis-"understanding."

Pam has failed to see her teaching broadly, from multiple perspectives, and very likely, she has not encouraged or invited the administrators to engage her work from the multiple perspectives that her efforts, like theirs, deserve. Put in the terms that John Dewey would use, Pam has understood the nature of her inquiry too narrowly and so has not been "responsible" to the complexity of her quest to give and get education.

❖ EXPLORING THE ISSUES

Relationships With Students

Martin uses the term "interactive empathy." Explain this concept in terms of how new teachers might react and think about their relationships with students. Is this way of conceptualizing one's work helpful or harmful? Explain your answer.

Relationships With Colleagues

Martin discusses Pam's personality and how her bias is apparent through her language, even manifesting itself in her work. How can "mis-alliances" between new teachers and school board personnel be avoided?

Reflection and Self-Confidence

What effect did the evaluator have on Pam's life? Why does she now feel fortified in her actions more than 30 years ago? How can theory support practice and therefore, teacher confidence?

❖ AUTHOR REFLECTION

Many years have passed since the event described in the case. Yet, when I reread the narrative, I reexperience the same pain, rage, and disbelief that accosted me as an ingénue. I ponder, what might I have done differently: chosen the *good class?* Prepared differently? Even now, I think not!

With more than 20 years of teaching behind me, I can compare the techie class with my present-day ones. And quite frankly, they don't seem too different. I don't believe that I haven't changed throughout the years and that I am perpetuating the same sorts of errors. Rather, I see in myself in those days the seed of a teacher who would flower. Now cognizant of John Dewey, Donald Schön, and Kurt Lewin, I am able to comprehend that my response to my techie class was appropriate, but the evaluator's one to me was not! Had I been more self-confident instead of self-effacing, I might have debated or pointed out the "whys" of my carefully planned, prepared, and executed class strategies. Had I known the names of the theorists and educational experts who tell us that that theory is substantiated in practice, I could have presented a defense that supported my teaching methods. At this early point in my career, however, I taught, as many of my colleagues have done, unaware that my practice had integrated the tenets of theoretical research.

But I was young, intimidated, and in spite of the fact that my teaching felt right—that I respected my students, their interests, and their satisfied reactions to my teaching and their learning—I did not speak out. The voice I heard spoke quietly to me, but not out loud, yet in the final analysis, I only straightened up pictures; I did not change a thing.

Still, I wish I had had the voice to speak up and justify my classroom instruction. It has taken me a long time to acknowledge that I had been a good teacher then.

❖ ENGAGING WITH THE COMMENTARIES

Mentoring Plans

Both Iain Munro and Elizabeth Campbell stress the need for support for new teachers. How do their ideas compare? Could you combine their approaches and suggest an effective way to communicate to the administration that a mentoring program might be advantageous to teachers new to schools.

New Teachers

Although three commentators are supportive of Pam and her abilities in the classroom, one is not. Through the lenses of the commentators, create a list of helpful suggestions for new teachers. Now, consider Jay Martin's perspective. How can all of these insights work toward improved relationships that benefit teacher confidence and performance in the classroom? After consideration of these views, construct a growth plan for Pam that would be applicable to other teachers new to the teaching profession.

Connecting Questions

The Connecting Questions located in the introduction highlight themes that are threaded throughout the cases. You may continue your exploration of the issues raised in this case by addressing those connections. For questions pertinent to this case, please see questions 1, 3, and 11.

❖ ADDITIONAL READINGS

Atkinson, D., & Dash, P. (2004). *Art in education*. Social and Critical Practice. (Landscapes: The arts, aesthetics, and education). *Volume 1*. Dordrecht, The Netherlands: Kluwer.

Examining how art education is situated in the field of social inquiry opens up perspectives from semiotics, hermeneutics, post-structuralism, and psychoanalysis realms. Language, discourse, and power are elements that are at play here.

Fuller, F. F., & Brown, O. H. (1975). Becoming a teacher. In K. Ryan (Ed.), *Teacher education: Seventy-fourth yearbook of the National Society for the Study of Education* (Part 2, pp. 25–52). Chicago: University of Chicago Press.

Written for people who are either interested or actively engaged in teacher education, this book focuses on many relevant areas of teacher education. It begins with a historical perspective, locating the major patterns of training and institutional arrangements in the United States. The second chapter provides research and theory and discusses why people choose to become teachers.

Goldhammer, R. (1969). *Clinical supervision: Special methods for the supervision of teachers.* New York: Holt, Rinehart & Winston.

Goldhammer presents a clinical approach to supervision. The author sees productive analogues: certain forms of teaching and of ego counseling. There are detailed images of supervision and methodological models that can be used for future preparation in terms of theoretical advancement, the creation of extensive case materials, and training films.

Hargreaves, A. (1994). *Changing teachers, changing times: Teachers' work and culture in the postmodern age.* New York: Teachers College Press.

This book focuses on how teachers and teaching have changed in recent years and assesses the changes teachers will face in the future. It examines how politicians and administrators want to effect change along with educational reforms and measures taken to accomplish that goal. This book examines how and why teachers actually do change and looks at what causes or inspires them to change.

Neilson, A. R. (Ed.). (1999). *Daily meaning: Counternarratives of teachers' work.* Mill Bay, BC: Bendall Books.

The stories of teachers in their everyday practice reveals an authentic picture of student-teacher relationships and teachers as individuals who observe, reflect, and consider societal impact on students. The inner voices of teachers ponder why they remain in teaching and endure the stresses of the profession.

Roth, R. A. (1998). *The role of the university in the preparation of teachers.* London: Falmer.

Strengthening teachers' knowledge base in universities, the usefulness of standards, and on-the-job learning are some of the issues dealt with in this book. The struggle continues regarding teacher preparation and the need for restucturing the entire system for meaningful teacher education. John Goodlad, Linda Darling-Hammond, and Gary Sykes provide cogent insights.

Shulman, J., & Colbert, J. (1988). *The intern teacher casebook.* San Francisco: WestEd.

The cases of interns focus on the struggles and challenges that these interns recall from their beginning teaching years. Commentaries add to the conversation and suggest helpful ways to think about issues.

Shulman, J., & Mesa-Bains, M. (Eds.). (1993). *Diversity in the classroom: Casebook for teachers and teacher-educators.* San Francisco: FarWest Lab.

The framework of Exploring the Case was adapted from this book.

Zeichner, K. (2003, April). The adequacies and inadequacies of three current strategies to recruit, prepare, and retain the best teachers for all students. *Teachers College Record, 105*(3), 490.

This essay analyzes the strengths and weaknesses of three of the major approaches to teacher education reform in the United States: the professionalization, the deregulation, and the social justice agendas. Although each of these approaches to reform has contributed in positive ways to improving teacher education to lessen the achievement gap in U.S. public schools, each possesses certain weaknesses that undermine goals.

Zembylas, M. (2004). The emotional characteristics of teaching: An ethnographic study of one teacher. *Teaching and Teacher Education, 20*(2), 185.

This article explores the emotions of an elementary school teacher during a 3-year research project. It examines relationships and the political context of the school. Field observations, in-depth interviews, an "emotion diary," and a collection of teaching documents point to complex tensions and challenges that all teachers experience. Power relations influence values, discourses, and beliefs in behavior practice. The article encourages readers to reflect on their assumptions, revise, and plan for classroom improvements.

9

Balancing the Needs
of All Students in an
Inclusive Classroom

In this case, an experienced teacher must decide how to balance the needs of all of her students when one boy presents a challenge. She feels frustrated by the walls of silence that have been constructed by colleagues, administrators, parents, other professionals, and policies. Case commentators Anna Ershler Richert, Lynne M. Cavazos, Tania Madfes, and Linda F. Rhone provide discourses that concern children who are different from their peers. They note issues of lack of support, the need to negotiate power, and teachers' professional responsibility.

❖ THINKING AHEAD

As you read this chapter, reflect on the following questions and issues:

The use of "she and he," while it may appear awkward to the reader, is intended to ensure the absence of gender bias.

- Consider the teacher's attitudes, experience, and knowledge. How does the teacher prepare for this particular class? What difficulties does the teacher foresee?
- Consider the contextual elements of the school and the classroom that influence the dilemmas faced by the teacher.
- What strategies does the teacher use to balance the needs of all members of the class?
- What does the teacher do to remedy the situation?
- Consider the teacher's frustration. What professional issues are at stake here?

"This is going to be fun! Scott is in our class."

My ears prick up. This is an early warning sign of an interesting classroom challenge, which might have long-term classroom management implications.

It is the first day of school, our very first meeting—a class of 35 advanced-enriched students enrolled in the 10th-grade Contemporary Government and World Concerns course. I sense the dominant male energy in the room as they jostle for position, just going through the door. I have been teaching this history program at this school for many years. I know these students will be energetic, verbal, involved, talented, highly skilled, and outward looking. These teenagers are always fun and a real joy to teach. They can be intellectually engaged and are ready to participate in all forms of learning. They are eager for success, marks are important to them, and most are prepared to work hard and experiment with new ideas.

I teach in a large urban center in a school of 2,200. We liken ourselves to a small town. The school is ethnically diverse, and its specialized programs and facilities draw students from the whole city. The school atmosphere is conducive to the academic and personal development of every student. It is a vibrant, noisy, "happening" place, and the school prides itself on providing an inclusive atmosphere where every child has the opportunity to excel. Courses are offered at the general, advanced, and advanced-enriched levels. Students are invited into the advanced-enriched program based on their academic achievement, creativity, and task commitment.

All I truly know at this moment is that there are 30 boys and 5 girls in this class, including the unknown quantity: Scott.

I meet Scott, and I know that I am confronted with my classroom challenge. He immediately fills my personal space. He is "nose to nose" when he is on the offensive, but he quickly retreats when I step forward. His constant interruptions during attendance demonstrate a lack of understanding of basic classroom procedures and dynamics. Initially, the other students are quiet, but soon, they needle him, turn away, or quietly try to provoke him. They are aware of the triggers that will set him off: "Did you see the article about the lap dancers in the newspaper?" But really, almost anything sets him off.

Eyebrows raise, heads turn to smirk or giggle at his outlandish take on what most consider commonplace. Issues about smoking, drug use, and sexual practices and orientation intrigue Scott. Surprisingly, there is a strong religious overtone to his comments. "You'll go to hell and be punished forever for smoking," he intones, with more than a hint of moral indignation. His body language is peculiar as well. He can be abrupt and threatening. It is obvious that he has no comprehension about how to create positive peer relationships. He rants or mumbles.

What is it about Scott? His behavior is so different from the usually noisy, aggressive, disruptive student that I have encountered during my long teaching career.

I continue to ponder the best course of action for this unusual young man. The class is always on tenterhooks, waiting for my response to Scott. He is going to require a great deal of patience and all of my parenting skills to deal effectively with his particular situation. I have questions for Guidance, his vice principal, the head of the advanced-enriched department, and possibly the local school team.

After the first few weeks of term with Scott burrowing into any plans I make for the class, I am aware that I am going to have to rethink some of my teaching strategies. I have 100 Tenth-grade students, and our plan is to create and hold our own model government and model United Nations. I utilize collaborative teaching strategies to cover large areas of material because classroom management and good peer relationships are critical for student success.

This is the situation: I need to integrate Scott into the classroom. I need to find a "place" for him in my student activities where he can shine and not disrupt the learning around him. I need to spend less classroom time helping him to manage his behavior. He has the ability to distract all of us from the task at hand. When he is absent, the class breathes a collective sigh of relief. I observe that the classroom dynamics are weakening as more and more students amuse themselves by engaging Scott in silly, disruptive banter. Yet I feel a need to reach out and discuss Scott with the class, to openly gain their support, but I realize that the issue of confidentiality would be compromised.

I need to know about Scott.

There are no answers forthcoming. His medical records and his diagnosis are confidential. There is no interaction, no response from his parents. I never meet them. There is no opportunity to consult with all of his teachers simultaneously. There is little support from Guidance; his Guidance teacher is bound by parental requests for silence. The head of the advanced-enriched program and the vice principal will only say that he has been placed in the program because his parents fear for his physical safety within the general school environment. As the year progresses, there are hints from others that he may suffer from a form of autism known as Asperger's Syndrome. I begin to wonder whether or not I have the right to know about Scott. Is a family's need for privacy greater than my need to know?

We still have to manage the daily program. Regular classes are improving. Scott and I meet daily for lunch for a few weeks. We come to a mutual understanding about his classroom behavior. Scott and I have developed small signals for each other—time for me to teach, and time for Scott to raise issues of concern. These issues must come from the newspaper and may not be related to smoking, drugs, or sexual behavior. In a way, they are loosely linked to my history course content. The class attempts to listen and discuss political issues initiated by his comments or conjectures. Although Scott grasps the facts, he finds their interrelationships difficult to comprehend. The other students perceive the threads of history, how past and present intermingle, and this baffles and annoys Scott.

But Scott also needs time to back out of potentially nasty encounters with his neighboring students. We decide that he will sit slightly apart from the others. He needs to maintain the integrity of his own space. The signals we have agreed on have some success, but he often forgets them as the year progresses. All of us are constrained by the sudden changes of his behavior. Our expectations for the year are becoming limited.

Yet we have established a structure to our daily classroom routines where Scott is not able to always interrupt and totally divert my intentions for study, and the class is more amenable to organizing our classroom simulations. The model government and model United Nations are excellent tools for discussion and for individual and group research. We are able to include Scott in some of the group work, and the class is satisfied that they will be able to earn their own marks. I have decided that group mark will not be influenced by any of Scott's work. His classmates even find a special role for him in our model government as Party Whip. Scott feels powerful, accepted, and an integral component of the model government. We choose a very strong Speaker of the House, and I am voted in as Sergeant at Arms. Their sense of humor is still intact.

The year passes. We have struggled with each other, and the program has suffered. My department head is concerned about the retention rate for our senior elective enriched history programs. Scott has found a precarious acceptance in class. He achieves limited academic success. He passes on his own merit with some extra weighting for appropriate classroom behavior. He has managed to complete all of his assignments. His arguments are thin, but since these students are to be evaluated as advanced-level students, and since he can grasp and organize the factual material, he is able to achieve 51 percent. He is very disappointed. He does not understand how little he understands, and he is angry.

My patience has worn thin, and I am not pleased with the year. The rest of the class has not received the attention that I feel is their due. All of Scott's teachers are frustrated with the lack of support from the administration, frustrated with the loss of teaching time while they struggled to mold his behavior to suit their classroom needs. His privacy was maintained—but there was a cost.

In retrospect, Scott was an invaluable lesson to all of us.

❖ EXPLORING THE CASE

A secondary school teacher with 28 years of experience wrote this case.

Identification

Identify the key facts of this case. What events are central to understanding this situation? Identify the dilemmas and tensions in this case. Explore the main aspects of each dilemma and tension.

Analysis

Analyze the issue(s) from the viewpoints of the different people in the case. What makes Scott's story unique? Consider the consequences of integrating a student like Scott with special needs into regular or special classes.

Evaluation

Examine critically the teacher's strategies for handling the challenge(s). Does the teacher depicted fulfill, fall short of, or surpass your notion of the role of a teacher?

Alternative Solutions

Were there alternative solutions or strategies available to deal with the teacher's dilemma? Generate alternative solutions to the ones presented in the narrative. Take into consideration risks, benefits, and long- and short-term consequences of each proposed action.

Reflection

At the conclusion of the case, the teacher ponders the role that Scott played in the lives of the other students. What new insight has been revealed? Has anything been resolved?

Changing Opinions

Consider your thoughts and assumptions at the beginning of the chapter. Who or what has caused you to consider a new way of thinking? How strongly do you still feel about your previous assumptions?

Synthesis

Synthesize your understanding of this case into a statement. What is this a case of?

Case Commentary by Anna Ershler Richert

The case, "Balancing the Needs of All Students in an Inclusive Classroom," raises many issues about what conditions exist in schools that make teaching and learning possible—or difficult, as the case may be. It also raises issues about professional responsibility that are particularly compelling, especially these days when the push in education is toward externally determined mandates and high-stakes accountability.

While reading this case, I kept wondering about Scott, the student who is the focus of this case, and the other students in the course. Who is responsible for the educational experience and learning outcomes of these students? We assume, of course, that it is his teacher, a 28-year veteran with notable teaching success. It is she or he who will be accountable in the end. As the author of the case, she or he positions her- or himself as responsible for Scott's success in the class just as she or he sees her- or himself as responsible for the success of the other students. I am quite certain that the school would see the teacher as responsible for Scott's and his classmates' success as well. How can we abide by a system that holds teachers professionally responsible for the learning outcomes of their students and then withholds information they need to do their work responsibly and well?

Scott's learning challenges present themselves the first day he arrives in class. Whereas they would probably be evident even to the inexperienced teacher, the case's veteran author speaks with the authority of experience when she or he says, "I meet Scott and I know that I am confronted with my classroom challenge. He immediately fills my personal space. He is 'nose to nose' when he is on the offensive, but he quickly retreats when I step forward. His constant interruptions during attendance demonstrate a lack of understanding of basic classroom procedures and dynamics."

As the opening days of school commence, the number of questions Scott's teacher has about him rise. Compared with other students whom she or he has known—a considerable number given this teacher's years of experience—Scott's behavior warrants special attention. He is awkward, loud, and unable to connect with his peers. He mumbles, rants, and occasionally uses abrupt and threatening language in class. As would be morally responsible for any professional confronted with a client (in this case a student) who exhibits troubling behavior that will affect her or his ability to do her or his work, the teacher wastes little time in seeking information about Scott. The teacher seeks information that she or he believes will help—actually allow her or him—to do her or his work.

What is remarkable in our profession is that this information can be withheld from the teacher. The teacher was not able to access Scott's medical diagnosis on the grounds that it was "confidential." Nor was the teacher able to access people who would know about Scott—his parents, for example—who would have been able to help make sense of the troubling behaviors observed. Instead, the teacher was kept in the dark. The teacher spent hours and days and weeks trying to understand Scott and determine what might help him learn. At the same time, the teacher had to manage and teach the other 34 students in the class who were not without their own learning needs, especially in this disrupted class.

If we are serious about making teachers professionally accountable for their work—which I believe we should be—we need to provide conditions that will allow them to do that work in professionally responsible ways. Mainstreaming children into "regular" classes requires that we provide teachers with knowledge of the students who are mainstreamed in. To teach well, teachers need to know their students well. They must have access to background information for all students, particularly those with special needs. Asking Scott's teacher to teach him while withholding information about him would be like asking an attorney to defend a client charged with driving through red lights without telling the attorney that the client is color-blind. It is irresponsible and unprofessional.

Whereas we can surmise that Scott's parents do not want the label of his medical diagnosis to affect his experience of school, we can see in this powerfully written case that label or not, Scott's condition affect not only his school success but that of his peers. Withholding information serves no one in this case. Scott, his classmates, and his teacher all deserve better.

❖ EXPLORING THE ISSUES

Working With Students With Special Needs

Richert asks, "How can we abide by a system that holds teachers professionally responsible for the learning outcomes of their students, and then withholds information they need to do their work responsibly and well?" How do teachers learn to cope when they must surmise and infer the source of student difficulties? If information is withheld, how should teachers augment their involvement with students whose backgrounds are not revealed?

Classroom Management

In Richert's second paragraph, she ponders, "Who is responsible for the educational experience and learning outcomes of these students?" The teacher in this case is very aware of the reaction of the other students in the class to Scott. When a child with special needs arrives in class, whether she or he is identified or not, how should a teacher balance the needs of the group against those requiring more assistance?

Case Commentary by Lynne M. Cavazos

Privacy, silence, lack of support, loss of teaching time, and disappointment are not the descriptors I expected in this case given the initial description of the school as a "vibrant, noisy, 'happening' place" that "prides itself on providing an inclusive atmosphere."

How is it possible for a school to be described in such contradictory terms? How is it possible that the creation of "Balancing the Needs of All Students in an Inclusive Classroom" actually supports an inclusive atmosphere for students, teachers, parents, and site administrators? The answer, I believe, lies in the fact that many schools have allowed "confidentiality" to become one of the walls that hinders professionals, teachers, counselors, and administrators from providing the support and assistance many students need both academically and socially.

With the current push for schools, especially secondary schools, to become collaborative learning communities with everyone working together to support student learning and achievement, I find it hard to believe that the school in the case study is a "happening place." It surely was not "happening" for Scott, for his teacher, or for the students in the 10th-grade social studies course.

As I read this case study, I became more and more frustrated by the lack of support given to this experienced teacher who clearly had been assigned a student with exceptional needs. This is an example of a veteran teacher who knows what information is needed, who has that information, and knows how her or his colleagues could collaboratively assess Scott's needs across different content areas. Nonetheless, the case author was prevented from obtaining the support she or he needed from the guidance counselor, the head of the advanced-enrichment department, Scott's parents, and site administrators.

What if Scott had been assigned to a first- or second-year teacher? How would a beginning teacher feel about her or his competency to support all students in learning and effectively manage a class with 30 boys and 5 girls, including an exceptional student like Scott? If a veteran teacher of 28 years has lost patience and is not pleased with the year, just imagine how devastated a new teacher would be! In this case study, student privacy was maintained but the cost was too high: for this veteran teacher, and for the students involved, especially given

Scott's disappointment and anger at his limited academic success and social acceptance.

I believe the case brings to the forefront why and how the use of privacy, silence, and confidentiality can be harmful to a school learning community. For a school to create an atmosphere that is "conducive to the academic and personal development of every student," the school must first create a strong learning community where collaboration and partnerships are the expectation and privacy and confidentiality are upheld but not withheld from professional teachers responsible and held accountable for the success of their students. If, as according to Hillary Rodham Clinton, it takes a village to raise a child, then I propose that it takes a caring learning community to develop students' academic and social skills and habits that will benefit them throughout their lives.

Students' parents are vital to a caring learning community. Although many high school students do not want their parents involved in schooling decisions, it is clear that the involvement of Scott's parents is essential if the dilemmas in this case are to be dismantled. Will it be difficult for school personnel to establish a respectful, supportive relationship with Scott's parents? Probably. Is it imperative for Scott and the teachers who work with him? Absolutely, and it is everyone's responsibility to create lines of communication with parents and find ways to involve them in the decision-making process. In his article "Creating a School Community," Eric Schaps (2003) identifies four beneficial community-building approaches that would help break down the *walls of silence* that currently exist in many high schools:

- Actively cultivate respectful, supportive relationships among students, teachers, and parents [I would add site administrators to this approach].
- Emphasize common purposes and ideals.
- Provide regular opportunities for service and cooperation.
- Provide developmentally appropriate opportunities for autonomy and influence.

❖ EXPLORING THE ISSUES

Partnerships

Cavazos looks beyond the classroom to the ethos of the school and questions why collaborative communities have not formed to support all learners. Where should teachers go to find support and resources for their investigations? How might staff members who teach students with special needs form a collaborative community?

Reflection

Cavazos worries about Scott's outcome had a first- or second-year teacher been his teacher. The teacher in this case works hard to ensure some success for Scott. Faced with a student like Scott, how should teachers prepare for working effectively with their classes, the school, and the student's parents? Were there benefits in including students like Scott in classes?

Case Commentary by Tania Madfes

As a former high school teacher, I empathized with the author of this case and understood the need to create order and routine in the classroom as a way to support the learning of all students. I also related to the teacher's frustrations. But it is as a parent that I found my real connection to this case and admiration for the author.

As a parent, I have expectations about how teachers will treat my children as well as teach them. This teacher did not say she or he needed to find a way to have Scott removed from the class so life would be easier. The teacher said she or he needed to integrate Scott into the classroom and find a place for him in the student activities where he could shine and not disrupt the learning around him. What a wonderful attitude about teaching as a social dynamic and the responsibility of a teacher to the *whole* child.

As the year progressed, the teacher found ways to meet with Scott and provide him with the kind of personalized attention he may have been craving. Together, they developed a set of signals so that instruction could proceed uninterrupted and Scott could still express himself. Scott's need for maintaining the integrity of his physical space was also acknowledged and honored. It appears that the students in the class also learned something about tolerance for those who may be different through watching the relationship between the teacher and the disruptive student. For it was his classmates who made it possible for Scott to be integrated into the group work and given a role that he could handle in the class project, making him feel "powerful, accepted, and an integral component of the model government."

The teacher's actions enabled Scott to become more accepted by his peers and to participate academically in an advanced-level class. As a parent, I entrust my children to the care of their teachers for almost 6 hours every day. I hope that during that time my children are treated well by the adults and the other children and I expect that they will learn not only the academic content but also the socialization skills they will need to become good citizens and good human beings. I would be pleased if my children were to have the privilege of being in this teacher's classroom.

❖ EXPLORING THE ISSUES

Inclusion Issues

Although Madfes is an educator, she provides the perspective of the parent here, one who endorses the work by the teacher in the case. Explain why the special care the teacher takes appeals to Madfes. What lessons might other teachers learn from this model?

Working With Students With Special Needs

Madfes suggests that many teachers find they develop familiar patterns of teaching, sets of steps that are repeated but with some variation. The teacher in this case does, in fact, provide variations for Scott. Do you think teachers should use routines to structure their classes, or should they be constantly implementing change?

Case Commentary by Linda F. Rhone

While reading this case, "Balancing the Needs of All Students in an Inclusive Classroom," there were several thoughts that resonated with me. First, it was the challenge of negotiating power in the classroom context. The teacher in this case faced having to negotiate power with one student in particular, Scott, then with the rest of the class. The teacher's courage and refusal to give up pondering the best course of action for this unique student is the essence of hope. I am reminded of the work of Mary Dilg (2003) entitled *Thriving in the Multicultural Classroom: Principles and Practices for Effective Teaching*. Dilg argued that

America's teachers would best serve the diverse populations of this century by understanding the diversities in their language, ethnicity, race, and religious beliefs. I believe these diversities would include learning styles and behavioral patterns.

This particular teacher's willingness to rethink her or his teaching strategies so that Scott could be incorporated into the classroom is as much understanding as any teacher could be asked to have! Her or his willingness to work collaboratively with her or his students is evident, as the entire class pondered ways to incorporate Scott in the classroom and maintain a classroom environment where everyone would be successful. The teacher's decision to use democratic teaching strategies that promoted collaboration between teacher and students and student and students promoted self-management and quality peer relationships.

Second, this teacher selected the model government and model United Nations teaching tools that centralized democracy and critical thinking, allowing each student to develop a voice and skills to better understand which types of behaviors would be conducive to their learning success and which types would hinder their individual and group learning success. Through these democratic teaching tools, Scott was able to participate in managing his own classroom behavior and his classmates were moved to find roles that allowed him to rechannel his energy from negative and disruptive behavior to more productive behavior. This also allowed him to receive acceptance among his peers, something he seemed to be striving for daily.

Because this case author lacked a collaborative learning community involving parents, other teachers, guidance counselors, and administrators to assist in discovering the best course of action for Scott, the teacher was moved to collaborate with the people who were most immediately involved—her or his students—and built trusting collaborative relationships with them. The teacher's actions are much like those advocated by Katherine Schultz (2003), who wrote *Listening: A Framework for Teaching Across Differences*.

Schultz argued that listening and building a trusting relationship were essential to meaningful teaching. The teacher in this case listened to the most challenging student, Scott, and her or his collaborative learning community—the students. They trusted each other and worked to create an environment where each could thrive for successful learning. The teacher's actions also mirrored the concepts advocated by the late Paulo Freire and other progressive educators around the world who believe that trust, mutual respect, and democratic teaching strategies are the essence of teaching and learning. For this teacher, her or his power over this class was far less important than empowering students to make the best choices for themselves.

Finally, this effective, thoughtful, and courageous teacher took advantage of teachable moments, as described by Schultz (2003), and subtle listening as a way to move all students in the classroom to success. It was clear that learning was and is a process still at work in her or his classroom. After almost three decades of teaching openness and willingness to rethink teaching strategies remains pivotal in the teaching of the students in her or his class. More important, maintaining a spirit of hope encourages me as a teacher educator. In essence, the teacher decided that Scott was worth her or his time and commitment. Though this teacher was clear in the final remarks that the program suffered due to the focus on unique students like Scott, the teacher was still willing to ponder ways to maximize the learning potential of all students. This teacher provides a voice of hope and insight to pre-service teachers, veteran teachers, administrators, and teacher-educators, as we all contemplate ways to incorporate the "Scotts" in our classrooms.

❖ EXPLORING THE ISSUES

Diversity

Rhone salutes the teacher's use of diverse thinking, assignments, activities, and so on to incorporate Scott into the class. How important are routines and consistency in dealing with students with special needs? When and why should teachers decide to institute change?

Collaborative Community

Rhone notes how the teacher created a collaborative community and refers to Paolo Freire's work as an exemplar. Was the environment in the case empowering for Scott? Or not? What values and elements of democracy are brought to the forefront in the case?

Teacher Identity

Rhone extols the teacher's personal attributes. How can teachers' passions and personal pursuits influence their professional lives?

❖ ENGAGING WITH THE COMMENTARIES

School Authority

Richert, Cavazos, and Rhone address a school environment in which silence, confidentiality, and privacy prevent open collaboration and conversations that would contribute to the ongoing development of children's education. Rhone refers to the situation as "negotiating power." Using the list by Eric Schaps, consider which points each commentator would endorse and why.

Perspective

This selection of commentaries is unique because it includes the voice and perspective of a parent. Contrast the attitude of Madfes with the parent in the story and speculate on the reasons the latter insisted on privacy. How does Madfes's commentary differ from the other commentators?

Connecting Questions

The Connecting Questions located in the introduction highlight themes that are threaded throughout the cases. You may continue your exploration of the issues raised in this case by addressing those connections. For questions pertinent to this case, please see questions 4, 6, and 9.

❖ ADDITIONAL READINGS

Benifhof, A. M. (1986). Using a spectrum of staff development activities to support inclusion. *Journal of Staff Development, 17*(3), 12–15.

The author examines ways for staff to comprehend how inclusion can occur successfully by tailoring programs to individual needs. There are model plans and individualized approaches with an example in one particular school district.

Finley, P. (1989). Malaise of the spirit: A case study. In J. Kleinfeld (Ed.), *Teaching cases in cross-cultural education.* Fairbanks: University of Alaska, Center for Cross Cultural Studies.

Finley describes an experienced high school teacher's dilemmas in a rural town in Alaska where severe tensions between white and Eskimo students and between community members and teachers are revealed in the classroom. Racial conflicts and issues of diversity are brought to light. The limitations of rules, routines, and principles are made obvious. Teachers decide how to cope effectively, considering practice versus theory and whether research-based knowledge is applicable to cross-cultural classrooms.

Friend, M., Bursuch, W., & Hutchinson, N. L. (1998). *Including exceptional students: A practical guide for classroom teachers* (Canadian ed.). Scarborough, ON: Allyn & Bacon.

The noncategorical approach to inclusion is the focus here. A model is presented to examine how all students might achieve success regardless of their specific category of exceptionality. The text's organization is helpful in sorting out information that pertains to strategies and resources. It presents a foundation in special education and encourages readers to apply that information in specific classroom situations.

McGee, J. J., & Menolascino, F. J. (2004). *Beyond gentle teaching: A nonaversive approach to helping those in need.* Dordrecht, The Netherlands: Kluwer.

With a view to collaboration and interdependence, this book encourages caregivers to change. Companionship, support, and interactive fulfillment are key.

Munby, H., & Hutchinson, N. (1998). Using experience to prepare teachers for inclusive classrooms: Teacher education and the epistemology of practice. *Teacher Education and Special Education, 21,* 75–82.

With a view to teacher preparation, the authors describe an innovative experience-based program and discuss inclusive education. The writers establish theoretical background with attention given to the nature of professional knowledge. Two case studies illustrate this approach.

Reynolds, M. C., Wang, M. C., & Walberg, H. J. (1987). The necessary restructuring of special and regular education. *Exceptional Children, 53,* 391–398.

The authors suggest that categories used in special education for mildly handicapped students are not always reliable. As indicators of particular forms of education, further scrutiny is required. Discrete categories may lead to disjointed school programs.

Shulman, J., & Mesa-Bains, M. (Eds.). (1993). *Diversity in the classroom: Casebook for teachers and teacher-educators.* San Francisco: FarWest Lab.
    The framework of Exploring the Case was adapted from this book.

Van Manen, M. (2003). On the epistemology of reflective practice. *Teachers and Teaching: Theory and Practice, 1*(1), 33–50.
    The author discusses the need for "tact" and knowing how to balance all the conflicting situations in a classroom that seem to occur simultaneously.

Wong, B. Y. L. (1996). *The abc's of learning disabilities.* Toronto, ON: Academic Press.
    This award-winning book examines strategies, definitions, insights, and planning for students who are identified as exceptional. It is a very helpful, practical guide.

10

Implications of
Student Cheating for
the Teaching Community

I n this case, when a teacher is alerted to evidence of cheating in class, she or he finds that solutions can be complicated. The case commentators Jean McNiff, Aria Razfar, Michael Manley-Casimir, and James McCracken focus on issues of equity, ethics, school policies, and collegial relationships.

❖ THINKING AHEAD

As you read this chapter, reflect on the following questions and issues:

- Consider the teacher's knowledge, experience, and values in this case.
- How does the teacher attempt to balance both teacher and student needs at the outset of the story?

The use of "she and he," while it may appear awkward to the reader, is intended to ensure the absence of gender bias.

- Do you think that this teacher has established clear, challenging, but achievable expectations?
- Consider the culture of the school and the community. Does either one play a role in this dilemma?
- What are the pressure points in the case?
- How does the teacher deal with the problem that has been discovered?

I bristle waiting for the 9 a.m. bell to ring. Already today, my car has been broken into, and the bill to repair the car window bashed in by the anonymous thief is shockingly high, but not high enough to risk reporting to the insurance company. The vice principal has assigned me double on-call supervision for the fourth day in a row. My lunch has disappeared somewhere between the parking lot and the office—and I have had to endure two telephone conversations with parents, both of which began amicably enough but quickly degenerated into the undisputed fact that my teaching had single-handedly been responsible for the total breakdown of family bliss! And now, the lunch period is filled with another acrimonious telephone encounter with a parent angry over my completely unacceptable policy of assessing a penalty for late assignments.

At 9 p.m. I remind myself that I should stop grading. But I convince myself that I must do just one more essay. Refreshed from reading a truly excellent essay, one that boasts great organization and wonderful sentence variety, I am revitalized with vicarious joy at a student's breakthrough in writing. Reaching for the next essay, I begin grading again. My eyes are lured to the following sentence near the end of the first paragraph: "Using elevated metaphors of evocative brilliance to illuminate the excesses of the human spirit. . . ."

These words slam into my emotional and intellectual solar plexus. Banging my fist down hard on the table, I curse. I curse the stars, the essay, the student; I curse myself!

It is almost 9:30 p.m. I know from experience it is not fair to me or to my students to grade past this hour, but if I don't finish this class set by tomorrow night, I shall be swamped when the new batch of essays from my graduating class comes pouring in on Wednesday. Why did I have to grade just one more? And now THIS!!! THIS is going to keep me up for another hour at least.

When the computer is booted up and the Google screen is fully displayed, I type in "elevated metaphors of evocative brilliance," click on

Go, and wait. In 3.7249 seconds, the indictment is flashed on the screen. When I click on the first entry and the page is displayed, the verdict confirms my suspicions. This essay is plagiarized. Not only the offending phrase, but also five whole paragraphs have also been stolen.

Print and try to go to bed, I command myself.

But after the day I've had, I am beginning to get mad. There is the nagging doubt that I am at fault. There is the crazy thought in my brain that when the student fails, the teacher is responsible: The assignment was too difficult, and they were forced to cheat. I stop myself from this too frequent self-deprecation and remind myself that some kids, some adults, some people cheat. Some kids are deeply affected by my beginning-of-the-year sermon on plagiarism. They understand when I say it is not only intellectual theft but also an affront to my intelligence, an insult to my abilities as an English teacher, a rude slap in the face of my professionalism for them to think I cannot recognize their unique voices when they write. Some hear and remember; others merely listen and forget. I know this is true when I teach the endless wonders of the nominative and objective case of pronouns, but shouldn't we expect more students to hear and to remember when we speak of, or attempt to teach values?

The next morning I take four plagiarized essays to my supportive department head. Despite the fact that this essay is worth 20 percent of the year's grade, students who cheat will receive a zero. Their graduating grades submitted to universities in 2 weeks will be severely affected. We call the students in separately and ask them to explain the similarity of their writing and the writing taken from the Web sites. Two students admit plagiarizing the essay outright and take responsibility for their actions and accept the explained consequences of their actions. The other two students are too shocked to speak or to weep, and then depart without acknowledging anything or exhibiting any remorse. These encounters are exhausting. They constitute some of the truly difficult moments in my life as a teacher.

But my satisfaction in dealing with a serious and unpleasant situation is short-lived.

There is a note in my box from the vice principal, Alice, when I return from spring break. She begins the meeting with, "When I was a teacher, I saw these plagiarism issues as black and white, but now that I am an administrator, I see very clearly the gray areas in these matters. You know there are always extenuating circumstances that we sometimes do not initially consider."

"Okay, if you want me to consider these extenuating circumstances, what are they?" I ask.

"As it was explained to me, they need to be kept confidential," replies a smug Alice.

"The extenuating circumstances? Or the need to keep them confidential? I don't understand, Alice, what was explained to you? And who did the explaining?" I am momentarily thrown off balance.

"I didn't interview the students. Jennifer, our principal, interviewed them, and she wants it kept confidential." She avoids making eye contact with me.

"The matter kept confidential? Or the extenuating circumstances kept confidential? Which one? And besides, if Jennifer wants it kept confidential (whatever the "it" is), why did she bring you into the loop?" I query. "She's the principal. Let her handle this."

"Oh, Jennifer doesn't want you discussing this with any staff member, not even members of your own department."

"Jennifer is putting a gag order on me?" I am aghast.

"That's how it was explained to me. There are extenuating circumstances involved. The principal has accepted them. She does not want the matter discussed further. She wants me to direct you to assign the students an 'incomplete' grade for the course. Jennifer wants them to receive an incomplete, so that's that. Understand?"

This thrust pierces my stunned brain. This is the second blow to my intellectual and emotional plexus I have sustained in this matter. I recover enough to seek a clarification: "You mean to tell me that all four students are to receive an incomplete for their documented plagiarism, and the principal wants me to assign that grade? Remember, it's not my policy. It's the department's policy and the school's policy. It's even printed in the student agenda!"

"Yes, change the grade to an incomplete. These are the directives to you from the principal, who is in charge of this matter." Like a robot, she is repeating verbatim the instructions that she parrots without any sign of the ethical dilemma that has been provoked. Suddenly, she gasps, incredulous. "What do you mean four?!! There are only two students involved."

In 5 minutes, I return to her office and spread out on her desk the four folders of evidence of plagiarism. It is her turn to be stunned. She uses her mouth to expel air much as a whale expels air through its blowhole. It is the only sound for a tense minute or two.

Since we both share the knowledge that a crucial part of the story has been withheld from each of us, I defy procedure and inform the vice principal that I intend to camp out in her office until I know every-thing she knows, and if she refuses to give me the full information, I will take the matter to the school board's ombudsman or a newspaper, whichever will hear me first. I am bluffing, but the ruse works and Alice cracks.

"Look, you know the climate out there has changed radically in the past few years, and the administration is required to . . . well, . . . well, pay more attention to the, the, the concerns of parents. The parents of these two graduating kids who, who, . . . uh, uh . . . did this thing have been all over the principal for the past 2 weeks, complaining about unfair punishment for a first-time offense, and this affecting their kids' chance at getting into university. And this year, we have double groups of graduates because the government has decided that kids need one less year of high school education. One of the kids' parents is a big shot lawyer with political connections, and the other is just a really great person who is a huge supporter of the school through the Parents' Council. The pressure is really intense to do something, to clear this matter up—cleanly. The principal wants to do what is right for the kids, and their future, and what she sees as being right for the school. Jennifer thinks the two of the accused have really, really learned their lesson over this, and she is sure they'll never do it again. Just change the grade." She looks me hard in the eyes, " . . . and let's get on with the new term. Okay?"

I don't know if I am beaten, or if I am beaten down. I don't know where my breath is coming from to make these sounds, but the words eventually come out slowly as if I am picking my way through a minefield:

"Let me get this straight. An incomplete for the two students whose parents put the pressure on the principal, and, and a zero for the kids who admitted to the plagiarism. Is that right?"

"Yes. That's right. Okay? I'm sorry." And maybe she is actually sorry.

As I leave the vice principal's office, the devil on my left shoulder reminds me there are only 5 short years left before I retire. On my right shoulder, I swear I hear an angel weeping.

❖ EXPLORING THE CASE

A secondary school teacher with 20 years of experience wrote this case.

Identification

Identify the key facts of this case. What factual events are central to understanding this situation? Identify the dilemmas and tensions in this case. Explore the main aspects of each dilemma and tension. Consider the dilemma from the various perspectives of the individuals involved in the case.

Analysis

Analyze the issue(s) from the viewpoints of the different people in the case. What steps does the teacher take to deal with the plagiarists? What problems does she or he encounter? How do her or his attempts to resolve the dilemmas lead to more dilemmas at a variety of levels? How ethically do all participants behave?

Evaluation

Examine critically the teacher's strategies for handling the challenge(s). Does the teacher depicted fulfill, fall short of, or surpass your notion of the role of a teacher?

Alternative Solutions

Were there alternative solutions or strategies available to deal with the dilemmas? Generate alternative solutions to the ones presented in the narrative. Take into consideration risks, benefits, and long- and short-term consequences of each proposed action.

Reflection

Although the teacher sadly reflects that she or he will be retiring in 5 years, she or he appears to be resigned to the outcomes of her or his actions at the story's conclusion. Does the teacher's concluding reflection provide a satisfying ending? Has anything been resolved?

Changing Opinions

Consider your thoughts and assumptions at the beginning of the chapter. Who or what has caused you to consider a new way of thinking? How strongly do you still feel about your previous assumptions?

Synthesis

Synthesize your understanding of this case into a statement. What is this a case of?

Case Commentary by Jean McNiff

I imagine that a response of many educators, on first reading this piece, would be, "What would I do in the same circumstances?" This was my first reaction. What would I do if I were faced with grave injustices and institutional cover-ups that constituted a flagrant denial of my own values of honesty and truth, the values I lived by in my efforts to contribute to what I understand to be a good social order? It has taken me some days to think through how I would choose, because choices carry consequences, and the consequences can often be severe.

Most educators, I believe, are people of considerable integrity who live by values such as honesty, truthfulness, beauty, and love, and most try to influence their colleagues and students to do the same. Yet something seems to happen in contemporary institutional life, where it is possible to perceive two sets of values at work—the values of education and the values of business. These are often in direct opposition to each other, and they tend to serve different interest groups. Educational practices that focus on encouraging others to think for themselves and to come together as equal participants in conversations about how to create futures in which everyone's capacities and situations are honored are often contradicted by business practices that focus on concentrating power and wealth into the hands of intellectual and corporate elites at the expense of others. Education and business, and the value systems that underpin them, are frequently incompatible. In my view, this is the greatest tragedy, since it is entirely possible to maintain high standards of integrity in schools and other education settings within financially viable structures and processes. When greed and power intrude, however, those potentials for fair and honest living go by the board—literally, in the case described in the story.

It is straightforward enough to write about social justice, as many philosophers do, as if justice is a phenomenon that can be theorized in abstract terms. Similarly, it is straightforward enough to generate abstract theories about democracy, freedom, and other high principles of living. The abstractions remain just that—abstractions that tell us how we should live without locating the ideas in living contexts that are always full of the inevitable problematic and contradictions of the daily living of real people who face intractable choices every day of their lives. Meryl Streep's character in the film *The Bridges of Madison County* echoes many philosophers in saying, "We are our choices." Yes, we are. How we live, as we make our choices, inspired and guided by the values we hold most precious, is one way of defining ourselves. We create our identity in company with others. Who we become very much depends on the choices we make. As educators, we are constantly faced with dilemmas about which educational commitments are nonnegotiable as we decide whether to resist or submit to institutional power and whether we are prepared to face the consequences of our actions. These decisions become our personal theories of right living.

What would I do? Would I compromise my integrity and my deeply held values of honesty and truth by deciding to remain silent and give in to the purchasing power of those who regard education as a market commodity available to privileged consumers, or would I stick to my principles and defy the wrath of institutional oligarchies by pressing for truth, using every avenue open to me, in the full knowledge of the kinds of consequences that would inevitably follow?

Since reading the piece, I have decided what my choice would be: not easy, not straightforward, but my choice, because this is how I understand my life.

❖ EXPLORING THE ISSUES

School Policies

How can school policies and systems be administered fairly and equitably? Can the models of business and education be conflated? Consider if and why schools would want to aim for a combined vision of education and business worlds? How might that combination be implemented if models were combined?

Self-Esteem

In the commentary, McNiff refers to how we create our own identities. What does McNiff (and Meryl Streep) mean by the sentence "We are our choices"? How might this sentence apply to teachers?

Ethical Behavior

McNiff says that people praise equity and justice. Although they may revere these qualities in the abstract sense, it is important for students to see how the abrogation of rights, such as plagiarism, works in practice, and who suffers or is violated in the process. How can ethical behavior be instilled at schools, and if violations occur, how might they be dealt with fairly, avoiding differing consequences for particular groups?

Ethical Decision Making

McNiff juxtaposes the realms of business and education, fearing the overlaps and the inconsistencies that grow from differing sets of values. Yet both models guide society. When students transgress, are the dual systems and philosophies in schools confusing for students because of the clash of paradigms? Is it possible for contradictions to be explained? If so, how?

Case Commentary by Aria Razfar

At the beginning of each course, when I introduce the course content and syllabus, I always declare the official policy on plagiarism and intellectual theft as handed down from official academic guidelines and the like. I have never actually pursued a student who I suspected of plagiarizing because I wasn't sure how to substantiate my hunch because I would have to be absolutely certain. The case of "Implications of Student Cheating for the Teaching Community" is a reminder of how technology has radically transformed how we engage long-standing issues such as plagiarism. I recently received an e-mail from a colleague suggesting the use of Google to catch students who are suspected of plagiarizing, which had never occurred to me before. Initially, I thought, "How clever; we'll show them [the students]." As a teacher and teacher-educator, I had always vehemently opposed such an oppositional discourse when it came to education. I thought to myself at that time and after reading this case, "Why would instructors police students in such ways?" I was reminded of Foucault's use of the metaphor of the panopticon and the teacher as an instrument of surveillance. While it is not a role that I think any instructor feels comfortable with, it seems like a necessary practice to ensure the sanctity of "academic integrity."

I have rarely thought about the underlying ideological and philosophical assumptions of this pillar of academic faith until I read the case of "Implications of Student Cheating for the Teaching Community." As a junior scholar, I have felt the elation of being "cited" in other people's work as well as the disappointment of others using "my" work without being "properly" credited. Given the embedded values of individualism, originality, and sole authorship that guide promotion in the academic world, is it little wonder that others and I have appropriated such values? After all, am I really the only author of "my" work, and what is "my" work anyway? Realistically, the writing we produce is always a conglomeration of voices engaged in a multivocal and multidirectional exchange—even when we sit alone behind our computers composing. At the same time, we need that sense of sole authorship to feel validated and legitimate. We hear that "collaboration" with other scholars, especially when a piece is cowritten, is marginalized in relation to single-author pieces. With respect to the case, one may ask: "Have students, teachers, and community members at large engaged in such discussions of core values?" My guess would be probably not.

The case of "Implications of Student Cheating for the Teaching Community" reminds us not only of the ethical and ideological tensions of educators but also of the institutional practices that disempower and debilitate them. The teacher in this case feels surrounded by parents, administrators, common thieves, and lastly her or his students, who have become intellectual thieves. The teacher's relationship with each segment of society is distant and confrontational. Amidst the chaos, the teacher remains heroic and the sole protector of sacred virtues, especially academic integrity. However, in the end, the teacher is powerless and compromises with those who wield the stick of authority, and after 20 years of teaching, she or he is painfully reminded that she or he is nothing but a cog in the machine of deceit. One wonders what reservoir of idealism the teacher draws from to remain steadfast. But I am left with a nagging question: Why doesn't the teacher stand up for her or his principles at the end and assign a zero to all of the implicated students? Does the teacher lack the agency? Obviously, the teacher doesn't because she or he acknowledges the choice between the devil's promise of only 5 years to retirement and the angel who is crying on her or his right shoulder.

As a professor who encourages projects that aim to address issues of social justice, I was reminded of the fundamental contradictions that exist between the systems in which our professional careers are based and the values we are trying to impart in classrooms and within ourselves as individuals. However, it is not sufficient to feel guilty—we need to strengthen those voices within ourselves and around ourselves that push us to take a moral stand. After all, we can't take retirement to the grave—but our ethical and moral stands will endure beyond us.

❖ EXPLORING THE ISSUES

Power Struggles

Razfar reflects that being an author and announcing that a piece of writing is yours alone is an empowering feeling, yet much of what is written and said has been collaborated on or constructed in concert with others, often even echoing voices heard before. That we actually write with our own hand and sign a document—does that mean the writer has sole ownership? How can schools teach individuals about the ethics of cheating if the above premise is true? Or is the above statement just a rationalization of plagiarists?

School Policies

Razfar points to the ethical and ideological tensions that occur in the story and in the school. How do institutional practices "disempower and debilitate" those tensions?

Teacher Responsibilities

Razfar wonders why the story's "hero" compromises in the end? Do you agree or disagree with Razfar's contention?

Collegial Relationships

The commentator points to the fact that the teacher is caught between the administration and the parents in this compelling narrative. Why would a school discriminate among cheaters and assign different consequences? What might be short- and long-term impacts for students, teachers, and the reputation of the school?

School Relationships

Razfar locates the "contradictions that exist between the systems in which our professional careers are based and the values we are trying to impart in classrooms and within ourselves as individuals." By ignoring the teacher, the administration is silencing an important link, not only for themselves, but also for the students. Why does the ruse of the teacher's intention to go public move the discussion forward? Has the teacher acted ethically? Did she or he have alternative choices?

Case Commentary by Michael Manley-Casimir

Abuse of Administrative Discretion

The analysis of cases such as "Implications of Student Cheating for the Teaching Community" always presents the difficulty of insufficient or unclear information. As a result, the reader and commentator must infer meaning from the reported story and impute meaning to the facts and circumstances of the case. Inevitably, such a process invites further comment and criticism.

This case presents several related facets that at first reading seem worthy of note. The first is the issue of the professional responsibility of the classroom teacher to act circumspectly in establishing and maintaining appropriate standards of academic honesty and to use fairness and impartiality in assessing suspected instances of plagiarism. The second concerns the role of the vice principal and principal in following published school policy in these matters and doing so in an even-handed, transparent, and consistent manner. The third, undercutting the others, concerns the way that each of the actors in the case use discretion and judgment in handling the instances of plagiarism; such could involve taking into consideration appropriate extenuating circumstances where such exist.

The way this story unfolds, however, leaves substantial doubt in my mind about the professional integrity of the school administrators, especially the principal in this case. The classroom teacher appears to have acted with due diligence and professional concern by ensuring that the essays from the four students, or parts thereof, were in fact plagiarized. Having established that, the teacher appropriately took the essays to the department head and together they confronted the students about their academic dishonesty. The effect, apparently following stated school policy, was the imposition of a zero grade for this essay—a serious sanction for the students since the essay constituted 20 percent of their grade and would negatively affect their graduating standing. At this stage, all four students appear to have been treated consistently and evenhandedly and no mention is made of extenuating circumstances.

Following spring break, however, the story changes. The principal, apparently giving in to parental pressure, instructs the vice principal to inform the classroom teacher to assign an incomplete status to two students, ostensibly on the grounds of extenuating circumstances. These circumstances are never stated and the other two students—whose parents did not, evidently, complain—are left with their zeros. What a grotesque abuse of administrative discretion on the part of the principal!

The bottom line in this case is that Jennifer, the principal, appears to have conceded to parental, political pressure and as a result committed an egregious abuse of administrative discretion. Such a judgment appears warranted on the grounds that she seems to have "trumped" the stated school policy respecting plagiarism by imposing her own reading on the events and issuing instructions to her vice principal that appear unsupported by good reasons or for that matter by any reasons. Through her actions, she also discounted the professional integrity of the classroom teacher who discovered the four cases of evident plagiarism. And by dealing only with the two cases involving students whose parents evidently complained rather than all four cases, she has perverted any sense of fairness in handling the cases.

❖ EXPLORING THE ISSUES

Social Justice

Manley-Casimir suggests that there are important gaps in the story, so the reader cannot get the entire picture. Yet Manley-Casimir contends that according to the details given, even the principal has not acted fairly. What inferences can be made about the relationship between community and school? Explore the students' belief in equity and social justice in school and society.

Power Struggles

Manley-Casimir questions the professional integrity of the principal in this case. In authoritarian rather than collaborative relationships, there will always be shifts in power. What redresses are there, checks and balances, for people—like this teacher—who are willing to act responsibly? What can a teacher do when faced with similar situations at a variety of levels in a school community?

Teacher Responsibilities

The principal and vice principal appear to "have conceded to parental, political pressure"; however, the teacher does not want to follow that example. What are a teacher's professional responsibilities when plagiarism is discovered? What does "personal integrity" mean for teachers who are aware of discriminatory practices in their school?

Case Commentary by James McCracken

The Quality of Mercy

> The quality of mercy is not strain'd.
> It droppeth as the gentle rain from heaven
> Upon the place beneath. It is twice blest:
> It blesseth him that gives and him that takes.

> —William Shakespeare

Unfortunately, there is much that is strained in the quality of mercy in this case. And indeed, what drops from above does not appear to be blessed.

The teacher-narrator describes a situation in which four students are caught plagiarizing: Two students admit the plagiarism and accept the consequences; the two other students do not admit plagiarism, and subsequently, parents protest the punishment. The principal determines that the latter two students will receive incompletes, which, in essence, nullifies the punishment. The principal's decision in this case raises a number of concerns.

First, it is clear from the teacher's narrative that she or he has explained what plagiarism is and how it will be dealt with in a "sermon on plagiarism" at the beginning of the course. The teacher clearly defines "intellectual theft" and "the affront to her or his intelligence" when students try to do this kind of thing. Moreover, it is noted that there is both a department and a school policy on plagiarism. Thus, the argument posed by parents that this is, indeed, a first offense and should be treated leniently is rather specious given the forewarning that has occurred.

Second, there is an obvious inconsistency of application of consequences in that it seems that the two students who accepted the punishment will not have their grade of zero changed. They will not receive the same "incomplete" as the two students who fought the consequence. It would appear that having a parent with political or social standing in the community is, indeed, an advantage at this school. This is a very dangerous message for any school administration to send to a school community, however unintentional.

Third, there are steps missing in the communication process. The teacher has followed an appropriate process by consulting with her or his department head and then meeting with each of the students in person. However, an obvious step has been missed. The principal and vice principal have not discussed the issue with the teacher before making the decision to award an "incomplete." Instead, there is an edict from the principal delivered by the vice principal.

The principal, it is said, "wants to do what is right for the kids, and their future, and what she sees as being right for the school." The problem here is that, in her well-meaning attempt to reduce the punishment and safeguard the grades for these two students, she is creating other potentially serious problems within the school. The two students in question may obtain better placements at university because of their higher grades, but two other serious problems result. First, this matter, most likely, will not remain confidential. Word will get out, and the message is clear: The first time you get caught plagiarizing, nothing bad happens. This weakens the department and school policy on plagiarism. Second, there is now a morale problem brewing in the English department that could spread to other academic departments.

In conclusion, it must be stated that the principal of the school is responsible for instruction and discipline of pupils in the school. She can direct teachers in many matters pertaining to instruction and evaluation. It is well within the purview of the principal to modify instruction, and this includes changing student grades. But this must be done prudently and only after much consultation. It is clear in this case that the principal has not followed this process. The teacher has not been given a respectful part in the process. She or he has been directed by a third party to change a grade, has not been given the reason for this edict, and is left embittered and confused. This is not the hallmark of effective communication. There will be times when a principal has to change a grade or make a decision that may not accord with a teacher's decision. It is hoped that when this happens, the principal is able to explain, to some extent, the reason for this change. The teacher and principal can then agree to disagree. At least, the teacher feels that she or he has been treated with a modicum of professional respect.

❖ EXPLORING THE ISSUES

Power Struggles

Why has McCracken begun with this particular quotation from Shakespeare? What has created "the strain" in the examples set out by this commentator?

Teacher Responsibilities

McCracken states, "It would appear that having a parent with political or social standing . . . is, indeed, an advantage at this school." How do preconceived ideas about students, school culture, and student backgrounds play a role in this teacher's reactions to unfolding events? Do you consider her or his expectations for both students and administration unfair or unrealistic?

Multiple Perspectives

McCracken is aware that the narrative is told and crafted from one particular point of view. Whose points of view are missing and why would those perspectives be helpful in determining "the truth" of the situation?

School Policies

In his last paragraph of his commentary, McCracken comments on the role of a principal in a school when teachers question authority: They must follow protocol in writing, speech, and action. How can you ensure that all voices have been heard and democratic processes have been followed so that justice is not only done, but also *seems* to have been done in school? What alternative models to the one presented in the narrative might you suggest that would more aptly respond to open discourses?

❖ ENGAGING WITH THE COMMENTARIES

Connecting Theory and Practice

McNiff talks about the need for contextual specificity, Razfar provides her "Google" example, and Manley-Casimir analyzes the concrete example in this story. Do the specific examples in practice make real the consequences on human lives and the consequences for those involved? Which commentator's response resonated most strongly with you? Why?

Ethical Decision Making

All commentators address ethics, responsibility, and professional judgment. Compare their positions. Which of these factors should be most heavily positioned in this discussion? What role should ethics (and whose ethics?) play in practice? Compare the conclusions reached by all of the commentators.

Power Struggles

McNiff explores the fundamental contradictions that exist between the systems in which teachers' professional careers are forged and "the values we are trying to impart in our classrooms and within ourselves as individuals." Examine how each commentator underpins his or her argument with that essential conflict.

Connecting Questions

The Connecting Questions located in the introduction highlight themes that are threaded throughout the cases. You may continue your exploration of the issues raised in this case by addressing those connections. For questions pertinent to this case, please see questions 2, 4, and 8.

❖ ADDITIONAL READINGS

Andriessen, J., Baker, M., & Suthers, D. (2004). *Confronting cognitions in computer-supported collaborative learning environments.* Dordrecht, The Netherlands: Kluwer.

The authors focus on pedagogical situations, task environments, and communication tools from which collaborative discussions can occur.

Analysis of theoretical models, empirical data, and Internet-based tools are discussed and situated in a variety of educational milieu.

Barrell, D., Fogarty, R., & Perkins, D. (1991). *How to teach for transfer: The mindful school*. Philadelphia, PA: Iri/Skylight Training & Publishing.

Campbell, E. (2003). *Ethical teacher*. Buckingham, UK: Open University Press.

Ethical Teacher examines teachers' beliefs and practices, noting the connections between the moral dimensions of schooling and professional ethics. The book presents the concept of ethical knowledge: that ethical knowledge relies on the teacher's awareness, understanding, and acceptance of the demands of moral agency and must be brought to the forefront of thinking about teaching.

Dewey, J. (1956). *The child and the curriculum* (Rev. ed.). Chicago: University of Chicago Press.

With a focus on educational theory, Dewey directs reader attention to assessments, past and present, and the practical applications of his ideas. In Philip W. Jackson's introduction, he explains why Dewey's ideas haven't been put into practice. This edition restores a "lost" chapter, dropped from the book by Dewey in 1915.

Eisner, E. (1970). *The enlightened eye: Qualitative inquiry and the enhancement of educational practice*. Upper Saddle River, NJ: Prentice Hall.

Eisner discusses the importance of appropriate curriculum planning, context, and the implication for schools. As a proponent of qualitative research, Eisner's approach always examines the role arts play in learning.

Fogarty, R., Perkins, D., & Barrell, D. (1991). *How to teach for transfer: The mindful school*. Philadelphia, PA: Iri/Skylight Training & Publishing.

The authors examine how teaching can be made meaningful, suggesting there are ways to transfer information from one realm of student experience to another.

Mills, H., & Donnelly, A. (2001). *The ground up: Creating a culture of inquiry*. Portsmouth, NH: Heinemann.

Exploring what was possible rather than typical for teachers and children in elementary education, the authors describe the goal of a small group of teachers, university partners, and a school district: to create a small-school partnership. This story demonstrates the potential of an educational partnership. This chronicle of an inquiry points to how a collaboration can promote learning and frame and inform curriculum, professional development, and continuous school renewal.

Palmer, P. J. (1998). *The courage to teach: Exploring the inner landscape of a teacher's life*. San Francisco: Jossey-Bass.

The Courage to Teach presents this premise: Good teaching comes from the identity and the integrity of the teacher. The author encourages teachers to reflect deeply. Palmer says that good teachers share one trait in that they are able to sustain a complex web of connections among themselves, their subjects, and their students, so that students can learn to model ethical behavior themselves. The connections made by good teachers are moral and spiritual when intellect and emotion converge.

Neilson, A. R. (Ed.). (1999). *Daily meaning: Counternarratives of teachers' work*. Mill Bay, BC: Bendall Books.

These stories are open and honest, revealing the many conflicts that arise in the classroom. Teachers' interactions and reflections respond to their students' plights in class and society.

Schön, D. (1987). *Educating the reflective practitioner*. San Francisco: Jossey-Bass.

Schön's remedy for higher education is learning by doing. He suggests that schools of higher learning teach skills of improvisation and problem framing by looking at the realms of the arts, crafts, athletics conservatories, athletics coaching, and craft apprenticeships. In all of these settings, a dialogue between student and "a coach" provides low-risk atmospheres that encourage creativity and integrity.

Schwab, J. J. (1973). The practical translation into curriculum. *School Review, 81,* 501–522.

J. J. Schwab continues his analysis of the commonplaces in education. His earlier articles in this series present new perspectives on curriculum improvement and focus on the incongruities in theory and practice. The "polyfocal" perspective teaches teachers how to consider diverse points of view and ask questions that elucidate meaning.

Shulman, J., & Mesa-Bains, M. (Eds.). (1993). *Diversity in the classroom: Casebook for teachers and teacher-educators*. San Francisco: FarWest Lab.

The framework of Exploring the Case was adapted from this book.

Shulman, L. S. (1986). Those who understand knowledge growth in teaching. *Educational Researcher, 15*(2), 4–14.

Shulman explains that the distinction between "knowledge" and "pedagogy" is a relatively recent development. Shulman discusses pedagogical content and forms of knowledge: propositional, case, and strategic. He focuses on the development of professional examinations and research-based programs of teacher education.

Sizer, T. R. (1984). *High school reform and the reform of teacher education.* Arlington, VA: Automobile Association of America.

Sizer's insights into reform and its impact on teacher education provide thoughtful reflection. Throughout his career, Sizer has continued to address schools as places of learning and joy along with the connections they have with real life and schoolwork.

Tom, A. (1984). *Teaching as a moral craft.* New York: Longman.

The past decade has seen many educational researchers, guided by Polanyi's (1969) inquiries into tacit knowledge, Schön's (1987) knowing-in-action, and the traditions of hermeneutic and phenomenological writings by Van Manen (1990). Tom looks at "performance-in-action" in classroom teaching. Attending to qualitative research, Tom says that researchers are moving toward conceptions that comprehend practice as a calling. He suggests that teaching can be a form of coaching (Sizer, 1984) or acting, a craft (Tom, 1984), or even artistic expression (Barrell, 1991; Eisner, 1979). Tom underpins his discussion with the notion that teaching is a "moral craft."

11

Challenges Teachers Face When Reentering the Classroom

In this case, a teacher who returns to teaching after several years of absence finds that she has difficulties controlling the classroom behavior until she unexpectedly receives support from one student. Case commentators Patrick M. Jenlink, Margaret Olson, and A. G. Rud confront a variety of issues in this case: effective classroom preparation, mentoring self-confidence, and student support.

❖ THINKING AHEAD

As you read this chapter, reflect on the following questions and issues:

- Compare the knowledge, skills, attitudes, and experience of the departing teacher and the permanent substitute teacher.

The use of "she and he," while it may appear awkward to the reader, is intended to ensure the absence of gender bias.

- Why is the permanent substitute teacher resentful of the original teacher's "mentoring"?
- Consider the differences in classroom management between the departing teacher and the permanent substitute teacher.
- What staff tensions are evident at the outset of the story, in particular between the department head and the principal?
- How might student behavior influence a teacher's confidence?

"Mrs. Spitzer, you must leave IMMEDIATELY."

It is as if the Red Sea has parted. All the teachers line the walls of both sides of the minuscule office when the principal, Mr. Greenstreet, strides in.

"It's a surprise to see you here. This makes twice in 4 years. What's the occasion?" sneers our department head. Obviously embarrassed, Mr. Greenstreet volleys back, "Well, yes, Donald, I've been busy, running the school, you know!" He continues, "There are German measles in the school and since Hannah (Spitzer) is pregnant, she must leave immediately." A thoroughly well-organized woman, Hannah, who does not believe anyone on earth can teach as well as she does, queries, "Who could replace me? I wasn't supposed to go on leave for 2½ months."

Caught at the outer reaches of the room, I am suddenly thrust into the dilemma when Ruth Holmes points at me. "Why not her? She did a fine job teaching ninth-grade Mythology."

"Okay, that's fine." Mr. Greenstreet, eager to exit the hostility of our office, turns and triumphantly vanishes. The department head, a man who in 2 short days has already commanded my respect, mutters under his breath. He has issues with the principal and does not veil his dislike.

Like a huge family, the English teachers gather around me, ready to assist and aid my sudden initiation into their midst. Lovely, warm Felicity pulls out binders with course outlines, suggestions, and assignments. Donald claps me on the shoulder, supportive and friendly. Only Hannah is standoffish, annoyed to have her plans abruptly undone. It feels good to have this sudden camaraderie of 15 teachers, in practical and emotional ways. I am secretly pleased and flattered that Ruth has designated me as a worthy candidate to replace Hannah, who is scowling, worrying about her pension if she leaves before the scheduled date.

Without any prior warning or preparation, I am flung into six new courses with 30 students in classes from 9th to 12th grades. Every night I read, read, and read, anxious to cover all the material. From her home, Hannah directs my assignments. Daily. Lesson plans are reviewed and critiqued by Hannah. Assignments are delivered faithfully to her house after school. Nightly criticisms by telephone of what I should be doing are shared. She always points out what is wrong with my takeover of every aspect of her classes.

Actually, I am not new to teaching. I had taught for 7 years before a brief hiatus during which time I returned to university to update my knowledge and develop professionally—something Hannah has not done in 10 or so years. This brusque return to teaching presents an intense trial by fire. I notice my left cheek has begun to twitch and burn. Hannah is driving me crazy.

Finally, I speak to Donald. I am exhausted by Hannah's abrasive mentoring, and I want to be in charge of my classes myself. I find her direction puerile and insulting. Donald says, "You are the teacher. Stop reporting to Hannah!" I am given a reprieve—at least in one area. The classes, except for one 12th-grade class, are going well, settling in with one rowdy exception.

I enter that class in trepidation every day, second period, dreading the students' rudeness. Some turn their backs and chairs away from me. Others ignore my presence. Harrison, a tall blond fellow, writes across the front blackboard "Happy Birthday Megan" and leads the class in a chorus of singing. I stand at the side of the class, helpless, a crooked smile forced on my face. I follow Harrison to his seat and reprimand him. He goes toe-to-toe, eyeball-to-eyeball with me, and I sense his violence as if he might explode and strike me for daring to challenge him. Sasha saunters up behind me.

"Hey, Miss, your sweater is on backwards."

Bravely, I continue to cross the threshold each day, reinforced by my colleagues' suggestions on how to subdue the beast. I am warned not to provoke Harrison. His reputation precedes him. By the end of every class, I am depleted, upset, angry, frustrated, and unable to find the key that will unlock the door to harmonious learning and mutual respect. But courageously, I continue to seek assistance from the other helpful English staff and department head, who assure me and tell me not to be so hard on myself.

We are beginning our work on *The Tempest*, and I already anticipate that it is not the stuff these adolescents' dreams are made of! No longer am I even the object of their games. I am merely an intrusion in the midst of their flirting, teasing, and socialization. So quickly, I have lost this group. Yet, I have no choice but to appear at 10:45 a.m. each day. In my hand, I clutch my lesson plan. I follow the steps carefully plotted to engage their interest (Ha! Who do I think I'm fooling?). There are the objectives, clearly laid out, well prepared the night before, and fortified by serious study and reflection. I have even sought media connections that might appeal to this teenage world.

But as predicted, Harrison and Sasha carry on as if there is no teacher in the class. I persevere, intent on delivering my lesson, ignored and useless, at the front of the class. Battered, I pray this lesson will somehow unlock their resistance and allow me to become a catalyst to a real learning community—one in which I can play a meaningful role. It's hard for me to believe that I once received a standing ovation for my teaching.

This day begins as all of the rest. I am becoming very anxious that someone in the hall will hear the commotion, enter, and reprimand the ineffectual being that is spouting off, obviously to herself, about Shakespeare.

The gods must be smiling on me because I observe John, at the very back of the class, raise his head from his sleepy pose and make eye contact with me. He sits up straight, cocks his head, and listens. *Listens.* He even raises his hand to ask a question. Is he going to ask a real question, or will he lampoon me again before his peers? Could he really be showing respect, or better still, interest? "Miss, do you think Caliban is the rightful owner of the island?"

There is a strange silence as all heads turn toward John to observe this weird phenomenon. Harrison is momentarily stunned. John is awaiting my response as I bounce his question back to him. "What do you think?"

"Caliban refuses to put up with Prospero; he's not like Ariel. Caliban won't take it . . ."

We become involved in a dialectic as we create knowledge about characters marginalized by new colonizers. He is actually listening to me. I build on his ideas. Back and forth we play, delighted and gleeful at the sand castles of arguments we construct and destroy. Only John and I are speaking. The others watch, entranced and amazed, surprised that we are really having fun. There is a ripple effect as John's peers, one by one, begin to open their books and look for the words he is now quoting. A bubble of happiness rises in me and almost catches in my throat. The social hall has been transformed into a place of learning. I must remain aloof, maintain control, but I am so excited that this group is becoming engaged in the discussion.

Sasha pinches Harrison's arm, but he shrugs her off, disinterestedly. I notice that almost all the students are focused on the friendly joust between John and myself.

Each day, I enter the class, really charged to teach, anticipating that John will provoke and engage me, and then his peers. Gradually, bored and begrudgingly, Sasha and Harrison either shut up or ignore me. I don't care because all the rest have made friends with Prospero, Miranda, and the other characters in the play, peering into their psyches, relating them to people they know. John has bolstered my pride and reawakened my confidence. I cannot help but wonder why John paid attention that day, but I am so grateful that he did.

Yet, in spite of John's avid interest, he refuses to turn in written assignments. In class, he dazzles with his comprehension and unique perspective, but he cannot extend his attention to collecting his ideas in print. I offer to work with him, but he only grins and says writing is hard for him, but that he really does enjoy my classes. At the end of term, with no essays, journal entries, or even paragraph answers submitted, John fails the course. I ask Donald if I can give him "the most improved student award" at the school assembly, but, of course, I know the answer.

John decides he will change schools for an arts-based program. I am disturbed that I have been unable to acknowledge or even pass this talented boy who smoothed out my return to teaching.

❖ EXPLORING THE CASE

This case was written by an experienced teacher returning to teach.

Identification

Identify the key facts of this case. What factual events are central to understanding this situation? Identify the dilemmas and tensions in this case. Explore the main aspects of each dilemma and tension.

Analysis

Analyze the issue(s) from the viewpoints of the different people in the case. How do the interactions between the teacher and the class raise issues that pertain to classroom management? Is the teacher helped or hindered by her colleagues? Describe the teacher's tensions?

Evaluation

Examine critically the teacher's strategies for handling the challenge(s) with the class and the staff. Does the teacher depicted fulfill, fall short of, or surpass your notion of the role of a teacher?

Alternative Solutions

Were there alternative solutions or strategies available to deal with the dilemma? Generate alternative solutions to the ones presented in the narrative. Take into consideration risks, benefits, and long- and short-term consequences of each proposed action.

Reflection

The teacher says that she is disturbed that "this talented boy" had not passed the course. How does the student's decision to change schools affect the teacher's thinking about this episode in her life?

Changing Opinions

Consider your thoughts and assumptions at the beginning of the chapter. Who or what has caused you to consider a new way of thinking? How strongly do you still feel about your previous assumptions?

Synthesis

Synthesize your understanding of this case into a statement. What is this a case of?

Case Commentary by Patrick M. Jenlink

The value of a case is premised, in large part, on what may be learned both explicitly and implicitly from the narrative themes that shape the story and provide a richly detailed context in which to situate individual and collective inquiry aimed at constructing meaning. Significantly, learning can be enhanced when a case demonstrates emerging relevance for the student and provides a realistic problem that challenges the student to examine the case, inquiring to understand what is problematic within an in situ context of teaching practice and experience.

The author of "Challenges Teachers Face When Reentering the Classroom" demonstrates what is problematic about reentering the classroom to teach. Teaching isn't easy under the best of all conditions, but it becomes even more challenging, as detailed in this case, when the substitute teacher must mediate the tensions of preparing six new courses against a backdrop of reporting to the departing teacher, Hannah Spitzer, who is assigned as a mentor. The narrative themes that emerge provide insight as to the often complex and dynamic nature of balancing a new teaching assignment with mentoring made problematic by issues of displacement and control. Classroom management emerges as a major theme in this case, made more problematic initially by what is termed as "puerile and insulting" direction provided by Hannah. Equally instructive in this case is the presence of disruptive forces in the classroom and the evolving tensions that pervade the climate of instruction, demonstrating the importance of teacher self-confidence as a mediating factor in addressing behavior issues.

It is interesting that the substitute teacher, in introducing the class to Shakespeare's *The Tempest*, situates herself and the class in a literary context that is reflective of emerging tensions, management issues, and questions of collegial support that plague the classroom. Herein lies a rich opportunity for the teacher to examine not only the essence of Shakespeare's Prospero, Miranda, Caliban, and the other characters' lives, but more important, to understand how students might be engaged in learning that has emerging relevance. The metaphorical and literal parallels between *The Tempest* and the classroom climate are important parallels. Such parallels could prove instructive to the substitute teacher as she self-critically reflects on how to address the tensions created by Harrison's acting out, John's unwillingness to address the writing expectations for the class, and her own expressions of anxiety and frustration that followed renewed confidence thanks to John. The importance of John's role in the class should provide a clear path of inquiry with respect to how support from a student within the classroom can work to facilitate the pedagogical transition from disruption to demonstrated interest and involvement on the part of other students.

"Challenges Teachers Face When Reentering the Classroom" demonstrates the importance of professional knowledge and the value of ethical treatment of a colleague, in this case, Hannah Spitzer's responsibility as a mentor. The difficulties of reentering a classroom are made explicit, and more important, prove instructive as the reader examines the challenging nature of teaching against a backdrop of professional standards.

❖ EXPLORING THE ISSUES

Classroom Dynamics

Jenlink suggests this case demonstrates the tensions that can occur when one teacher replaces another. Students who are taught by two teachers with conflicting instructional styles might find this situation difficult to navigate. Why does a change in context alter structure and milieu when the permanent substitute teacher attempts to take over this class? Why might disruption be waiting to happen in this case? Do you think "disruptive forces" already existed before the entry of the new teacher? How else might this situation have been managed?

Power Struggles

In the second paragraph, Jenlink notes that the permanent substitute teacher appears to be struggling with the students and with her own sense of authority. What similarities exist between *The Tempest* and this classroom situation? How can a teacher look to students like John for support? How else might a teacher in this situation deal with issues of and challenges to his or her authority?

Support Networks

Jenlink questions Hannah's responsibility as a mentor in his final paragraph. Although Hannah's mentoring had a negative effect on this teacher, the rest of the staff in the English department was supportive. How might the staff and the administration have improved the transition stage for the permanent substitute teacher?

Case Commentary by Margaret Olson

From at least as far back as Aristotle, stories provide one of the primary ways we learn about, share, examine, and make sense of our own and others' ethical and moral stance. Within education, "teaching is complicated by the nature of education-related problems that are especially messy, overlap, and come in clusters rather than rows" (Bullough & Baughman, 1997, p. 131). This complexity mostly leads to ethical dilemmas rather than solutions.

I was struck by the multitude of stories, each with its own ethical dilemma, that were encapsulated within this case and was reminded of Randall's (1995) comment that "our life, it turns out, is not one story but many, a plethora of stories in fact, both stories within us and stories we are, in turn, within" (p. 185). The teacher-author of this case found herself on the periphery of some and at the center of others leading to different simultaneous yet often mutually exclusive ethical dilemmas. Being storied by Ruth as a "fine teacher" quickly placed her as a potential main character in the replacement story being authored by Mr. Greenstreet. No one appeared to consult with either the teacher-author or Hannah about how they would story this abrupt shift in authority. While the teacher-author felt honored to be storied by Ruth as worthy to work with students, she was also led to create a story about Hannah, a colleague and the teacher she would be replacing, that was not professionally flattering. Here an ethical dilemma emerges: "How can one be or become a good teacher and at the same time value this quality in others who may teach very differently? How can we respect diversity in students or expect students to respect the diversity of their peers if we cannot respect it in colleagues?"

Perhaps this lack of valuing diversity is rooted in our recent Western, individualistic focus. Although each of these stories was integrally interwoven within and across a variety of individuals, as Randall tells us, "Every side in every conflict is telling a different story" (1995, p. 107). Being "worthy" to teach led initially to conflicts with Hannah over what worthy teaching might look like and also to conflict with students when one class in particular did not appear to value the way their new teacher was attempting to play a meaningful role. Yet, underlying the differences within this case, each teacher involved seemed to be attempting to live her or his own version of "Who's in charge here?" oblivious that they were indeed part of a complex web of interwoven stories. There appeared to be little sense of shared authorship except by students. The teacher-author appeared to assume that she needed to be the "catalyst to a real learning community." However, when John, a student, became that catalyst, the teacher-author was thrilled, yet continued to believe that she needed to "remain aloof, maintain control." I wonder how long this pervasive story of the ethic of "rugged individualism," perpetuated within our schools for and by teachers and students, will continue to work against the ethic of relational knowing in a context of diversity.

❖ EXPLORING THE ISSUES

Teacher Confidence

Olson frames her discussion by thinking in terms of the usefulness of the story to learn, share, and make sense of our lives. In what ways do narratives enable teachers to learn and grow from their own inquiries based on real-life problems?

Classroom Dynamics

Olson comments on the abrupt shift in authority. What other parts of the teacher's "story" should have fortified her to become her own authority in this classroom? Why do you think she remains "aloof" to the most disruptive students?

Ethical Responsibility

Bullough and Baughman's quotation notes the messy, clustered, overlapping problems that occur in education. What ethical questions arise because of the eruption of measles in the school? How has the permanent substitute teacher's narrative been changed by the outbreak?

Diversity

Olson asks, "How can one be or become a good teacher and at the same time value this quality in others who may teach differently?" How does this question point to acceptance of diversity in teaching methods? Are we too influenced by "our recent Western, individualistic focus" to combine different approaches in teaching?

Case Commentary by A. G. Rud

I read this case with more than professional interest, as I had returned to full-time teaching a year ago after a series of administrative assignments. I learned as much from what the author described as from the silences and missing perspectives in the text.

I felt the author's inner torment from the inability to engage the two uninterested students, Harrison and Sasha, while I also sensed her vulnerability to John, the one student who did evince interest in the class. I keep alive hope that my students' minds will be ignited by what I teach, much as this author does.

But such an expectation can be fragile. Recently, a student came to me and said that class material had not "stuck" for him, thus accounting for his poor performance on an exam. I wanted to know why topics in the cultural foundations of education, on immigrant education, Froebel and the kindergarten movement—a favorite of mine—or even simple extrapolation of Hegel's dialectic to educational issues and classroom practice, had not stuck for him. I was taken aback by his use of "stick with," as this indicated to me that he had tried to learn it, but it did not excite him enough to warrant its attachment to his mind. He did not share my excitement about the topics.

I sense further vulnerability in the author, brought about by the "abrasive mentoring" behavior of Hannah, the teacher she is to replace. The author appears almost infantilized by this teacher, having to enact what seems to be a recapitulation of student teaching, complete with detailed instructions and heavy-handed advice. But it is hard not to be so vulnerable upon the "Challenges Teachers Face When Reentering the Classroom." When I resumed teaching, part of my assignment was a course I had never taught before. I was dependent on notes by colleagues, and I looked to my younger teaching assistants for guidance, seeking a surefire way to reach students as if teaching could be done a priori. I had forgotten about the enormous and sustained effort that good teaching demands.

This fecund case raises questions and further issues. Although the author works hard to engage students, perhaps she gave too much attention to John, the student who responded to her presentations. Could she have brought the other students into the fold and really tried harder to work with Harrison and Sasha to get them to be part of the community of inquiry?

Was there something in Shakespeare that would have excited these students as well? Why didn't they make a connection to the play? I wonder about how a set curriculum that prescribes Shakespeare may not allow the students' own interests to be part of the initial equation. I wanted to hear from Harrison and Sasha, beyond their drift to boredom and antisocial behavior.

The case ends with a lament about John, the student who smoothed the author's return to teaching. Although he moved on to another school, I would see this as a success, rather than as the loss or absence. John is realizing the Deweyan goal of education as the continual process of learning. The author helped this student find a more appropriate arts-based curriculum.

❖ EXPLORING THE ISSUES

Gaps and Omissions

With only the teacher's voice to relate the story, we only hear and see through her eyes. Rud addresses the missing perspectives, gaps, and silences in the narrative. What would those perspectives provide? Conversely, why are those omissions important for you as a reader?

Self-Knowledge

Rud senses the teacher's "vulnerability" to John. The teacher does not seem to know herself why John suddenly connected; yet, in the end, John does not pass the course. In his final paragraph, Rud directs our attention to John Dewey's approach to education. How does Dewey provide a perspective that might fortify teachers whose students do not always attain success in ways traditionally accepted?

❖ ENGAGING WITH THE COMMENTARIES

Classroom Management

Each commentator examines classroom management from a unique perspective. Compare and contrast their views. Could their insights be combined to suggest a remedy for the teacher in this case?

Ethical Behavior

Both Jenlink and Olson discuss the ethics of behavior. One commentator's focus is theoretical while the other's is practical. Compare their differently focused discussions.

Student Behavior

In each response, the commentators refer to the role John plays in the classroom context. Compare and contrast John as the pivotal change that transforms learning for the students and control for the teacher. Is there a way for teachers to create a situation in which students like John can affect their classes?

Connecting Questions

The Connecting Questions located in the introduction highlight themes that are threaded throughout the cases. You may continue your exploration of the issues raised in this case by addressing those connections. For questions pertinent to this case, please see questions 3 and 5.

❖ ADDITIONAL READINGS

Arhar, J. M., Holly, M. L., & Kasten, W. C. (2001). *Action research for teachers: Traveling the yellow brick road.* Upper Saddle River, NJ: Prentice Hall.

This practical book is a guide to conducting action research in educational settings. It uses metaphors from the *Wizard of Oz* throughout: Dorothy's journey as key. Offering step-by-step guidance through the action research process, complete coverage of theories, and real-life examples, the authors present teachers with tools for action research. In addition, theory is examined in four action research studies in a variety of contexts, grade levels, age-groups, and disciplines.

Bosner, G. (1987). Addressing the problem of elsewhereness: A case for action research in schools. In D. Goswami & P. Stillman (Eds.), *Reclaiming the classroom: Teacher research as an agency for change* (pp. 4–13). Portsmouth, NH: Boynton/Cook.

The thesis here is that all English teachers should be involved in ongoing research in the classroom.

Cochran-Smith, M., & Lyttle, S. L. (1999). Relationships of knowledge and practice: Teacher learning communities. In A. Iran-Nejad & P. D. Pearson (Eds.), *Review of research in education, 24* (pp. 249–305). Washington, DC: American Educational Research Association.

The authors point out the difference of what "knowing more" and "teaching better" means in terms of change efforts. There are distinctions explained among "knowledge-for-practice," "knowledge-in-practice," and "knowledge-of-practice." The chapter considers various change initiatives related to teacher learning. The writers explain that in spite of some strategies sounding similar, they are, in fact, quite different and have quite distinct impacts on the everyday lives of students and teachers.

Connelly, F. M., & Clandinin, D. J. (2000). *Narrative inquiry.* New York: Teachers College Press.
    Narrative inquiry can be central to gathering the human dimension in research because it captures more than statistics and numbers. In this text, Connelly and Clandinin discuss how narrative exploration can be used in educational and social science research. Their useful book offers new and practical ideas for conducting fieldwork, composing field notes, and conveying research results. The authors use many stories and examples to illustrate their process.

Hutchinson, N. (1998). Reflecting critically on teaching to encourage critical reflection. In M. L. Hamilton (Ed.), *Reconceptualizing teaching practice: Self-study in teacher education* (pp. 124–139). London: Falmer Press.

Kroll, L., Cossey, R., Donahue, D., Galquera, T., LaBoskey, V., Richert, A. E., & Tucher, P. (2004). *Teaching as principled practice: Managing complexity for social justice.* Thousand Oaks, CA: Sage.
    This book, complete with questions, is guided by four principles: morality; teaching as an act of inquiry and reflection; learning as developmental and constructive process; and teaching as a collegial and political activity. The authors give examples that aid in clarifying their principles and are applicable to action research. The text is a catalyst to insights, reflections, and meaningful discussions.

Newman, J. M. (1991). *Interwoven conversations: Learning and teaching through critical reflection.* Toronto: OISE.

Perkins, D. N. & Saloman, G. (1988). Teaching for Transfer. *Educational Leadership, 46*(1).

Sarason, S. B. (1993). *You are thinking of teaching? Opportunities, problems, realities.* San Francisco: Jossey-Bass.

Shulman, J., & Mesa-Bains, M. (Eds.). (1993). *Diversity in the classroom: Casebook for teachers and teacher-educators.* San Francisco: FarWest Lab.
    The framework of Exploring the Case was adapted from this book.

Sizer, T. R. (1994). *High school reform and the reform of teacher education.* Arlington, VA: Automobile Association of America.

Sizer's insights into reform and its impact on teacher education provide thoughtful reflection. Throughout his career, Sizer has continued to address schools as places of learning and joy along with the connections they have with real life and schoolwork.

Talbert, J. E., & McLaughlin, M. W. (1993). Understanding teaching in context. In D. K. Cohen, M. W. McLaughlin, & J. E. Talbert (Eds.), *Teaching for understanding: Challenges for policy and practice* (pp. 167–206). San Francisco: Jossey-Bass.

The authors, who are leading experts in teaching and policy research, provide examples of what teaching for understanding entails. They describe how to foster, sustain, and support the knowledge, capacity, and professional beliefs essential for teachers. They dispute the "teach and test" approach in favor of meaningful reflection on classroom life and relationships with students. They diagnose elements in schools that are prohibitive or enhancing.

Westheimer, J., & Kahne, J. (2003, September). Teaching democracy: What schools need to do. *Phi Delta Kappan, 85*(1).

In studying 10 educational programs that purport to develop democratic citizens, the authors say that civic commitments, capacities, and connections aid in promoting thinking about democracy in schools. They critique the constant testing and messages of curriculum reform, lauding Elliot Eisner's approach to learning that extends beyond the classroom to life.

12

Developing Appropriate Boundaries With a Troubled Student

I n this case, a teacher considers the role she or he plays in the life of a troubled adolescent. Case commentators John Loughran, Ardra L. Cole, Allen T. Pearson, and Janine Remillard discuss issues of student relationships, expectations, and the personal involvement of a sensitive teacher. Building trust, often a difficult endeavor, permits both teacher and student to probe their own lives to examine why they act as they do.

❖ THINKING AHEAD

As you read this chapter, reflect on the following issues:

- Consider the skills, attitudes, experience, and knowledge of the teacher.

The use of "she and he," while it may appear awkward to the reader, is intended to ensure the absence of gender bias.

- Consider the contextual issues.
- Identify the problems and pressures that are disturbing Mel.
- List the dilemmas the teacher must face regarding Mel.

There was an uneasy silence in the almost empty classroom. Mel looked downward before she spoke. "I need to talk." There was a tremor in her voice, and I knew that something important was to follow.

"I was wondering if you have this friend, and she's into drugs big-time, and she tells you she wants to get off them, what do you do? I don't know how to help her."

So typical of Mel. She was the type of kid who always thought of others first. I had known her for 5 years when she had come from outside the district to attend our school because it was a Gifted Center. Even in the first days of our ninth-grade English class, I could tell that her choice to join the gifted class was not an easy one. There was shyness about her, and I could see she felt awkward moving in her own skin. Growth spurts do that sometimes. But I knew she belonged here, in this class. I could see how much she loved to learn, and for the most part, it came easily to her. Now she was in the home stretch, her final semester of high school.

She was the type of kid who takes time to know. In fact, it was only when I taught her a second time in my 11th-grade Media class that I discovered her intense passion for horses. She was an accomplished rider who committed herself totally to the sport, winning local and provincial competitions. I also learned then that Mel, a high-performance individual, had no respect for failure—especially her own. The way she talked, I could picture Mel and her horse, groundless together. Riding simply spoke to who she was. I think that's why she loved writing, because no one need speak; yet at the same time, she could be connected to the unspoken rhythms in her own life.

"I think she wants help."

I told her I would get some information about drug programs in our community from the guidance office, and that I would get back to her.

Later, that same evening, a small surge pulsed from deep within me, grew like a wave, and pressed hard against my chest. I knew in an instant that the troubled teen that Mel had alluded to was, in fact, her. Questions flooded my mind. How should I broach the subject without jeopardizing her trust in me? If my hunch were true, what was my role to be?

The next morning I went directly to the head of guidance at our school. Joan was a strong advocate of students, especially for those with exceptionalities. We shared a natural rapport, and I respected Joan's judgment. I told her about the situation, while protecting the anonymity of the student. However, as I began to tell the story, I realized that I had come here as much for myself as for Mel. I needed a space to think out loud and examine my own lack of knowledge. I wasn't even aware of my legal responsibilities regarding disclosure, but Joan calmly reassured me that, from her perspective, the girl was in no immediate danger to herself or others.

But these were uncharted waters for me. I was not a trained counselor, and I realized I had assumed a significant role in Mel's story.

Upon reflection, I knew Mel trusted me and that the foundation of that trust had begun 5 years earlier in my ninth-grade English gifted class. I was proud that I always situated my students in the center of their own learning. We often ended our class discussions in literature by making connections to our own lives. We respected everyone's input and considered seriously the diverse voices that were encouraged in my class. All voices belonged, and so, when students would, over time, raise their concerns and explore their frustrations about being labeled "gifted," I would be part of that discussion.

Mel must have seen then that I honored the voices of my students by truly listening and affirming their struggles. How could I honor her voice now?

I had a clear sense that she had a place for me on this journey. I knew I was not interested in becoming a "professional pal," but what was an appropriate distance to serve her needs? As I talked, a picture began to form in my mind:

"What if I could serve as a bridge for her?"

A bridge to resources and a bridge back to her family.

Mel had grown up in a high-performance home. She was the gifted daughter of gifted parents. Her mom was an accomplished doctor and writer. Her dad was a professional engineer. Mel's older sister, Sarah, was developmentally delayed, and Mel grew up watching the quiet devotion of her parents to Sarah's special needs. Mel confided that she felt guilty for being the "smart one." She worked hard not to give her parents trouble. It was difficult to reconcile the two conflicting pictures of Mel—the good child and the drug user.

I was glad the next day that our graduating English class backed on to lunch, and there was a chance to talk. I circled the hard edges of exposing "her friend's" identity for a short time, and then I took the leap.

"Mel, I have this gut feeling that the person we are talking about is you."

Simply, she said, "Yes."

Since that day, I have often wondered about the way she hid herself inside the story. Perhaps it was a clever strategy to give her the chance to see if she indeed trusted me, and to determine if she really wanted help. In a curious way, I sensed that she needed to test me: the highly intuitive child checking on the teacher's own level of unspoken awareness. How difficult for Mel to expose for the very first time her own sense of failure to another adult.

Over time, I learned many things. She told me that she had been progressively smoking more dope each day for over 2 years. She smoked at home in the basement, and she smoked in the washrooms. Her friends readily accepted her into the group: "Mel was cool." They shared an unspoken habit, and closeness was measured by how often they smoked together. Support was defined by helping a friend get more weed. Belonging was tied to a single need. This was friendship at no cost.

I was relieved when Mel finally decided to tell Joan about her situation. This was a good sign because she was beginning to build a network of support inside the school. However, there was nothing calm about this journey.

That first week that she stopped taking drugs, she entered my classroom while I was teaching. Her face was pale. Her hands trembled.

"I can't do this," she whispered. "It's just too hard."

I was in the middle of teaching a class and directed her to Joan's office. After she left, I took a deep breath, returned to my room, and continued the lesson. But in front of my students, I was troubled by Mel's physical well-being.

Thank goodness for the solid support of colleagues. I hurried to see Joan that day. She reported that Mel was not sleeping well, and that she had stopped eating. Keeping her secret was becoming more and more difficult at home. We both agreed that Mel must talk to her mom as soon as possible.

That same week, Mel confided how easy it was to fabricate lies in order to trick her parents. I knew Mel trusted me because I spoke from the center of my conviction. Much later, she confessed that she liked that I challenged her.

"They think I'm at a friend's house when I'm really at a rave. They never suspect a thing."

"As a parent myself, Mel, I have to tell you that parents want what's best for their children. Up to this point, you've given them no cause to mistrust you."

"They've always trusted me. Given me the freedom to figure things out on my own."

"Why was that?"

"Because I could be trusted. They had confidence in me."

"And now you have lied to them for over 2 years, and see them as fools for not figuring it out? You said you trusted me. That's why you came to me in the first place. Mel, talk to your mom. Give your parents the chance to really support you—not just when things are going well, but when things are going badly."

One week later, she revealed the truth to her mom. Shortly after, I met with Mel and her mom at the mom's request. As soon as we shook hands, I observed that she was a high-energy woman who had a plan of action. She gave Mel the latest research on drugs and a crash course in the physiology of addiction. She put her in touch with a professional counselor, and for that I was thankful.

There was nothing easy in Mel's relationship with her mom. There was a strain in the mother's look, a detachment in her voice. She wanted so badly a clean solution to such a complex problem. When she told me that she always valued "an honest and open relationship with her daughter," I noticed that Mel immediately looked down. For me, the mother had a simple request: to be a connection in her daughter's school day, to listen, and to support.

Mel and I walked every day during my prep period, usually for about one-half hour. I think she felt freer to speak her mind when we walked side by side, never making eye contact, but going in one direction. Our walks continued for three months, leading up to graduation.

As I listened to Mel's story, I was reminded of the importance of understanding the special needs and backgrounds of students, particularly my gifted students. As I learned more about Mel's predicament, my attitude began to change.

I was troubled by my school's approach to gifted education. As early as eighth grade, secondary schools were actively recruiting these talented students.

Our principal had recently been promoted, and he saw his role as instilling pride in his school by "showcasing" the talents and accomplishments of the gifted students to the larger community. He blithely promoted our school's image of excellence on the backs of these students.

I have been teaching these gifted students for over 15 years now, and attitudes that stereotype them—the image of the dream class— doesn't change easily. Even yesterday in the staff room, a senior teacher told me that it must be nice to teach these students: "They show up every day, do what they're told, and teach themselves."

I was furious. I wanted to challenge her, but just wasn't up for it. I was too tired. My thoughts had returned to Mel, the gifted, Mel, the horsewoman, Mel, the troubled.

In all of my conversations with Mel, one moment stands out:

"Remember you said life is like sailing. You need to grab hold of the rigging, take charge of the boat. I think I know what you mean now."

"That's good to hear, Mel."

"Remember how I told you I felt I was in a fog."

"Yeah, I remember."

"Well, the fog is starting to rise."

"And what do you see?"

"I'm a long way from shore."

"You always were, Mel. But now, you finally know it for the first time."

And she began to cry.

Mel started to keep a journal and began to write more. She said that even William, her horse, knew that she was more connected to her "real self."

Even though Mel graduated clean that spring, I can't say that she has totally recovered. I hear from her in university, and she tells me that when stress gets bad, she finds her way back to drugs. Perhaps those currents will always pull her.

Since that time, however, I have tried to apply what I have learned. I gave a workshop last February at our professional development day, challenging the myths of teaching the gifted. I am currently leading the mentorship program at our school, and for next year, I have decided to form a staff gifted team to identify the specific learning needs of at-risk students.

Time locates timeliness.

There are moments in our teaching careers we don't choose. They choose us. And what of the role of the teacher beyond the mechanics of the classroom, the routines that organize our comings and goings? Sometimes we are forced to leave the safe harbor, to set sail for a short time with another, to nudge with our listening care, toward this simple wish—that we all may know our singular uniqueness and accept our place of belonging on this good earth. And groundless becomes grounded in this new understanding.

❖ EXPLORING THE CASE

A secondary school teacher with 20 years of experience wrote this case.

Identification

Identify the key facts of this case. What events are central to understanding this situation? Identify the dilemmas and tensions in this case. Explore the main aspects of each dilemma and tension.

Analysis

Analyze the issue(s) from the viewpoints of the different people in the case. What is Mel's story? Does she represent the typical gifted student? As you begin to reread this case, consider whether or not the teacher depicted fulfills, falls short of, or surpasses your notion of the role of a teacher.

Evaluation

Examine critically the teacher's strategies for handling the challenge(s) with Mel. Does the teacher depicted fulfill, fall short of, or surpass your notion of the role of a teacher?

Alternative Solutions

Were there alternative solutions or strategies available to deal with the dilemma(s)? Generate alternative solutions to the ones presented in the narrative. Take into consideration risks, benefits, and long- and short-term consequences of each proposed action.

Reflection

The teacher is very philosophical at the end of the story, moving outward to thoughts on education and its place in the larger scheme of life. Has anything been resolved or learned through this experience with Mel?

Changing Opinions

Consider your thoughts and assumptions at the beginning of the chapter. Who or what has caused you to consider a new way of thinking? How strongly do you still feel about your previous assumptions?

Synthesis

Synthesize your understanding of this case into a statement. What is this a case of?

Case Commentary by John Loughran

Teaching is about relationships. It takes a good deal of trust for a student to risk displaying vulnerability where learning is concerned, especially when the risk is underpinned by feelings of doubt, hesitation, or inadequacy.

Good teachers respond well to these feelings when their students venture a question or a tentative response in class. Good teachers feel their students' sense of uncertainty and react in supportive and respectful ways to encourage the learning that they know will occur as a result of an open admission of confusion, difficulty, or lack of understanding.

In the rush and bustle of classroom interactions, good teachers build their relationships through everything they do. But what happens when interactions are not bound up in the classroom? What happens when the learning is not about math or science or some other school subject? Do the same empathetic responses come to the fore? Does the change in context change one's behaviors?

I would argue that good teachers' behaviors do not change because good teachers respond appropriately regardless of the context because they genuinely care for their students. It is this very point that is at the heart of the interactions between Mel and her teacher.

Mel takes the risk of speaking up. She displays her vulnerability. She asks for help from someone she trusts, but she or he is not just someone, she or he is her teacher. Mel risks her vulnerability because her teacher understands the importance of relationships and has purposefully worked to build them. The teacher knows Mel. The teacher knows her situation. The teacher knows how to respond to the *intuitive child when checking on his or her own level of unspoken awareness.*

For a high achiever like Mel, it must have been with a great sense of trepidation that she admitted to her apparent sense of personal failure. But she did so because she needed help, help that first and foremost was sought from her teacher.

If there were ever any questions about the significance of the role of the teacher, this case dispels them. This case reminds us all of why the profession is so important and why teachers are such a valued resource in our world.

For Mel's teacher, the situation in which she or he found her- or himself and the thoughtful and caring way in which she or he handled it did not lead to a false sense of self-importance, or to a broadcasting of her or his skills and abilities. The teacher's experience of working with Mel led her or him to reflect on her or his practice, her or his attitude toward other students with specific learning needs, and to a questioning of the taken-for-granted aspects of the myths about teaching the gifted.

For Mel, finding ways of being comfortable with herself as a gifted learner required confronting some of her own inadequacies and misgivings. Fortunately, she had someone she could trust to turn to when she was ready to ask for help.

Just as Mel's teacher's skills came to the fore when needed in this special case, so too they undoubtedly come consistently to the fore lesson after lesson. Day after day in the school environment, teachers are continually needed to encourage other students to take risks in their learning so that they might grow in their unique ways as they come to learn about their sense of belonging on this good earth.

The role of teacher should not be taken lightly. Too much of what teachers do really matters.

❖ EXPLORING THE ISSUES

Professional Conduct

Loughran reflects that good teaching is built on trust; however, there are often emotional dimensions that occlude understanding of the situations students bring with them. In addition, relationships outside of the classroom are important factors that also add stress to the life of a teacher. Should teachers extend the boundaries of the classroom?

Student Responsibility

In the fifth paragraph, Loughran states that Mel has taken risks in opening herself to the teacher. Why does she take this risk, and is there evidence of her growth and development because of her relationship with her teacher? Why would status as an exceptional, "gifted" student add to student pressure?

Case Commentary by Ardra L. Cole

The kind and level of commitment of Mel's teacher, depicted in this case, is a reality of teachers' work. In the run of a normal day, teachers draw on multiple forms and sources of knowledge to carry out their various and complex roles and responsibilities. They access subject matter knowledge as well as general and subject-specific pedagogical knowledge. They look to research and relevant professional literature; rely on the wisdom of experience and practice; and make use of personal learnings and intuitions. They negotiate complex interactions with students, parents, peers, administrators, and others and are mindful of how to operate within the bureaucratic structures of schools, communities, school boards, and professional and political regulatory bodies.

Some of the most challenging roles (e.g., social worker, counselor) teachers carry out as part of their daily work demand knowledge and expertise that are seldom included as an explicit part of any professional education and development program. Neither do these roles appear in formal, public descriptions of teachers' work. And yet teachers are expected by students, parents, policymakers, and the public to assume a complexity of roles with little or no acknowledgment or support.

Much of what teachers do is invisible not only to the public but also, sadly, to each other. Teachers carry out much of their work behind closed classroom doors with little or no intellectual or emotional support. The busyness of schools, crowded days and curriculum, pressures to evaluate, extracurricular demands, and a host of other chores keep teachers separated from their colleagues and tied to the exigencies of their work. Conversations with peers remain relatively superficial; conversations about perplexing matters of teaching and learning seldom happen. Teachers have little opportunity to be and work together, share ideas and knowledge about each other's work, help one another become better teachers, and bring to bear their substantial collective wisdom for the betterment of students and themselves. There is scant time for professional, collegial, or even friendly exchanges. Although career-long professional learning is (yet another) explicit expectation of teachers, there is often neither time nor opportunity in everyday teaching life for any kind of collegial or reflective engagement.

As pressures on students, families, and communities mount, so, too, do the demands on and expectations of schools and teachers. Coping with role complexity and the numerous and growing responsibilities and demands associated with both teaching and being a teacher is a primary source of teacher stress and burnout. If teachers are to live and teach in good health, we—everyone invested in education—must work together to foster conditions that respect teachers' work and facilitate teacher learning.

❖ EXPLORING THE ISSUES

Teachers' Roles

Cole points to the daily work of being a teacher: from carrying out multiple tasks and responsibilities to negotiating "complex interactions with students, parents, peers, administrators and others." She adds that much of the work is "invisible." How does this teacher react to the demands on her or his time? Is she or he able to elicit support from colleagues, and why is that satisfying or not satisfying? Where does Cole suggest teachers look for support in their increasingly difficult work?

Professional Conduct

Cole comments on the "reality" of teachers' work. What does she mean by that phrase? What do inquiry, research, and negotiation have to do with that work, particularly in the classroom?

Case Commentary by Allen T. Pearson

The case study on the role of the teacher introduces many ideas and themes, all of which are very tempting for this commentary. I am struck, in particular, by the number of times that the word "trust" appears. The concept of trust is central to the role of the teacher but is only discussed in one sort of context. Parents, in sending their children to school, entrust their children's safety to teachers. It is, of course, both the professional and legal responsibility of teachers to honor this trust. Not ensuring the safety and well-being of the children in their charge is one of the greatest misdeeds a teacher can commit. It is this particular sense of trust that one reads about the most.

But although the safety of children is an area in which trust is required and written about, I believe that the academic trust that children must have in their teachers is just as important. If students did not trust that what their teachers say is correct, sensible, worth paying attention to, or worthy of consideration, no learning could take place in a classroom. Teachers are in a position of academic authority, but that authority only holds when students place trust in their teachers. This form of trust is not difficult to earn. Students come to school predisposed to trust that their teachers know what they are talking about. But if, in the rare case, this trust is lost, the teacher can achieve no learning with her or his students.

It seems to me that this initial grounding of trust that makes teaching possible can evolve and develop to the mature and deep form of trust that we see in this case study. There, Mel felt she could trust her teacher more than her parents in disclosing her personal problems. And this is not an uncommon phenomenon. But it is always challenging for a teacher. The initial trust in the teacher as an authority deepens into a more intimate trust of a confidante. The philosopher Annette Baier once wrote, "Trust is much easier to maintain than it is to get started and is never hard to destroy." Teachers know this, and this can be a difficult challenge in cases like this. Mel trusted her teacher, who knew that the wrong step could destroy that trust with very serious consequences for Mel. The joy in reading this case is that the teacher was able to maintain Mel's trust during her difficult time.

In general, trust creates vulnerability. When a student trusts a teacher, it is always possible for the teacher to exercise ill will and harm the student. But in trusting the teacher, the student believes that this potential harm will not occur. So, success in teaching requires that the teacher allow this vulnerability and not betray it. This case study shows very clearly this important moral dimension of teaching and reminds us of the complex ethical responsibility we have for the welfare of our students.

❖ EXPLORING THE ISSUES

Trust

Pearson speculates on what trust can mean. Give examples of the kinds of trust a teacher should develop in a classroom, in a school, and in a school community. Why is it essential that trust in the teacher-student relationship not be betrayed?

School Policies

Pearson again cites the importance of trust that schools must maintain to function responsibly in the community. What role do school policies play in protecting the relationships between students and teachers?

Case Commentary by Janine Remillard

The case of Mel's teacher is a powerful reminder of the real characteristics of quality teaching. It stands in sharp contrast to current calls for highly qualified teachers where quality is defined by credentials and student achievement scores. This case paints a portrait of the work of teaching that cannot be captured in courses taken or degrees conferred. It tells a compelling story of a teacher of over 15 years who managed to keep her or his students and their humanness at the center of her or his teaching.

The author characterizes the choices made as she or he came to the assistance of a student struggling with drug addiction as part of the role of the teacher that is well "beyond the mechanics of the classroom." As the teacher notes, it is one of those moments in teaching that is not chosen by the teacher, but which chooses her or him. Clearly these events and how they unfold in the lives and work of teachers are not planned, but a close look at this teacher's response to this particular moment in teaching reveals much about characteristics of quality teaching that are applicable well beyond the single instance.

When Mel approached the teacher about helping a "friend" get off drugs, the teacher did not hesitate to offer assistance. But this teacher did more. The teacher's deep caring for the young student led her or him to the realization that Mel was the troubled friend. The relation-ship the teacher had established and her or his deep respect for the student allowed her or him to hear what the student wanted to say, not just what she said. This kind of listening was the first step in being able to reach out to Mel.

The teacher's approach to offering assistance is also worthy of note. Rather than positioning her- or himself as her savior, the teacher guided Mel to the resources and people she needed to garner support. As the teacher put it, she or he served as a bridge for Mel, not only to her family but also to the guidance counselor and to herself, connect-ing her to her own strengths and desires.

And through this process, the teacher acted as a steady fellow trav-eler in Mel's journey. The teacher was available to listen and talk. The teacher supported her as she faced her own struggle. The teacher didn't deny that it was Mel's challenge to meet, but the teacher made it clear that Mel was not alone.

And finally, like all good teachers, this teacher used her or his experience with Mel to learn more about her or his students, her- or himself as a teacher, and about her or his values as an educator. Not only did the teacher begin to see through the "myth of the gifted child," but also the teacher took actions in her or his practice to promote real change in the school.

This case illustrates the way these qualities were central to this teacher's effort to support a young student in her hour of personal need. Yet, it is not difficult to see that these characteristics underlie all dimensions of high-quality teaching, including the academic. The more teachers are able to listen openly to their students and recognize the insights, understandings, or emotions they may not fully express, the more likely they are to meet students on their own terms. I think of this as generous listening. As teachers, we often find ourselves lis-tening for the ideas behind the words that our students say. And as we work to move students to new learning, we must serve as bridges to new worlds and capabilities. As it was for Mel, the journey is the student's to make. But, as teachers, we can provide pathways that guide them and connect them to tools and resources including, as is often the case, those they already have. Moreover, as Mel's teacher did, we can accompany students as they journey. We can walk beside them, supporting them through struggles, and taking pleasure in their victories.

Most important, the mark of a highly qualified teacher is in what she or he makes of these encounters with students; it is in the way experiences with students cause us to reflect on who we are and what matters most in our work. Mel's teacher reminds us, "There are moments in our teaching careers we don't choose. They choose us." But what is most essential about these moments is what we choose to do with them.

❖ EXPLORING THE ISSUES

Teacher-Student Relationships

The teacher in the case reflects that events are often not chosen; they choose us. Remillard concurs with this insight. How teachers respond in difficult situations teaches many lessons beyond the scope of managing classrooms, grading papers, and communicating with parents. Consider the care and involvement that exemplary teachers exude and how that stance can improve or influence development of a collaborative school environment.

Privacy Issues

Remillard says that a "teacher's approach to offering assistance is also worthy of note." Drug use and drinking are two areas of societal concern, especially for adolescents. How should teachers address or offer assistance regarding these issues in class or in school forums? What paths should be taken when "the friend" turns out to be a student in your class? What moral dilemmas are involved in disclosure? Evaluate whether or not the teacher in this case acted ethically and prudently for her- or himself and Mel.

❖ ENGAGING WITH THE COMMENTARIES

Expectations

Both Cole and Remillard address expectations of students and teachers, as well as those expectations prescribed by others as "professional behavior." Compare the expectations as described by the commentators and explain which set of expectations is hardest to fulfill.

Are there similarities for both groups, and what is the strongest motivation for setting new expectations?

Teacher-Student Relationships

Pearson and Loughran discuss risk taking, vulnerability, and trust in the relationship between Mel and the teacher. What elements from each commentary speak to the deepening of teachers' reflection and philosophical stance? How might a student like Mel affect your own personal philosophy about teaching?

Connecting Questions

The Connecting Questions located in the introduction highlight themes that are threaded throughout the cases. You may continue your exploration of the issues raised in this case by addressing those connections. For questions pertinent to this case, please see questions 5, 6, and 10.

❖ ADDITIONAL READINGS

Baier, A. (1985). *Postures of the mind: Essays on mind and morals.* Minneapolis: University of Minnesota Press.
    Baier takes a thoughtful look at theory, justice, trust, and shared responsibility in these essays.

British Columbia Ministry of Education. (1995). *Gifted education: A resource guide for teachers.* Victoria, BC: Author.
    This is a practical guide that highlights strategies, funding, and working with educational partners.

Cochran-Smith, M. (2002). Learning and unlearning: The education of teacher educators. *Teaching and Teacher Education, 19,* 5–28.
    The author discusses the notion of "stance"—how teachers continue to grow in new situations, facing their assumptions and learning from them to continue to interact and reflect sensitively with students and themselves.

Hargreaves, A., Earl, L., & Ryan, J. (1996). *Schooling for change.* Bristol, PA: Falmer.

Based on international research, the authors discuss how schooling can be improved for adolescents. They address school cultures, systems of support, organizations that foster good teaching and learning, curriculum frameworks, and alternative assessments.

Hutchinson, N. L., & Levesque, N. L. (1996). Educating exceptional adolescents: Social contexts and social implications [Special theme issue]. *Exceptionality Education Canada, 6*(3/4).

This journal features many well-researched articles that examine myriad issues that concern students with special needs, including gifted students.

McIntyre, D. J., & O'Hair, M. J. (1996). *The reflective roles of the classroom teacher.* Belmont, CA: Wadsworth.

The authors present a variety of teaching skills and techniques to foster reflection in the classroom.

Richert, A. E. (1990). Teaching teachers to reflect: A consideration of programs structure. *Journal of Curriculum Studies, 22*(6), 509–527.

Richert's focus is always on practice and working with narratives that aid teachers in the art of reflection. The author discusses the need for "tact" and knowing how to balance all the conflicting situations in a classroom that seem to occur simultaneously.

Shulman, J., & Mesa-Bains, M. (Eds.). (1993). *Diversity in the classroom: Casebook for teachers and teacher-educators.* San Francisco: FarWest Lab.

The framework of Exploring the Case was adapted from this book.

Van Manen, M. (2003). On the epistemology of reflective practice. *Teachers and Teaching: Theory and Practice, 1*(1), 33–50.

Van Manen discusses the need for reflection and the development of professional judgment in balancing the needs of all participants in the classroom.

Wong, B. Y. L. (1996). *The abc's of learning disabilities.* Toronto, ON: Academic Press.

This award-winning book examines strategies, definitions, insights, and planning for students who are identified as exceptional. It is a very helpful, practical guide.

13

School Politics
Divide a Community

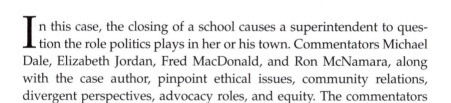

In this case, the closing of a school causes a superintendent to question the role politics plays in her or his town. Commentators Michael Dale, Elizabeth Jordan, Fred MacDonald, and Ron McNamara, along with the case author, pinpoint ethical issues, community relations, divergent perspectives, advocacy roles, and equity. The commentators discuss the difficulty of navigating "the cruel world of politics."

❖ THINKING AHEAD

As you read this chapter, reflect on the following questions and issues:

- Why would problems naturally occur when decisions must be made to alter a school's funding formula?
- What is the writer's background, and consider if the problems presented might be specific to only a small community.

The use of "she and he," while it may appear awkward to the reader, is intended to ensure the absence of gender bias.

- List the dilemmas that confront the writer. What guides this educator's philosophy, and why would it be at odds with the desires of other stakeholders?
- Compare the perspectives of the diverse stakeholders and explain why each holds a particular point of view.

Amalgamation of school boards! New funding formula! New curriculum! Redefining of school board membership! Will the upheaval ever stop?

I have been an educator for over three decades, and I have come to accept change, but never in such great proportions. There were periods of time during school reform that completely overwhelmed me as I pondered how everything would unfold and how all of the pieces would fit together. In addition to imposed adjustments, I had accepted the challenging role of Superintendent of Program and Schools for the Red River District School Board in September 1998. This new position was the culmination of my years as a teacher, vice principal, and principal in the system. After my appointment, I discovered that I would be responsible for the management of massive restructuring on a larger scale for the next 4 years.

The funding formula was based on student enrollment, and with revenues and resources drying up, declining enrollment added to the list of other impacts on the system. The numbers of special education teachers were being reduced, and principals and vice principals were being given more teaching responsibilities—much in opposition, I might add, to the board's dictum of strict adherence to the 24.5 pupils to 1 teacher ratio, which caused an uneven distribution in class size. Low numbers in one class due to special programming increased the numbers disproportionately in other classes.

In smaller communities, most schools were constructed to house between 200 and 300 students. With many schools significantly under-enrolled, the capacity of each school did not often reflect the board's target number. How could I prevent schools from closing, balance all of the reform issues, and hold strong to my philosophy that "kids come first."

Our board commissioned senior administration to prepare a report that addressed the issue of excess space. In collaboration with principals and managers, senior staff examined the "below capacity" ratings of our schools. Internal struggles tugged at me as I wrestled with my staff to determine which approach would provide the best learning experiences for students. Always, an ever-decreasing cash flow and student populations plagued me.

After months of struggle, data collection, model building, and group interactions, the committee was ready to move forward with its report to the trustees, which provided the choice of six options. The committee suggested reconfiguring elementary schools into pre-kindergarten-to-eighth-grade schools, thereby closing seven schools, including one secondary school. At the time of the report's release, many trustees appeared to be in compliance with the report, recognizing that if the system were to survive, schools must close. The path mapped out by the report would decrease the cost of operating schools, and the existing resources applied to the system would improve leadership allocation to schools, along with improved resources in all of our buildings.

The communities, however, held quite a different point of view. Although they gave lip service to the notion that changes were inevitable, what they really meant was "not in my backyard."

The next stage in the process involved public consultation. Sixteen community study groups were established with a trustee as chair and five additional members from each school community and myself, a superintendent, designated as a resource for these groups. I was well valued by some of the groups that understood the rationale of the report, yet to others, who opposed our report, the word "resource" meant "the enemy," as they perceived attacks on the status quo. Interactions at that level caused attacks on the system, and accusations that the administration had falsified information in an attempt to deceive the public. Public forums screamed "flawed report" with pleas to the trustees to "send it back to ensure information was correct." Instead of authentic data, the emotional outcry of "not in my backyard" dominated any other voices trying to explain the reasons for allocations.

The local press gloated and ran daily front-page headlines attacking the administration and making us the target. In addition, the controversy created a split between the study groups and the resource. The press's slanderous affronts orchestrated a direction that would bring about the desired result of proving the *flawed* nature of the report and providing convincing evidence. They strongly implied those school communities' wishes and not the "kids first" should be implemented, the latter being the intended result of the recommendations of senior administration.

I was caught in a balancing act of determining when to become a driving force and when to steer the process. With most of the groups, all I had to do was provide a direction for the talks; but in one group, there was a definite aversion to my involvement in the process: I was the enemy, and they strongly suggested it wasn't necessary for me to attend all of the meetings. They were quite capable of proceeding on their own. It was, however, the same group that had allotted their time to criticizing the report. I would never abandon that group, even though my workday of 14 to 16 hours, fulfilling my regular duties, might have given me an excuse for not attending those rather unpleasant evening meetings. But I met my responsibilities to the end.

The attacks became very strong and pointed at times, and I was flooded with a variety of emotions. When the guns were all pointed in my direction, I had to decide if I would pull off the gloves and start the duel immediately, or retreat and leave the group to its own nefarious devices. For me, professionalism had to reign supreme in the overall picture, and somehow I was able to maintain my composure and present the data and facts in response to their accusations. I kept reminding myself that I must remain objective throughout the entire ordeal and project an image of neutrality, always aware the final decision was not mine, but the trustees'.

Before long, it became evident that the pressures of the community were causing a change of heart in the trustees. I watched it unfold in the study groups as I evaluated their comments in both the informal and formal arenas of politics. The pedagogical view of "what is best for students" was overshadowed by "what is the most popular opinion in the community" and "how will the communities be affected by school closure." The latter two ideas began to pull their political weight, and I became less and less sure how these issues would be resolved.

With the conclusion of public consultation, decision day was drawing near. The tension heightened as the stage was filled with diverse stakeholders and their personal plotlines. For 2 weeks, presentations that varied from high-profile reports complete with PowerPoint razzle-dazzle presentations to low-keyed productions of community opinion continued at the board.

My energy drained.

Five of the 16 study groups accepted that it was a reasonable reconfiguration that would result in closing two schools, and the others would be amalgamated. All other groups were adamant that nothing would change in their own backyards.

Then came the fateful night in March when the board made the final decision. All the conflict was behind, and I, along with other members of the senior administration, prepared to respect the trustees' decision. However, reciprocating respect did not seem to be the order of that day. The crowds of public that gathered to watch the events unfold defined the atmosphere of the meeting. Growing tension mounted as Trustee Ambush, a former teacher in the system, led the parade to browbeat the senior administration publicly. He perceived the moment as a golden opportunity. Through his attempt at being a crowd pleaser, Mr. Ambush, uttering derogatory comments against the administration, pronounced, "This whole process is some devious plot by senior administration to decimate the educational system."

That cut to the very heart of my being.

Once again, my emotions screamed to react. Internally, I raged: "How dare anyone make such a devastating indictment of the hardworking group that composed the senior administration team?" We had labored long and grueling hours, testing and retesting the system to determine what was best for kids. We had never done anything lightly or flippantly.

But once again, professionalism prevailed. I continued to play my part, showing respect for the process and keeping my mouth tightly shut. I focused on the fact that we had done the right thing, and the report proved it.

However, the incriminating remarks were far from finished. The next week in the local newspaper, Trustee Ambush was quoted as saying, "If the board was a corporation, the trustees and senior administration would have been fired months ago!" Perhaps I should have taken comfort in the fact that the trustees had become the target of his attack; but no, that wasn't my style. I felt this was a further attack on my credibility.

Later, when challenged on the issue, the same trustee nonchalantly sloughed it off. "It's only politics," he sneered, "Don't take it so personal [sic]." I suppose that we were learning that the world of politics is a cruel world. I had been an educator for years and always recognized the reality of politics in education, but I had never felt so close to the firing line.

When the final vote was taken, it was close: five to four. Five trustees voting to appease the crowd while four brave souls stayed the course in an attempt to do what was right for kids and the system. The result of this small war was that only two schools were closed, and the rest under consideration for closure stayed open: a lot of effort for naught.

Interestingly, the issues remain, and the process resumes all over again next year. Yet, the silver lining was the trustees taking more responsibility. That showed their desire to change the policy to reflect different stages of development in the system.

We'll see how it all works. I'll be reading about the process in the papers this time because I'm retiring come June.

❖ EXPLORING THE CASE

A superintendent officer with over 30 years of experience wrote this case.

Identification

Identify the key facts of this case. What factual events are central to understanding this situation? Identify the dilemmas and tensions in this case. Explore the main aspects of each dilemma and tension.

Analysis

Analyze the issue(s) from the viewpoints of the different people in the case. Why does the writer feel personal responsibility in defending her or his views in a public forum?

Evaluation

Examine critically the superintendent's strategies for handling the challenge(s). Does the superintendent depicted fulfill, fall short of, or surpass your notion of the role of a superintendent?

Alternative Solutions

Were there alternative solutions or strategies available to deal with the dilemma? Generate alternative solutions to the ones presented in the narrative. Take into consideration risks, benefits, and long- and short-term consequences of each proposed action.

Reflection

The superintendent appears to be glad that she or he is retiring in June. Is she or he satisfied with the outcome of events? Has anything been resolved?

Changing Opinions

Consider your thoughts and assumptions at the beginning of the chapter. Who or what has caused you to consider a new way of thinking? How strongly do you still feel about your previous assumptions?

Synthesis

Synthesize your understanding of this case into a statement. What is this a case of?

Case Commentary by Michael Dale

Frustration, exasperation, anger, resignation, perhaps even despair are the emotional tones that ring aloud through this narrative. I refer here not solely, and not even primarily, to the "emotional outcry" of the community and the local press the superintendent describes, but to the superintendent's own emotions as revealed through this narrative account. This might strike readers as an odd place to begin commentary on this case study concerning the decision-making process around school consolidations and closings. However, I think we are reminded as we read this case study that working as a school administrator, as well as teaching, is emotional and intellectual labor. If philosophers such as Martha Nussbaum are correct in arguing that "emotions are suffused with intelligence and discernment" and "contain in themselves an awareness of value or importance," we cannot simply dismiss them as we consider the soundness and goodness and justice of judgments made and decisions rendered.

The superintendent's anger at the communities' disagreement with and criticisms of the senior administration report to the trustees, anger at the "gloating" local press's "slanderous affronts" of that report, and finally anger at Trustee Ambush's "derogatory comments against the administration" who wrote the report rests on the judgment that the committee's recommendations were in the best interests of the students ("kids come first"). The superintendent asserts that the recommendations were "right for this kids and the system," but we need to examine more thoughtfully this very question: How do we as teachers and administrators determine what is in the best interests of the students? Although the superintendent narrating this case baldly pits the school communities' wishes against the alleged "kids first" report and recommendations, we should look more carefully at these communities' desire not to close schools. I imagine that the parents and community members who spoke against the recommendations of the committee also believed that their reasoning was based on what was in the best interests of the children and adolescents of their communities. And when Trustee Ambush ("a former teacher in the system") criticizes the report as a "plot by senior administration to decimate the educational system," we might charitably probe whether he too is working from a conception of what is best for the students and teachers in the system. Even if the superintendent was able to "project an image of neutrality" during community meetings, we should not lose sight of the fact that the report itself embodied a value judgment.

The ethical reasoning and moral judgment necessary to answer the question of what is in the best interests of students is accompanied in this case study by the question of how decision-making power should be shared in democratic communities. In this case, the trustees clearly possessed the ultimate decision-making power after receiving the committee's recommendation and listening to the communities' voices. Should the trustees possess this ultimate power? How should decision-making power be shared among teachers, students, administrators, and parents in educational matters?

Finally, I think we should pay attention to the circumstances and context in which this scenario takes place. Funding is based on student enrollment, and as student enrollments at particular schools decline, money becomes scarce and small communities in particular seem to be most adversely affected. Rather than being told of spacious schools with plenty of room for children and teachers to move about, we read of "excess space." It is worthwhile asking whether the funding formula itself is in the best interests of the students. Furthermore, the commissioned senior administration committee appears to have been charged with increasing the efficiency of the system. Despite increasing pressures to view education as a business, teaching and learning are not business relationships, nor should knowledge and understanding be understood as commodities exchanged between teachers and learners. We should carefully consider the extent to which demands for an "efficient system efficiently delivering instruction" distorts the true nature of education and the relationships between teachers and learners.

❖ EXPLORING THE ISSUES

Negotiating Power

Dale quotes Martha Nussbaum's comment that "emotions are suffused with intelligence and discernment [and] contain in themselves an awareness of value or importance." Identify the values at stake here. What are the emotional issues and the reasons that motivate the speeches and reports of each stakeholder?

Advocacy Roles

Although the slogans "kids first" and "what is best for students" are touted over and over again by a variety of speakers, Dale questions who really has the interests of the students at heart. Why are the realms of politics and education at odds?

School Politics

Dale questions how demands for an "efficient system delivering instruction" will affect the relationships between teachers and students. How should ethical reasoning and moral judgment be instituted as part of the debate?

Case Commentary by Elizabeth Jordan

Since I was able to take three different perspectives, this was a very hard commentary to write. I have chosen to briefly give all three viewpoints.

From the perspective of a parent, one of the last things I want for my child is to be confronted with an unexpected change such as the closing of his school. While I may accept that there are financial considerations, I am going to argue that the financial burden should be spread over the entire school district and not be reflected only in my son's school. Personally, my husband and I deliberately moved into this community because of the school and the school system. I too would be hard-pressed to remain calm if this event loomed over our family.

When the report to the trustees was submitted with six options, one in particular was singled out—closing seven schools. Only at this point was it opened to public consultation. From a parent's point of view, decisions were already in place. Parents may be consulted and feel they have input, but the report they were discussing had identified a single option. My first reaction to reading about this process was, "Why bother? You've already decided." Asking for comments and allowing the parents to become part of the overall process at this stage probably had the opposite effect. Parents were trying to make sure it wasn't their school that was closed. The entire "not in my backyard" element was probably introduced at this point.

From the perspective of an educator, I sympathize with this district and the teachers. Trying to stretch a budget beyond reasonable limits makes it very difficult for classrooms to run effectively and efficiently. The support system within a school is essential if we hold our students' well-being and learning as the primary goals of education. Often budget cuts need to be made and hard decisions are often required from administrators. If that means closing a school so resources can be adequately reallocated to provide for the students, then perhaps it should be done. Thought and care must be taken to ensure all students and teachers are adequately considered. Once these items have been taken into consideration, then closing a school may make an enormous difference for the entire school district in terms of service to students and teachers. It appears that administrators had worked hard to ensure all aspects of these areas were considered and the most logical choice was closing seven schools.

From the perspective of an elected official, I see this as a politically emotional, explosive item. Not only was the general topic one that required very careful handling, but also the process exacerbated the whole problem. Too much was done "in-house," within the district system. By the time it went for public input, everyone was sensitized to the intended or anticipated result. The focus of closing seven schools was brought before the public prior to allowing them the opportunity to see the data that had led up to the final decisions.

One of the first things politicians learn is that newspapers are in the business of selling papers. I suspect that more newspapers were sold because they focused on the emotional side of this issue, rather than if they had emphasized a balanced view. From a political viewpoint, this should come as no surprise. Neither should the reaction of the politically motivated Trustee Ambush. Many politicians are so aware of the "need to be reelected" that they will shift opinions according to what will get votes. This person was right. The administrator should not have taken it personally; this trustee would do it to anyone who blocked his rise in politics.

I feel that this administrator really did care too much. This is why she or he was so hurt and offended by the political dealings. The case writer is an educator, not a politician.

❖ EXPLORING THE ISSUES

Divergent Perspectives

Jordan sets out several distinct perspectives, from several points of view. Compare and contrast those viewpoints. Identify the issues that are relevant to each perspective.

School Politics

Jordan notes the politics involved in Trustee Ambush's approach. In his conversation with the author of the case, Trustee Ambush says, "It's just politics." (Also, see the concluding sentence in the commentary). What does the above statement mean, in particular to the students and the writer, whose credibility has been impugned? What role do the media play in the debate?

Leadership

Jordan concurs that in life and politics, tough choices must be made. When there are budget cuts, how are educators able to maintain focus on student learning and well-being as primary goals?

Professional Integrity

We are led to believe that the arguments that the writer makes are genuine. Why might she or he be ill equipped to take on or refute professional politicians on an equal playing field? Reflect on Jordan's final statement in the prior commentary. "The case writer is an educator, not a politician." What kinds of rhetoric affect styles of communication with specific groups?

Case Commentary by Fred MacDonald

Few would be surprised that the slogans and phrases used by education reformers and governments to advocate a particular reform agenda or to introduce a set of policy initiatives have been carefully and deliberately chosen to heighten their impact and significance. In the United States, report titles such as "A Nation at Risk" and "No Child Left Behind," or in Ontario, Canada, the provincial government's blueprint for education that "Puts Students First" or its "For the Love of Learning: Report of the Royal Commission on Learning" are carefully chosen so that their authors are able to define and set the boundaries within which others are expected to make sense of the reform agenda or policy initiative. Too frequently and too easily, perhaps, these slogans and phrases used in such titles become part of the popular commonsense vocabulary of the government, the media, the public, and educators alike.

The dilemma(s) presented in the case "School Politics Divide a Community" included in this casebook provide(s) an opportunity to examine how such slogans become so pervasive and commonplace that they are drawn upon by administrators as they make educational decisions. This particular case illustrates the powerful influence the language of educational slogans can have on us and how contests over the multiple interpretations of such slogans can be the root cause of many of the dilemmas that confront us in education.

In this case, the narrator laments her or his inability to reconcile what she or he understands as competing conflicts of student needs and political promises in her or his position as Superintendent of Program and Schools to "prevent schools from closing, balance all of the reform issues, and hold strong to [her or his] philosophy that 'kids come first.'" No matter how it is phrased—by the government's "putting students first" or the superintendent's "kids come first" or the public's desire to put their own children's interests first by challenging proposed school closings in their local communities—all who are interested in the educational welfare of students purport to know what is best for them, frequently to the exclusion of others' interests, which are, perhaps, equally valid.

This case illustrates very clearly the importance of confronting, questioning, and criticizing the ambiguous meaning of the slogans that bombard us in education. The ease with which the narrator glosses over and dismisses the "emotional outcry of 'not in my backyard'" in favor of authentic "data collection, model building, and group interactions" and the "pedagogical view of 'what is best for students'" illustrates the importance of attending to and examining our assumptions. Do we really know what is best for students, and if we think we do, how do we know it? The adoption of such hollow and unexamined slogans as "kids come [putting students] first" as either an educational philosophy or government policy direction should prompt in us an uneasiness and discomfort. In my view, the creation, rapid adoption, and frequent deployment of such slogans by governments, educational administrators, and others, including teachers, result unfortunately in the oversimplification of highly complex educational issues.

❖ EXPLORING THE ISSUES

Reflection

MacDonald suggests that the case writer has been on a roller coaster ride in which she or he has been publicly demeaned. Although she or he concludes in relief that she or he will be retiring, how might she or he restore and salvage her or his sense of self in education? How does she or he see a positive outcome (two ways)?

Professional Integrity

It is important to identify why reform agendas and accompanying documents define and address specific issues, particularly in the allocation of monies. Why would a slogan like "No Child Left Behind" create leverage for government's decision to make changes? How does MacDonald's suggestion to unravel the meaning of slogans aid in learning about our assumptions?

Political Slogans

MacDonald reasons that educational decisions are often made in the exclusion of the rights of those who should be served—in this case, the students. Who has influenced those decisions and why? What does MacDonald offer as a way to rebut the meaningless slogans that often guide action?

Case Commentary by Ron McNamara

The writer, now retired, was a newly appointed superintendent in a newly amalgamated school board at the time of the writing of this case. She or he considers her- or himself a seasoned veteran of the educational system with over 30 years of service as a teacher and administrator. The superintendent's thorough analysis of the data, searching for the best solution, certainly epitomizes knowledge of policies and procedures along with community norms to guide decisions. The superintendent was actively involved in a reflection of her or his practice and her or his beliefs throughout the process.

The problem encountered in a small community is reflective of all school communities when a school is slated for closure. I have been involved in similar circumstances as we closed seven schools and each school community fought bitterly in an effort to save their school. Five years later, divisions still remain between trustees and members of our school communities. The children have adapted quite well, but the adults still have the deep scars from the battles won and lost at the board table.

Problems will naturally occur when decisions are made to alter funding formulas because a "one size fits all" approach to funding education just doesn't fit. Although sharing some similarities, the regions are quite distinct. What works well for the staff and students in a small town does not necessarily work well in a big city. Moving to a common funding formula benefited some boards and severely handicapped others. Regional priorities, even when identified through a wide-scale consultation process, are not perfectly reflective of the local communities. For example, in some areas where competition for skilled workers is intense, boards were forced to pay high salaries to attract competent workers. This same problem might not have existed in other areas, which made the "fitting" of operational expenditures into a regional model difficult, if not impossible.

The writer in this case faces a major dilemma that challenges the core reason that she or he chose to be an educator and on which she or he bases her or his decision making—"kids come first." The superintendent believes that she or he has done her or his best to adhere to her or his beliefs under the circumstances. Whereas introducing controversial reforms is challenging, the superintendent feels comfortable knowing she or he has maintained her or his original focus; yet the diverse stakeholders also believe that they, too, are doing what is in the best interest of the students in their communities.

Superintendents must skillfully navigate through the maze of stakeholders, all of whom have their own agendas to push. It requires "thick skin" and sharp negotiating skills to be successful. Knowing when to speak and when to listen can prevent one from committing fatal career mistakes.

Many of the outcomes in this case might have been avoided if the standards of practice had been adhered to by district administration. Many issues arose because of years of distrust of senior administration. However, a constantly changing administration will inevitably cause disruptions or changes in approaches to problems, even those believed to be resolved. Perhaps consultation before developing the report might have alleviated some of the disputes. In spite of the frustration expressed by the writer, she or he continually exercised professional judgment and integrity throughout the process.

❖ EXPLORING THE ISSUES

Leadership

Review the case writer's qualifications and experience in education. How does McNamara suggest that a superintendent "skillfully navigate through the maze of stakeholders"? How could an effective leader champion her or his community and retain her or his ethics? Compare the personal experience of McNamara and the superintendent in the case. What do they share?

Equity

McNamara questions a "one size fits all" approach to determining funding formulas. How should decisions on an issue that could apply to diverse regions, rural and urban areas, be made responsibly? Why would the "one size fits all" approach be problematic for diverse communities?

Reflection

The superintendent is now able to identify the pitfalls that were not obvious when she or he was living this experience. What does she or he now propose as a remedy?

❖ AUTHOR REFLECTION

In rereading, I reflected on the events that took place in my career that are represented in this case. First, it helps me see what needed to be corrected in the process that was established to allow these things to unfold—namely policy—and how that needs to change. Second, I hope it will help others in a similar position to be aware of some of the challenges out there. I would also hope that those who are responsible for educational leadership courses and programs would be able to use this in preparation of candidates for superintendent positions.

I believe my study, along with all of the others that have been compiled in this book, will form a professional memory that will be preserved to allow others to learn through the lens of those who have gone before. Case studies bring theory and practice into the same room to stimulate thinking that makes teachers the professionals that all of us strive to be.

❖ ENGAGING WITH THE COMMENTARIES

Ethics

Both MacDonald and Dale take aim at the lack of ethics involved in this political issue that will affect real human beings in real classrooms. Compare their discussion of the rhetoric and the questions they pose that expose the self-interest of the parties involved in the volley of words. What might MacDonald and Dale think about this statement: "The process resumes all over next year"?

Personal Connections

Compare the emotional quality of the commentaries and note where the commentators have connected the case to their own personal histories as educators, parents, and so on, particularly in Jordan's and McNamara's responses. Do those personal connections aid in your understanding of the issues at stake? Or do these reflections merely cloud or allow the commentator to be self-indulgent?

Connecting Questions

The Connecting Questions located in the introduction highlight themes that are threaded throughout the cases. You may continue your exploration of the issues raised in this case by addressing those connections. For questions pertinent to this case, please see questions 2 and 9.

❖ ADDITIONAL READINGS

Cunningham, W. G., & Cordera, P. (2004). *Educational leadership: A problem-based approach.* San Francisco: Jossey-Bass.
  With coverage of key leadership topics that include critical thinking, ethics, best practices, and field-situated scenarios, this book reflects on past changes and thinking in educational administration. Multiple perspectives challenge readers to synthesize the material and relate their contentions to real-life dilemmas. The approach is problem based. There is a focus on diversity.

Elmore, R. (2000). *Building a new structure for school leadership.* Washington, DC: The Albert Shanker Institute.
  Elmore explores issues of structure and leadership in public education. At the same time, he explains the pitfalls of public funding for private schools. He encourages educators to study the schools whose leaders and best practices have been established for meeting high standards. The report features successful efforts in which exemplary superintendents and principals have fostered teachers' exemplary instruction.

Fullan, M. (2001). *Leading in a culture of change.* San Francisco: Jossey-Bass.
  Fullan suggests that good leadership is not innate and that one must learn to lead by mastering five core competencies. By discussing the business, nonprofit, and public sectors, the author examines leaders who face new and daunting challenges in technology and sudden shifts in the marketplace, along with crises in the public arena. This book provides insights into the dynamics of change and the role of leadership in managing and coping. Leaders must know how to motivate and mobilize. Fullan focuses on broader moral purpose, cultivating relationships, sharing knowledge, and setting a vision and context for creating coherence in organizations.

Fullan, M. (2001). *The meaning of educational change* (3rd ed.). New York: Teachers College Press.
  This new edition maintains the key structure and context of former editions. Part 1 presents an overview of educational change. Part 2

examines change at the local level. Part 3 deals with educational change at the regional and national levels. Both small and big pictures of change alternate to maintain the theme. The author clearly articulates the contradictory and paradoxical nature of change. He provides practical ideas on the processes and procedures to effect large-scale change.

Greenleaf, R. (1996). On becoming a servant leader. In D. M. Frick & L. C. Spears (Eds.), *On becoming a servant leader: The private writings of Robert K. Greenleaf.* San Francisco: Jossey-Bass.

Greenleaf's collection of previously unpublished works spans 50 years and shares his personal and professional philosophy, which postulates that true leaders are those who lead by serving others. His topics delve into power relationships, ethics, management, and organization. Practical suggestions are offered.

Katz, M. S., Noddings, N., & Strike, K. A. (Eds.). (1999). *Justice and caring: The search for common ground in education.* New York: Teachers College Press.

This book looks at the tension between care and justice as moral orientations. This well-known group of authors, whose focus is ethics and caring, contribute to the reader's comprehension that moral orientations can work together to produce wiser and more practical policies and practices. Problems at every level of education are presented. Tough questions in theory, practice, and policy making are raised for thoughtful consideration. The authors use real-life situations to illustrate how collaboration rather than competition can promote solutions of justice and care, complementing both moral theory and practice.

Kouzes, J. M., & Posner, B. (2002). *The leadership challenge.* San Francisco: Jossey-Bass.

The authors address research on ordinary people achieving "individual leadership standards of excellence." They suggest the following: Model the way, inspire a shared vision, challenge the process, enable others to act, encourage the heart. These contentions are reexamined in the context of the postmillennium. They say, "People make extraordinary things happen by liberating the leader within everyone."

Neher, W. (2004). *Organizational communication: Challenges of change, diversity, and continuity.* San Francisco: Jossey-Bass.

This text provides an extensive overview of the major theories of organizational communication. Neher explores ethics and globalization, technological change, and increasing diversity in organizations. In this new organizational communication text, the approach is student-centered, theoretical, and case based. Neher uses critical, interpretive, functionalist, and managerial conceptions for his arguments.

Nussbaum, M. (2001). *Upheavals of thought: The intelligence of emotions.* Cambridge, UK: Cambridge University Press.

In Nussbaum's probing examination of need and recognition, such topics as personal point of view, belief, evaluation, judgment, and even animal emotions are discussed.

Owens, R. (2004). *Organizational behavior in education: Adaptive leadership and school reform.* San Francisco: Jossey-Bass.

This hands-on book encourages readers to develop and create a plan for implementing school reform. Major emphasis in this edition is on the No Child Left Behind Act of 2001. The organizational nature of culture, diversity, leadership, motivation, change, conflict, and decision making along with the need to maintain high standards are all considered.

Shulman, J., & Mesa-Bains, M. (Eds.). (1993). *Diversity in the classroom: Casebook for teachers and teacher-educators.* San Francisco: FarWest Lab.

The framework of Exploring the Case was adapted from this book.

Silver, P. (1986). Case records: A reflective approach to administrator development. *Theory Into Practice, 25*(3), 161–167.

This article explores the importance of maintaining case records in educational administration. It analyzes the documents in a variety of perspectives and suggests a period of reflection. The authors recommend intellectual engagement that is enhanced with the increase in professional involvement.

References

Banks, J. A. (2003). *Teaching strategies for ethnic studies* (7th ed.). Boston: Allyn & Bacon.

Barrell, D., Fogarty, R. & Perkins, D. (1991). *How to teach for transfer: The mindful school.* Philadelphia, PA: Iri/Skylight Training & Publishing.

Berthoff, A. E. (1982). *Forming, thinking, writing: Composing the imagination.* Portsmouth, NH: Boynton/Cook.

Bidari, A., & Ijaz, M. A. (1992). *Changing perspectives: A resource guide for antiracist and ethnocultural-equity education: All divisions and OACs.* Toronto, ON: Ministry of Education.

Biklen, S., & Pollard, D. (Eds.). (1993). *Gender and education: National Society for the Study of Education Yearbook.* Chicago: University of Chicago Press.

Boler, M., & Zembylas, M. (2003). Discomforting truths: The emotional terrain of understanding difference. In P. Trifona (Ed.), *Pedagogies of difference: Rethinking education for social change* (pp. 110–136). New York: Routledge Falmer.

Britzman, D. (1991). *Practice makes practice: A critical study of learning to teach.* Albany: State University of New York Press.

Bullivant, J. A. (1993). Multicultural education: Characteristics and goals. In J. A. Banks & C. M. Banks (Eds.), *Multicultural education: Issues and perspectives* (2nd ed., pp. 3–28). Boston: Allyn & Bacon.

Bullough, R. V., Jr., & Baughman, K. (1997). *First-year teacher eight years later: An inquiry into teacher development.* New York: Teachers College Press.

Bullough, R. V., & Pinnegar, S. (2001). Guidelines for quality in autobiographical forms of self-study research. *Educational Researcher, 30*(3), 13–21.

Butler, J. (1993). *Bodies that matter: On the discursive limits of sex.* New York: Routledge.

Campbell, E. (2003). *The ethical teacher.* Maidenhead, UK: Open University Press.

Clandinin, D. J., Davies, A., Hogan, P., & Kennard, B. (1993). *Learning to teach: Teaching to learn.* New York: Teachers College Press.

Connelly, F. M., & Clandinin, D. J. (1999). *Shaping a professional identity.* New York: Teachers College Press.

Dilg, M. (2003). *Thriving in the multicultural classroom: Principles and practices for effective teaching.* New York: Teachers College Press.

Doyle, W. (1990). Classroom knowledge as a foundation for teaching. *Teachers College Record, 91*, 347–360.

Eisner, Elliot W. (1997) *The enlightened eye: Qualitative inquiry and the enhancement of educational practice* (2nd Ed.). New York: Merrill Publishing Company.

Fine, M. (1988). Sexuality, schooling and adolescent females: The missing discourse of desire. *Harvard Educational Review, 58*, 29–53.

Gardner, H. (1999). *The disciplined mind: What all students should understand.* New York: Simon & Schuster.

Harrington, H., & Garrison, J. (1992). Cases as shared inquiry: A dialogical model of teacher preparation. *American Educational Research Journal, 29*(4), 715–735.

Haynes, C. C., & Thomas, O. (2001). *Finding common ground: A guide to religious liberty in public schools.* Nashville, TN: First Amendment Center.

Hidi, S., & Harackiewicz, J. M. (2000). Motivating the academically unmotivated: Critical issues for the 21st century. *Review of Educational Research, 70*(2), 151–179.

Hutchings, P. (1993). *Using cases to improve college teaching: A guide to more reflective practice.* Washington, DC: American Association for Higher Learning.

Madfes, T. J., & Shulman, J. (2002). *Dilemmas in professional practice: A case-based approach to improving practice.* San Francisco: WestEd.

McNiff, J., Lomax, P., & Whitehead, J. (2003). *You and your action research project* (2nd ed.). London: Falmer.

Merseth, K. (1991). *Cases and case methods in teacher education: Handbook on teacher education.* New York: Macmillan.

Nord, W. A., & Haynes, C. C. (1998). *Taking religion seriously across the curriculum.* Alexandria, VA: Association for Supervision and Curriculum Development.

Ontario College of Teachers. (2000). *Ethical standards for the teaching profession.* Toronto, ON: Author.

Ontario College of Teachers. (2000). *Standards of practice for the teaching profession.* Toronto, ON: Author.

Polanyi, Michael (1969). *Knowing and being.* Edited with an introduction by Marjorie Grene. Chicago: Univeristy of Chicago Press.

Randall, W. L. (1995). *The stories we are: An essay on self-creation.* Toronto, ON: University of Toronto Press.

Schaps, E. (2003, March). Creating Educational Leadership. *Caring Schools, 60*(6), 31–33.

Schön, D. A. (1987). *Educating the reflective practitioner: Toward a new design for teaching and learning in the professions.* San Francisco: Jossey-Bass.

Schultz, K. (2003). *Listening: A framework for teaching across differences.* New York: Teachers College Press.

Shulman, J., Whittaker, A., & Lew, M. (2002). *Using assessments to teach for understanding: A casebook for educators*. New York: Teachers College Press.

Shulman, L. S. (1986). Those who understand: Knowledge growth in teaching. *Educational Researcher, 15*(4), 4–14.

Shulman, L. S. (1992). Toward a pedagogy of cases. In J. H. Shulman (Ed.), *Case methods in teacher education* (pp. 1–30). New York: Teachers College Press.

Shulman, L. S. (1996). Just in case: Reflections on learning from experience. In J. A. Colbert, P. Desberg, & K. Trimble (Eds.), *The case for education: Contemporary approaches for using case methods* (pp. 197–217). Needham Heights, MA: Allyn & Bacon.

Sizer, T. R. (1984). *High School reform and the reform of teacher education*. Arlington, VA: Automobile Association of America.

Sykes, G., & Bird, T. (1992). *Teacher education and the case idea: NCRTL special report*. East Lansing: Michigan State University Press.

Tharp, R. G., Estrada, P., Dalton, S., & Yamauchi, L. (2000). *Teaching transformed: Achieving excellence, fairness, inclusion and harmony*. Boulder, CO: Westview.

Tom, A. (1984). *Teaching as a moral craft*. New York: Longman.

Van Manen, M. (2003). On the epistemology of reflective practice. *Teachers and Teaching: Theory and Practice, 1*(1), 33–50.

Weinstein, C. S., & Mignano, A. J. (2003). *Elementary classroom management* (3rd ed.). New York: McGraw-Hill.

Index

About the Editors

Patricia F. Goldblatt (EdD, Ontario Institute for Studies in Education [OISE]/University of Toronto [curriculum]; MA, BEd, and BA, University of Toronto) has been an educator for more than 30 years, teaching art and English to high school students. In her work at the Ontario College of Teachers, Goldblatt has been responsible for policy development and research activities in standards of practice, ethical standards, and teacher professional learning. Her work has involved a variety of initiatives, including the revision of course programs for in-service teachers provincewide in such diverse areas as special education, visual arts, and religious education. In particular, Goldblatt introduced case methodology to the college as a way to connect the standards with teachers' practice in Ontario. Her writing on multiculturalism, women's studies, art education, literature, and, most recently, cases as a teaching tool has appeared in journals in Europe, Britain, Asia, the United States, and Canada. Patricia has also presented scholarly papers locally, nationally, and internationally.

Déirdre Smith (MEd, Brock University [teaching and learning]; BEd and BA, York University; and BEd Ontario Institute for Study of Education [OISE]/University of Toronto) is Manager, Standards of Practice and Education at the Ontario College of Teachers. In this capacity, she leads a team responsible for the development and maintenance of standards of practice, ethical standards and a provincial professional learning framework for the 190,000 members of Ontario's teaching profession. Coordinating policy development and research in teacher education has led to the development of provincial inquiry based pedagogical and curriculum resources for pre-service and in-service teacher education. Déirdre's experience as a school principal, curriculum coordinator, classroom teacher, adult educator and child and youth counselor inform her work in teacher education, policy development and research.

About the Contributors

Becky M. Atkinson is a doctoral candidate in Education Research at the University of Alabama in Birmingham. She teaches foundations and science methods in the Teacher Education program at Samford University, also in Birmingham.

Paul Axelrod is Dean of the Faculty of Education at York University in Toronto, Ontario.

David Booth is a Professor at the Ontario Institute for Studies in Education of the University of Toronto (OISE/UT).

Harold Brathwaite is the former Director of Education for the Peel District School Board and Senior Adviser to the President of Seneca College in Toronto, Ontario.

Elizabeth Campbell is an Associate Professor at the Ontario Institute for Studies in Education of the University of Toronto (OISE/UT).

Lynne M. Cavazos is Director of the Teacher Education Program at the Gevirtz Graduate School of Education at the University of California, Santa Barbara.

D. Jean Clandinin is a Professor and Director of the Centre for Research for Teacher Education and Development at the University of Alberta in Edmonton.

Ardra L. Cole is Professor in the College of Education at the Ontario Institute for Studies in Education of the University of Toronto (OISE/UT).

Cheryl J. Craig is an Associate Professor in the College of Education at the University of Houston in Texas.

Michael Dale is a Professor in the College of Education at Appalachian State University in Boone, North Carolina.

Poonam C. Dev is an Assistant Professor in the School of Education at Nazareth College of Rochester, New York.

Janna Dresden is a first-grade teacher in Athens, Georgia.

William J. Hunter is Dean of the School of Education at the University of Ontario Institute of Technology in Oshawa, Ontario.

Nancy L. Hutchinson is a Professor on the Faculty of Education at Queen's University at Kingston, Ontario.

Nathalia Jaramillo is a doctoral candidate at the University of California, Los Angeles.

Patrick M. Jenlink is Director of the Educational Research Center in the Department of Secondary Education and Educational Leadership at Stephen F. Austin State University, Nacogdoches, Texas.

Anne Jordan is a Professor and Associate Chair at the Ontario Institute for Studies in Education of the University of Toronto (OISE/UT).

Elizabeth Jordan is the Coordinator for Diplomas in Special Education and Infant Development, Supported Child Care at the University of British Columbia in Vancouver.

Judith Lessow-Hurley is a Professor of Elementary Education in the College of Education at San Jose State University, California.

Barbara B. Levin is an Associate Professor in the Department of Curriculum and Instruction at the University of North Carolina at Greensboro.

John Loughran is Director of Pre-service Education and Professional Development at the Faculty of Education at Monash University in Clayton, Victoria, Australia.

Fred MacDonald is a secondary school teacher and doctoral candidate at the Ontario Institute for Studies in Education of the University of Toronto (OISE/UT).

Tania Madfes is a senior researcher at WestEd in San Francisco, California.

Michael Manley-Casimir is Dean of Education at Brock University in St. Catharines, Ontario.

Jay Martin is the Edward S. Gould Professor of Humanities at Claremont McKenna College and Claremont Graduate University in California.

James McCracken is Director of Education at Ottawa-Carleton Catholic School Board in Ontario.

Peter McLaren is a Professor of Education at the Graduate School of Education and Information Studies at the University of California, Los Angeles.

Ron McNamara is a Principal in Windsor-Essex Catholic District School Board in Ontario.

Jean McNiff is an independent researcher in Dublin, Ireland.

Janet L. Miller is a Professor at Teachers College, Columbia University, New York.

Lyn Miller-Lachmann is Editor-in-Chief of *MultiCultural Review.*

Ellen Moir is Executive Director of the New Teacher Center at the University of California, Santa Cruz.

Iain Munro is on the Faculty of Education at Queen's University at Kingston, Ontario.

Margaret Olson is an Assistant Professor in the School of Education at Saint Francis Xavier University in Antigonish, Nova Scotia.

Becky Wai-Ling Packard is an Assistant Professor in the Department of Psychology and Education at Mount Holyoke College, South Hadley, Massachusetts.

Allen T. Pearson is Dean of the Faculty of Education at the University of Western Ontario in London.

Stefinee Pinnegar is a teacher educator and educational researcher at Brigham Young University, Provo, Utah.

Aria Razfar is a Professor in the Faculty of Education at Whittier College in California.

Janine Remillard is an Assistant Professor at the University of Pennsylvania in Philadelphia.

Linda F. Rhone is a Visiting Assistant Professor at Shepherd College, Shepherdstown, West Virginia.

Anna Ershler Richert is a Professor of Education at Mills College in Oakland, California.

Joy S. Ritchie is a Professor of Education at the University of Nebraska at Lincoln.

Jerry Lee Rosiek is an Associate Professor of Educational Research at the University of Alabama in Birmingham.

A. G. Rud is an Associate Professor in the Faculty in the Department of Educational Studies at Purdue University, Lafayette, Indiana.

Tom Russell is a Professor on the Faculty of Education at Queen's University at Kingston, Ontario.

Rita Silverman is a Professor in the School of Education at Pace University in New York.

Frances Squire is a retired educator and part-time Professor at Ottawa University in Ontario.

Robert E. Stake is Director at the Center for Instructional Research and Curriculum Evaluation at the University of Illinois at Urbana-Champaign.

Deborah J. Trumbull is an Associate Professor at Cornell University in Ithaca, New York.

Kristopher Wells is on the Faculty of Education at the Centre for Research for Teacher Education and Development at the University of Alberta in Edmonton.

Andrea K. Whittaker is on the Faculty of Education at San Jose State University in California.

Ron Wideman is Associate Dean of Education and on the Faculty of Education at Nipissing University in North Bay, Ontario.

David E. Wilson is a Professor of Education at the University of Nebraska at Lincoln.